GLORY, TROUBLE,

AND RENAISSANCE AT THE

ROBERT S. PEABODY

MUSEUM OF ARCHAEOLOGY

*Critical Studies in the
History of Anthropology*

SERIES EDITORS

Regna Darnell
Stephen O. Murray

Glory, Trouble, and Renaissance at the Robert S. Peabody Museum of Archaeology

EDITED AND WITH AN INTRODUCTION BY

Malinda Stafford Blustain and Ryan J. Wheeler

UNIVERSITY OF NEBRASKA PRESS | LINCOLN AND LONDON

This volume has been published with support from Peter T. Hetzler, MD, (Phillips Academy Class of 1972) in honor of his father, Peter Hetzler (Phillips Academy Class of 1945) to whom the Peabody meant so much.

Library of Congress Cataloging-in-Publication Data
Names: Blustain, Malinda Stafford, editor. | Wheeler, Ryan J., editor.
Title: Glory, trouble, and renaissance at the Robert S. Peabody
Museum of Archaeology / edited and with an introduction by
Malinda Stafford Blustain and Ryan J. Wheeler.
Description: Lincoln: University of Nebraska Press, 2018. |
Series: Critical studies in the history of anthropology | Includes
bibliographical references and index. |
Identifiers: LCCN 2017026968 (print)
LCCN 2017029986 (ebook)
ISBN 9781496204158 (cloth: alkaline paper)
ISBN 9781496205414 (epub)
ISBN 9781496205421 (mobi)
ISBN 9781496205438 (pdf)
Subjects: LCSH: Robert S. Peabody Museum
of Archaeology—History. | Indians of North
America—Museums—History. | Indians of North
America—Material culture—Collectors and
collecting—History. | Archaeological museums and
collections—Massachusetts—Andover—History. | United
States—Antiquities—Collectors and collecting—History. |
Robert S. Peabody Museum of Archaeology—Officials and
employees—Biography.
Classification: LCC E76.86.A53 (ebook) | LCC E76.86.A53 G45 2018
(print) | DDC 970.004/97—dc23
lc record available at https://lccn.loc.gov/2017026968

Set in Arno by Mikala R Kolander.
Designed by N. Putens.

Contents

Illustrations

Series Editors' Introduction

The Peabody museums at Harvard, Yale, and Salem are better known than the Andover museum, the history of which is catalogued in this volume. Although institutional histories tend to be limited to major institutions, this creates a gap; there is a more general history of museums in the professionalization of anthropology and archaeology that calls for a range of cases varying in scale, personnel, and mandate. The Robert S. Peabody Museum is distinct from the other philanthropic Peabody family enterprises. Its association with Phillips Academy, a distinguished prep school, rather than with a university, colors the pedagogy as well as the collections policy, expedition history, and display priorities. The Addison Gallery of American Art, also at Phillips Academy, frames the institution's notion of how young scholars might experience the past and its artistic representations.

The presence of some "outsized" figures over the history of the museum meant that it carried more influence in the larger profession of American archaeology than its size or sponsorship might suggest. The authors of the various chapters in this book cover the history in ways that are personal as well as descriptive, with a good flavoring of anecdote and controversy, including several rebirths after near-closure. The essays are not designed to provide a systematic critical history, but in sum they deliver material that easily falls within a wider comparative frame.

Antiquarian archaeologist Warren K. Moorehead, the first curator, explored major sites and cultures from Maine to the American Southwest. He clashed with A. V. Kidder, who joined the museum in 1915, advocated scientific stratigraphic methods, and pioneered collaborations in the American Southwest through the Pecos conferences. Then there was Richard S. "Scotty" MacNeish, a colorful character who was often at the center of controversy regarding his pre-Clovis finds and his ideas about the earliest agriculture. And we learn about the museum's active role in implementing the Native American Graves Protection and Repatriation Act in collaboration with Native American communities. Moorehead, though an amateur, was the one who established relationships with Native American leaders, Red Cloud and Poundmaker among them.

Archaeologists have long been interested in the history of their relatively young discipline. These essays also speak to historians of science and local/public historians, and illustrations enhance the book's appeal. The narrative line is basically chronological, carrying the story and allowing a maximum range of voices, including those of students, to address the institution's role. Themes criss-cross as the story unfolds, and all the threads seem to come together in the cumulative contemporary appreciation that the institution and its supporters have for their own history and place in larger histories.

Regna Darnell, co-editor

Acknowledgments

We are happy to acknowledge the efforts of the many people who contributed to the symposium and to crafting the present volume. We are grateful to Marshall P. Cloyd, Phillips Academy Class of 1958, for his great generosity and intuitive grasp of what the Peabody has meant to North American archaeology and its potential to shape the worldview of present and future Phillips Academy students. His leadership during the past two decades has been the single most critical factor ensuring the museum's current success.

The Peabody Advisory Committee, chaired by Marshall Cloyd until July 2014, has been instrumental in guiding the museum, and each of its members—present and past—deserves heartfelt thanks: Elizabeth Artz Beim, Benjamin Burke, Barbara Callahan, Linda S. Cordell, Marcelle A. Doheny, Jenny Elkus, Jeremiah C. Hagler, Peter Hetzler, Agnes Hsu-Tang, Heather Dunbar Lucas, Bruno Marino, Tristin Moone, James B. Richardson III, Daniel H. Sandweiss, Kuni S. Schmertzler, Abigail Seldin, Donald Slater, David Hurst Thomas, Sandra A. Urie, and *ex officio* members Gail M. Mansfield, Peter Ramsey, Thom Lockerby, Rebecca M. Sykes, John E. Rogers, and Trish Russell.

We are deeply indebted to Matthew Bokovoy, senior acquisitions editor, Heather Stauffer, editorial assistant, and Joeth Zucco, senior project editor at the University of Nebraska Press, as well as Regna Darnell and Stephen O. Murray, series editors for Nebraska's Critical Studies in the History of Anthropology. We also thank copyeditor Sally Antrobus for her diligence and care in improving consistency and finding and correcting errors and omissions in the final manuscript. Special thanks to Jane G. Libby and Don Abbott for their initial work on the volume during the editing phase and to Sharon Magnuson for additional editing. The comments provided by anonymous reviewers have improved this volume immensely and we thank them for their time and wise guidance.

FIG. 1. Peabody Museum after 2011 renovation. Photo by Donald A. Slater, for the Robert S. Peabody Museum of Archaeology.

Introduction

PRESENT AND PAST AT THE ROBERT S. PEABODY

MUSEUM OF ARCHAEOLOGY

Malinda Stafford Blustain and Ryan J. Wheeler

This volume is unusual in several respects. The subject, the Robert S. Peabody Museum of Archaeology, is part of Phillips Academy in Andover, Massachusetts, an independent boarding high school. As far as we can tell, there are no other similar institutions that are part of secondary schools, at least in the United States. It is worth mentioning that Phillips Academy also is the home of the Addison Gallery of American Art. Together these two cultural centers make Phillips Academy unique among its peers.

Also unusual is that a museum of its size merits an institutional history. The Peabody has always been much smaller than its bigger relations at Harvard, Yale, and in Salem, Massachusetts. At the outset and for much of its history there have been only a handful of staff members at any given time, despite collections that now number over 500,000 objects. The building itself is less than 15,000 square feet (fig. 1). Despite the small footprint and small staff, the Peabody has been associated with some outsized characters of American archaeology, who are introduced in the following pages. Many knowledgeable readers will recognize the names Moorehead, Kidder, and MacNeish but may be surprised to learn of their association with Andover's Peabody Museum.

Our museum is frequently confused with the much larger institutions that share the Peabody name. The Peabody Museum of Archaeology and Ethnology (Harvard), Peabody Museum of Natural History (Yale), and the

Peabody Essex Museum in Salem all originated with wealthy philanthropist George Peabody. Many visitors ask about the connection with these larger and better known museums. There is a genealogical connection. The Andover museum was founded by George's nephew, Robert S. Peabody. Robert (Phillips Academy Class of 1857) founded our institution in 1901 with three goals in mind: to introduce the students of Phillips Academy to the world of archaeology, to promote archaeological research, and to provide a place for students to gather.

The essays making up this volume were first presented at the symposium titled "Rising from the Ashes: Glory, Trouble and Renaissance at the Robert S. Peabody Museum of Archaeology," held at the 76th annual meeting of the Society for American Archaeology in Sacramento, California, on April 2, 2011 (fig. 2). Organized by Malinda Blustain while she was director of the museum, the symposium was a celebration of the renaissance that occurred when the school and museum found common interests in student and faculty engagement, after the dark times that faced the Peabody in 2002, when dwindling financial assets led parent institution Phillips Academy to consider closing the museum and dispersing collections. Besides conveying this history, the symposium presentations include the reflections of students, faculty, administrators, and others from beyond the confines of the museum or academy.

Chapter 1, by Nate Hamilton and the late Eugene Winter, provides a biographical overview of the personnel of the Peabody from two men long connected with it. Gene reminisced about a time when he was ten or eleven years old and rode his bike—without his parents' knowledge or permission—from his home in Lowell to Andover to visit the Peabody. He probably didn't know it at the time, but this was in the early days of the Massachusetts Archaeological Society, an organization that the Peabody was instrumental in founding. Later Gene would serve as president of MAS and worked closely with Peabody personnel. Like Gene, Nate has had a long association with the Peabody and has worked to analyze some of our Maine collections and to provide field opportunities for Andover students and alumni. Their chapter provides a snapshot of the trends and tensions that characterized Americanist archaeology during the twentieth century.

FIG. 2. Presenters at the 2011 Society for American Archaeology symposium, Rising from the Ashes: Glory, Trouble and Renaissance at the Robert S. Peabody Museum of Archaeology. Back row, from left: Hillary Abé, Jerry Hagler, Gene Winter, Jim Bradley, Jim Richardson, Nate Hamilton, J. M. Adovasio, and Brian Robinson; front row, from left: Kristi Gilleon, Chris Toya, Mary Eubanks, Lindsay Randall, Becky Sykes, Abigail Seldin, Claire Gallou, Malinda Blustain, Linda Cordell, and Donald Slater. Photographic collection of the Robert S. Peabody Museum of Archaeology.

This is most apparent in the differences between Warren Moorehead—the Peabody's first curator—and Alfred Kidder, hired in 1915 to commence a new southwestern expedition for Phillips Academy. Moorehead was strongly antiquarian in his endeavors, perhaps even more so than his peers, while Kidder was interested in a new kind of archaeology that unified the work of stratigraphic excavation with ethnographic analogy and physical anthropology. What is interesting about the seemingly dichotomous relationship between antiquarian and scientist is that Moorehead's concern about contemporary American Indians and the relationship between professional and avocational archaeologists strongly colored the Peabody's future, especially in response to the Native American Graves Protection and Repatriation Act of 1990.

Chapter 2 by Jim Richardson and Jim Adovasio looks at the Peabody's history from the perspective of research on the settlement of the New World. Jim Richardson, like Nate Hamilton and Gene Winter, can claim a long association with the Peabody—he tells a story of making an initial visit to Andover during his honeymoon in 1961 to see the museum and meet Byers and Johnson. The Peabody's involvement in questions of antiquity and timing of New World settlement happened largely during the second half of the twentieth century. In the 1950s Douglas Byers and Fred Johnson—the museum director and curator, respectively—aided avocational archaeologists who had discovered the Bull Brook site during quarrying operations in Ipswich, Massachusetts. In the 1960s Byers excavated at the Debert site in Nova Scotia, continuing his interest in early sites. At Bull Brook, significantly, it was the relationship between professionals and avocational archaeologists that led to the preservation of important information about the site.

During this same period curator Johnson was involved in the American Anthropological Association's radiocarbon committee and assisted in introducing this new technique to the world of archaeology. Likewise, Richard "Scotty" MacNeish, who had first recorded the Debert site, worked closely with Byers and Johnson in Mexico before assuming the directorship of the Peabody in the late 1960s. It is not surprising that the larger-than-life MacNeish challenged the assumed antiquity of humans in the New World with his work in Ayacucho, Peru, where he claimed he had evidence of Pleistocene megafauna in association with humans and pre-Clovis tools. His interest in the early end of the American chronology continued with work in Belize and New Mexico, where he again suggested that he had evidence of human occupation before 50,000. While MacNeish's particular evidence for pre-Clovis remains in dispute, his investigations and the work of Byers and Johnson give a local glimpse into the discourse around Clovis and the timing and mechanism of the settlement of the New World, ideas that are playing out at the macro level in archaeology and the popular media.

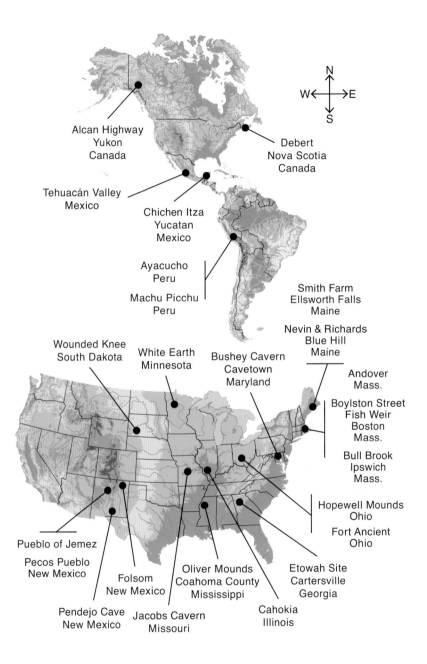

FIG. 3. Map showing many of the places and archaeological sites mentioned in the text. Map by Stephen Gleason Design.

In chapter 3 the late Linda Cordell explores Alfred Kidder's role as director of the Peabody Museum's southwestern expedition and the implications for American archaeology and the museum. Kidder's work at Pecos was the largest undertaking of the Peabody prior to Scotty MacNeish's Tehuacán Valley project in the 1960s (see figure 3 for many of the places and sites mentioned in the volume). It is interesting to consider how Kidder and MacNeish bookend the twentieth-century history of the Peabody, both undertaking massive projects that helped shape the theory and methods of contemporary and future archaeologists. The internal decision to focus on Kidder's Pecos project also represented a significant departure from Robert S. Peabody's wishes that the program include instruction and research. The exclusive focus on research set the stage for future crises, as the Peabody had fewer and fewer connections to its parent institution. At the same time, Kidder's Pecos project provided an opportunity in the 1990s to forge our deepest and most meaningful connections with American Indian communities because of this shared history. Kidder's work left an indelible mark on the world of southwestern archaeology—from ideas about chronology to the Pecos Conference—and likewise marked a significant turning point in the history of the museum, one that shifted the focus from students and teaching to pure research.

The late Brian Robinson, the acknowledged expert on the archaeology of the Bull Brook site and Maine's Moorehead burial tradition, was well placed to write chapter 4, which explores the Peabody's role in the history of northeastern archaeology. Robinson focuses on the work that Moorehead did, primarily in Maine in relation to the so-called "Red Paint" burials, now understood to represent an Archaic burial tradition found in Maine, the Canadian Maritimes, and neighboring areas. Much of Robinson's discussion focuses on the intricate networks that Moorehead established in the Northeast, a practice also discerned in the work of Doug Byers and Fred Johnson in their more than thirty years staffing the Peabody, as represented by projects at the Boylston Street Fish Weir, Cape Cod and Martha's Vineyard, and continued work in Maine, much of which was published in the museum's "blue book" research series between 1940 and 1979. Brian's own work—much of which has centered on positioning the

Moorehead Burial Tradition—has also involved a lot of bridge building with the Wabanaki peoples of Maine.

In chapter 6 Mary Eubanks provides a retrospective on Scotty Mac-Neish's Tehuacán Archaeological-Botanical Project of the 1960s. Mary is an alumna of Abbot Academy (Class of 1965), the private girls' school that merged with Phillips Academy in 1973. Later Mary worked with MacNeish and some of his collaborators as she pursued her own research on corn genetics. In many ways MacNeish's Tehuacán and Ayacucho projects mirror Kidder's Pecos project, representing major undertakings of our relatively tiny institution that reflected the broader refocusing of archaeological investigation and scholarship. Tehuacán and Ayacucho, like Pecos, continue to be influential projects that contemporary scholars revisit on a regular basis. Perhaps most fascinating is that MacNeish's work was central to scientific debate about the origins of corn, a debate that inspired others to continue the search successfully in other regions and push back the dates for domesticated corn to some 8,500 years ago. MacNeish's botanical collections—some of which are housed at the Peabody—are still accessed by scientists interested in corn domestication and evolution.

Scotty MacNeish's pugilistic style was not confined to the boxing ring or scientific debate but extended into his relationship with the museum's parent institution, Phillips Academy. As Malinda Blustain discusses in chapter 7, the academy didn't always appreciate Scotty's direct style, despite student interest and his accolades in the archaeological and anthropological community. Tales from alumni who took classes with MacNeish or his curators, or who ventured to Mexico and Peru on his projects, demonstrate his skill at inspiring an interest in travel, world cultures, and history. But it wasn't enough. Spending on field projects, dwindling endowment funds, and disputes over maintenance and insurance led to increasing tension between the Peabody and Phillips Academy. Blustain's account in chapter 7 sets the stage for MacNeish's unhappy departure in 1983 and the near death experience of the museum at that time, as well as the backstory for the similar episode that played out twenty years later during Jim Bradley's tenure as director. Perhaps the most exciting part of the story, however, is the efforts by the museum, the school, and the archaeological community

to return to Robert Peabody's vision of an institution that provided archaeological instruction and programming to high school students. Today that
relationship seems obvious and inevitable, but in 2002 getting faculty to
cross the street with their students was anything but straightforward.
One of the pioneers—instructor in history Marcelle Doheny—was the
first to deploy museum collections in her classes, demonstrating to her
colleagues the value of hands-on learning and teaching with objects. Marcelle is still formulating new courses, taught in conjunction with Peabody
staff members and heavily relying on museum collections to inspire and
enliven discussion, as in her recent senior elective Race and Identity in
Indian Country.

One of the most significant events in the recent history of the Peabody
was the passage of the Native American Graves Protection and Repatriation Act (NAGPRA) in 1990. Jim Bradley, the museum's director from
1990 to 2001, explores NAGPRA in a very personal reflection in chapter 8,
sharing his account of the repatriation of nearly two thousand individuals and associated funerary objects from Pecos Pueblo by their modern
descendants from the Pueblo of Jemez. The farsighted and progressive
approach to NAGPRA taken by Jim as director and Leah Rosenmeier as
the museum's repatriation coordinator helped shape the institution that we
know today: one that has prioritized descendant communities over objects.
After a decade of NAGPRA—by the time of the Pecos repatriation—the
literature of institutional experiences with the act was limited. With the
25th anniversary of NAGPRA this has changed, but there is still room
for more reflection on the repatriation experience from the institutions
involved and, more important, from the tribes. Even today Pecos is regarded
as the largest repatriation under NAGPRA, but it exists within a broader
context of large and small consultations by the Peabody, primarily during
the tenure of Jim and Leah in the 1990s. Notable are the consultations
concerned with Warren Moorehead's collections from Etowah, Georgia,
and the Museum's Maine holdings. Both presented their own challenges
and, like Pecos, involved other institutions. The museum's NAGPRA files
indicate that the Etowah consultations were challenging because they
involved groups that had been forcibly removed to Indian Territory—now

Oklahoma—and that consensus building, especially around final disposition, was difficult. Ongoing scholarship in southeastern archaeology and traditional beliefs lined up in many cases, aiding some of the questions around affiliation. Ultimately the consultation resulted in affiliation to five tribes—the Alabama-Quassarte Tribal Town, Kialegee Tribal Town, Muscogee (Creek) Nation, Poarch Band of Creek Indians of Alabama, and Thlopthlocco Tribal Town—though decisions about repatriation remain unresolved. In Maine it was difficult to align archaeological theories and data with the views of the Wabanaki, and divergent institutional approaches to NAGPRA and the lack of a site-by-site approach magnified the differences in thinking among tribal representatives and the museum personnel. The so-called 1,000-year rule—issued by the Maine Historic Preservation Commission—further complicated matters. Despite these challenges, a significant number of NAGPRA collections at the Peabody were repatriated to the Maine tribes. A new request in 2011 allowed conversation and consultation to resume regarding the oldest remains and funerary objects—those from the Moorehead burial tradition. Collections split with other institutions continue to frustrate tribal repatriation efforts, but the museum affiliated the funerary objects from the Nevin site and saw their repatriation in 2015.

Chapters 9, 10, and 11 provide a glimpse of the current role of the Peabody Museum in the broader academic world of Phillips Academy. In many ways we have returned to Robert Peabody's vision of the museum as a place where high school students encounter archaeology and anthropology and everything these disciplines have to offer. Today most students at the school come to the museum with their classes. Others are involved in the work duty program, performing all the behind-the-scenes collections duties familiar to those at a small museum, while others go on expeditionary learning programs or conduct independent research projects. Chapter 9, by Curator of Education Lindsay Randall and Pueblo of Jemez tribal archaeologist Chris Toya, explores the Pecos Pathways program, an outgrowth of the NAGPRA consultations of the 1990s. Here students from Jemez and Andover come together to explore archaeology and history in both New Mexico and Boston. Phillips Academy instructor of history and social science Donald Slater and Nate Hamilton, in chapter 11, look at some of the other expeditionary learning programs offered by the museum, from excavations at the Rebecca Nurse Homestead in Danvers, Massachusetts to adventure travel programs in Mexico and Peru. In chapter 10 biology instructor Jerry Hagler looks at the ways in which Phillips Academy students engage with the museum. Most interesting is that the approach is not one that focuses on teaching archaeology classes, which is the most prevalent avenue to archaeology in the classroom, at least in the United States. Educators at the Peabody have focused on using the concepts, methods, and objects of archaeology and anthropology to support the school's existing curriculum. At Phillips Academy students' lives are packed full with academics, music, sports, clubs, and more, leaving little room for add-ons. By finding ways in which archaeology can inform math, music, art, English, the sciences, and more, we have found our way into many classes across the curriculum, hosting well over a thousand students per year for class visits. In academic year 2016–17 at least three term-long classes were being taught at the Peabody—Human Origins, which Hagler discusses in chapter 10, along with Marcelle Doheny's Race and Identity in Indian Country and Donald Slater's Maya Cosmos.

The final chapter includes six essays by faculty members, recent alumni, and friends who provide their stories and reflections on the museum's recent history. These touch on Native American experiences, the value of archaeology in multidisciplinary teaching, and student responses to work duty, trips, and independent projects. The perspectives in chapter 12, along with the museum's experience in collaborative and expeditionary learning, have helped inform the strategic directions for the immediate future, with major themes including Collaborative Learning, Decolonizing Museums, Sustainable Outreach, and Collections Stewardship. Much of our future focus draws on our history—the collections, both archaeological and ethnographic, are central to the classes and lessons offered—as well as reflecting Robert Peabody's vision for an institution that engaged high school students with the still young discipline of archaeology.

Chapter 1

A Biographical History of the Robert S. Peabody Museum of Archaeology

Nathan D. Hamilton and Eugene C. Winter Jr.

The Robert S. Peabody Museum of Archaeology has been at the vanguard of North American archaeological method and theory since its founding in 1901. It was involved in the founding of the Society for American Archaeology (SAA), a professional organization for American archaeologists. Museum personnel developed a systematic approach to excavation that employed stratigraphic principles to unify regional chronologies and initiated the use of radiocarbon as an absolute dating technique. They focused on environmental reconstruction, devising innovative interdisciplinary collaborations to research agricultural origins and the development of societal complexity. This legacy gives the museum unique stature in scientific innovation as well as in education and public archaeology initiatives that focus on Phillips Academy and its outreach to both scholarly and indigenous communities.

This chapter provides an overview of the museum's directors and staff and their general contributions to the development and history of the institution. Research agendas, select areas of field investigation, field and laboratory methods utilized, and contributions to the field of archaeology are briefly discussed.

The history of any museum is really the story of the people who worked there and what they studied and learned concerning the artifacts and collections that it holds and exhibits. The founder and donor of the museum was Robert Singleton Peabody (fig. 4). A Phillips Academy graduate, Peabody reflected upon his own educational experience. He wanted students at Phillips Academy to be aware of the science of archaeology, quipping that its very existence was "a specimen fact I did not learn in my four years." He further wrote, "Cultivated, educated life has, at least, one side not bounded by Divinity, Law, or Medicine; and to excite interest with whatever knowledge might be gained, at the earliest possible period of student life" was a goal of the museum (Robert S. Peabody to Trustees of Phillips Academy, March 6, 1901, pages 4–5, Robert S. Peabody Museum of Archaeology, Founder records).

Robert S. Peabody—the Founder

Robert Singleton Peabody (1837–1904) graduated from Phillips Academy, Class of 1857, and then attended law school at Harvard (Moorehead 1906). At Phillips Academy he cultivated a talent for classical languages, as attested by frequent quotes in later correspondence, and graduated at the head of his class. A favorite nephew of self-made man and philanthropist George Peabody, Robert established a lucrative law practice in Vermont prior to relocating to Germantown, a neighborhood in the northwestern part of Philadelphia. A patent registration in the museum archive for a paddle-boat suggests he had diverse interests, which may have included inventions.

He established a rapport with Warren Moorehead, the author of a newspaper article on the Moundbuilders, relating a boyhood interest in Indian artifacts and the desire to amass a larger collection. Like Moorehead, Peabody was from Ohio, and they shared an enthusiasm for relics. Moorehead aided Peabody with his interest in collecting American Indian artifacts, helping him to amass some 38,000 objects by the close of the nineteenth century. Later in life Peabody considered donating his collection to the Harvard Peabody, established by his uncle in 1866 (Parker 1971, 155–56); Moorehead (1938, 9) relates that a meeting between Peabody and Frederic Ward Putnam, Harvard Peabody's chairman, did not go well, leading ultimately to the founding of the museum in Andover and a substantial endowment to Phillips Academy, tallying over $500,000 at one point (roughly $13 million in today's dollars). Richardson and Adovasio (this

FIG. 4. Robert Singleton Peabody, founder of the museum. Photographic collection of the Robert S. Peabody Museum of Archaeology.

volume) explain that Peabody may have been angling for a position for Moorehead. Considering Putnam's prior experience with Moorehead in connection with collecting expeditions for the 1893 Columbian Exposition, he may have been disinclined to consider such an appointment (see Snead 2016).

Peabody's keen interest in archaeology was fostered by collecting activities, family connections, and personal friends. Phillips Academy's newly founded Department of Archaeology reflected Robert Peabody's strong personal interest in field research, collections activities, books, and above all else the teaching and practice of archaeology. Peabody's vision for the museum, as related by Moorehead (1906, 1938), was threefold: to foster an interest in archaeology and American Indians among the boys at his alma mater, to encourage research on his collections, and to provide social spaces for the academy's students. At age sixty-four he provided his personal funds to build a museum and established a clear agreement of understanding. A general objective of the museum was the curation and display of his collection. Equally important, the new museum building was to serve as a meeting place where students and interested citizens could discover the emerging field of archaeology. The building itself was designed by Boston's preeminent architect Guy Lowell, who designed other important buildings of the time, including the iconic Museum of Fine Arts in Boston. Lowell's archaeology building was similar to other colonial revival buildings, with a grand staircase and large exhibition rooms off a central hall (Faxon 2000, 105–7). An article in the *Phillipian*, the Phillips Academy student newspaper, on May 1, 1903, describes some of the spaces, including the lecture hall and library on the second level and the meeting spaces for students in the basement. Earlier photos show many large wood and glass cases filled with stone tools and other objects.

Back issues of the *Phillipian* indicate that many student organizations had space in the new museum building, including the camera club, chess club, debating society, various music clubs, and the like. The museum housed a reading room as well—pleas in the *Phillipian* for the return of books indicate that Sir Arthur Conan Doyle was popular—reserved as a smoking lounge for older boys, and the basement included a grill room.

Sadly, our view of Robert S. Peabody is limited, and while he lived to see the museum building completed, his failing health prevented any real enjoyment of his munificent gift. It is clear, however, that he was an extremely astute lawyer and businessman, based not only on his handling of his late uncle's estate but also from the complex nature of the endowment that he created in his archaeological gift to Phillips Academy. One unusual provision required that the donor and his wife, Margaret, should remain anonymous (Robert S. Peabody to Trustees of Phillips Academy, March 6, 1901, Robert S. Peabody Museum of Archaeology, Founder records).

With the opening of the Department of Archaeology, the Peabody family legacy grew and asserted its strong role in archaeology in America and throughout the world. In spring 1901 Robert's eldest son, Charles, was appointed the first honorary director of the museum. At its opening dedication ceremonies Charles, without mentioning his father's name, references the original gift letter, which states, "It is possible that at some future time there might be in your hands . . . sufficient funds to justify in the judgment of your Board an addition to the present archaeological foundation of one or more branches of cognate science, as Ethnology or Paleontology, etc." (Robert S. Peabody to Trustees of Phillips Academy, March 6, 1901, page 4, Robert S. Peabody Museum of Archaeology, Founder records).

Charles Peabody—Honorary Director

Charles Peabody (1867–1939) was born in Rutland, Vermont, but he did not attend high school in Andover as his father had (MacCurdy 1948). He attended the Germantown Academy in Philadelphia, the University of Pennsylvania, and in 1893 completed a PhD program in philology at Harvard; his Harvard classmates included George Reisner, who went on to an influential career in archaeology. Stephen Williams (1999, 3) speculates that philology at the time was probably a combination of classical and Middle Eastern languages and may have included Old World archaeology and biblical studies.

In a May 1900 letter Charles exhorted his father that he would like nothing better than a position at Phillips Academy and the newly proposed

Department of Archaeology, but that he understood how perceptions of nepotism might limit his involvement (Charles Peabody to Robert S. Peabody, May 22, 1900, Robert S. Peabody Museum of Archaeology, Robert S. Peabody correspondence). He was, however, involved in the construction of the museum building and advised his father that part of his role was keeping "an impetuous" Moorehead in line (Charles Peabody to Robert S. Peabody, March 31, 1901, Robert S. Peabody Museum of Archaeology, Robert S. Peabody correspondence). Charles was ultimately appointed honorary director of the museum; annual reports indicate he received no salary. (Moorehead consistently blacked out the word "honorary" on the museum stationery and always referred to Peabody as the director.) Peabody maintained his residence at 197 Brattle Street in Cambridge, near Harvard, where he was an instructor in European archaeology.

Moorehead and Peabody exchanged frequent correspondence regarding matters of teaching archaeology classes, the day-to-day operation of the museum, and more ambitious plans for an expanded museum facility. Peabody and Moorehead collaborated on a number of early projects, including their analysis of gorgets, hematite artifacts, and excavations at Jacob's Cavern in Missouri, and Peabody provided underwriting for Moorehead's monumental two-volume *The Stone Age in North America*. Peabody was frequently out of the country, spending considerable time in France, where he investigated European Paleolithic sites. For example, Harvey Bricker (2002, 278) notes that Peabody and George Grant Mac-Curdy were traveling companions in Europe in 1908 and 1912.

His archaeological interests in the United States, however, were decidedly southern and southeastern. In many ways Charles Peabody exemplified his father's goals, uniting an interest in the archaeology of Europe and the Americas. He engaged in field research and excavated mounds and caves or rockshelters in the southeastern United States (Browman and Williams 2013, 216–19; Williams 1999). Early work at Jacob's Cavern, Missouri (1903), demonstrated his commitment to greater control in excavation and to precise recordkeeping in order to understand distribution and patterns of artifacts. At Jacob's Cavern, Peabody ensured excavation control by employing a unit-delineated grid system. An integral aspect of his research was the establishment of a publication record. The first report published by the museum (1904) was his report on Jacob's Cavern. Peabody's interest in emerging theories of archaeology is reflected in his work at cave sites, both in France and the United States.

Along with his early stratigraphic work at Jacob's Cavern, Peabody conducted excavations in 1901, 1902, and 1918 in Mississippi, as well as mound excavations in North Carolina and an investigation of Bushey Cavern near Cavetown, Maryland. David Browman (2002, 251–52) and others have recognized Peabody's early application of the stratigraphic method, learned from his friend and Harvard mentor Frederic Ward Putnam, with notable examples at some of the sites already mentioned. Browman (2002, 251–52) further notes that George Reisner's work in the Old World and continued success with the stratigraphic method by Charles Peabody and Roland Dixon may well have inspired Alfred V. Kidder's pioneering work at Pecos, New Mexico. Perhaps it is fitting that one of our few photographs of Charles Peabody is at Pecos in 1916, next to a stratigraphic column (Kidder 1958, fig. 72e). Peabody and his daughter Caryl spent two weeks as visitors to the Pecos project that year (Charles Peabody to Warren K. Moorehead, July 20, 1916, on the letterhead of the Andover Pecos Expedition, Valley Ranch, New Mexico, Robert S. Peabody Museum of Archaeology, Warren K. Moorehead records).

After World War I Charles returned to France, where he, along with Louis Henri Martin, George Grant MacCurdy and Glenn Bartlett MacCurdy, established the American School in France for Prehistoric Studies, which was affiliated with the Archaeological Institute of America. Disagreements with MacCurdy, Aleš Hrdlička, and others involved in the school led to his withdrawal of support as the organization was renamed the American School of Prehistoric Research and its aims broadened and refocused (MacCurdy 1948; Petraglia and Potts 2004, 25, 28, 30–31). In 1923 Peabody made his home permanently in France, resigning from his position as honorary director of the Peabody. However, he maintained friendly ties with the museum; for example, just a few years before his death he was still corresponding with Moorehead and Douglas Byers at the Peabody, arranging for an exchange of European and American specimens.

Warren K. Moorehead and the "Old School"

A personal friend of Robert Peabody, Warren King Moorehead had acquired collections for him during the 1890s, prior to the founding of the museum. He was appointed the first curator of the department by Peabody and worked alongside Charles Peabody until he was appointed the museum's second director in 1924 (see Robinson, this volume). Moorehead left an indelible stamp on the museum. Perhaps his greatest contribution was extensive regional surveys conducted primarily in the eastern United States. His association with the Peabody family and the museum had spanned nearly four decades when he stepped down in 1938, a year prior to his death. His large-scale archaeological surveys and excavations included the Arkansas River Valley, northwest Georgia, and coastal and interior Maine.

Warren King Moorehead (1866–1939) was born in Sienna, Italy, the son of a Presbyterian minister, but grew up in Ohio, where he cultivated a lifelong interest in archaeology and American Indians (Byers 1939; Kelly in Moorehead 2000a). Throughout his career he was a prolific excavator and author, writing an almost dizzying number of articles and books. Some of these works, like the two-volume *The Stone Age in North America* (1910), highlighted the artifact collections of a widespread network of collectors and antiquarians. Christenson (2011) concisely summarizes Moorehead's early career:

> By the time he was twenty-two (1888) he was arguing for the preservation of Fort Ancient [Ohio], exhibiting his collection at the Cincinnati Centennial Exposition, hiring Irishmen to dig for him, being buried alive and severely injured in the collapse of a trench, and, most significantly, was invited by Thomas Wilson, Curator of Anthropology at the Smithsonian Institution, to bring his collection to Washington, D.C., to study.

James Knipmeyer (2006) illuminates a little-known episode in Moorehead's career, when, in 1892, he led an ill-fated and poorly organized expedition "in search of a lost race" for a new magazine called the *Illustrated American*. Moorehead and his party visited one hundred archaeological sites—most of them unknown to the world of science—between Durango, Colorado, and Comb Ridge, Utah. Unfortunately Moorehead had to pony up personal funds to cover expedition costs, and the notes, photographs, and maps from the project were lost in a fire; but Moorehead's expedition was one of the first to explore what would later be known as the Anasazi culture. James Snead (2016) provides more detail on this venture, in which Moorehead was apparently working for multiple interests, including both the publisher of the *Illustrated American* and Frederic Ward Putnam, who had commissioned Moorehead to collect artifacts for display at the 1893 Chicago World's Fair. Moorehead's correspondence from his time at Phillips Academy shows that he frequently engaged in schemes to accumulate and sell artifacts, often with similarly unpleasant results. Despite his earlier misadventures, he returned to the Southwest again in 1897 for his patron Robert S. Peabody, and many of the artifacts from that expedition are preserved in the museum's collections.

As a correspondent for the *Illustrated American*, Moorehead found himself in the Dakotas in the weeks and days leading up to the Wounded Knee massacre. It was here that he began his lifelong friendship with Lakota chief Red Cloud and his family (Moorehead 1902, 10–11). He also dabbled in archaeological publishing, acquiring the *Archaeologist* in 1893 and the *Antiquarian* (renamed the *American Archaeologist*) in 1896; unfortunately these publishing endeavors were unsuccessful, but they helped broaden Moorehead's contacts with professional and avocational archaeologists, building on his Midwest and Washington DC networks (Christenson 2011; Kelly in Moorehead 2000a). After his time at the Smithsonian and his work on the Columbian Exposition of 1893 he served as curator of the Ohio Archaeological Society until ill health took him back to the Southwest.

Moorehead began his association with Robert S. Peabody in 1896, providing several collections of American Indian artifacts (Moorehead 1906, 1938). He reminisces about his lengthy discussions at Peabody's Adirondack cabin and at his home in Germantown, Philadelphia, which provided the germ of the idea of a Department of Archaeology at Phillips Academy. Moorehead left Ohio in 1897, spending time in Arizona to recuperate from tuberculosis. At this time Peabody financed Moorehead's reconnaissance surveys in the warmer and drier Southwest, perhaps an attempt to revisit his early expedition for the *Illustrated American*, accumulating artifacts from Chaco Canyon, the La Plata Valley, and the Salt River Valley. Continued health issues confined Moorehead to Saranac, New York, for the winters of 1899, 1900, and 1901, where he remained in close contact with Peabody and continued to publish books. Moorehead was Peabody's choice as the first curator of the new Phillips Academy Department of Archaeology and succeeded Charles Peabody as director early in 1924 (Telegraph from Warren K. Moorehead to James H. Ropes, January 25, 1924, sent from Natchez, Mississippi, Robert S. Peabody Museum of Archaeology, Warren K. Moorehead records). As soon as Moorehead was appointed curator of the fledgling museum he was tasked with arranging insurance and transportation of the founder's artifact collection from Philadelphia to Andover. He also surveyed the students of Phillips Academy, assessing interest in new courses in archaeology, and as the new museum had yet to be built, he soon set the young men to unpacking and studying the collection in the old gym. During the first decades both Moorehead and Peabody did offer courses, though these were discontinued in 1919 at the recommendation of the Peabody oversight committee, which sought to refocus the institution on research rather than expansion of exhibits or education.

Moorehead's principal interest was in the archaeology of eastern North America, and his fieldwork targeted important sites like Fort Ancient and the Hopewell mound group in Ohio, Etowah in Georgia, and Cahokia in Illinois. In at least two cases—Fort Ancient and Cahokia—Moorehead was intimately involved in efforts to preserve these sites through public acquisition.

The lack of formal training plagued Moorehead throughout his career. Charles Peabody, in correspondence with his father, Robert S. Peabody, laments this deficiency (although Moorehead did receive several honorary degrees, including an honorary master's degree from Dartmouth College in New Hampshire).

Moorehead's antiquarian approach also attracted persistent criticism. Douglas Byers (1939, 288) wrote that rather than addressing the broader archaeological questions being investigated by mid-twentieth-century professionals, Moorehead's primary interest remained in artifacts, demonstrating that he was still of the "Old School." John Kelly (in Moorehead 2000a), in his introduction to a new edition of Moorehead's Cahokia reports, gives a detailed overview of the push for preservation and the archaeology, noting that efforts resulted in the creation of a 144-acre state park in 1925 that included Monks Mound and other features of the much larger site. Moorehead's multiple field seasons at Cahokia, however, led Kelly (in Moorehead 2000a, 47–48) to conclude that "his expertise was not that of a careful excavator or analyst" and that his major contribution was the preservation of part of the site. Despite his detractors, Moorehead forged a long and illustrious career as curator, and then director, of the Peabody. His efforts to preserve Fort Ancient and Cahokia led to declaration of both as state parks and to their being listed as National Historic Landmarks. Cahokia has since been elevated to a UNESCO World Heritage Site, and both the Cahokia and Etowah publications have been reprinted (Moorehead 2000a, 2000b).

Criticism of his methods by leading scholars came to the notice of the administration of Phillips Academy, which may have led them to limit the scope and scale of his investigations. In one instance he recounts how Roland Dixon, the eminent Harvard anthropologist and member of the 1914 advisory committee on archaeology, redirected his Maine archaeological explorations, diverting him from excavations to reconnaissance survey (Brief outline of a conversation between Principal Alfred E. Stearns and Curator Warren K. Moorehead, February 6, 1919, Robert S. Peabody Museum of Archaeology, Warren K. Moorehead records). This seemingly random intrusion makes sense in light of Dixon's work for the National Research Council in promoting state archaeological surveys (O'Brien and Lyman 2001, 3). In fact, the appointment of the special oversight committee by the Phillips Academy Board of Trustees in 1912 rankled no end with Moorehead, and he presented numerous alternatives to the recommendations being developed by the committee (for example, a document titled "Curator's Analysis of the Putnam Committee Report," February 20, 1914, Robert S. Peabody Museum of Archaeology, Warren K. Moorehead records). The committee was an illustrious one, including Franz Boas of Columbia; Frederic Ward Putnam of the Harvard Peabody,

Hiram Bingham III of Yale University, and William Henry Holmes of the Bureau of American Ethnology. In one instance Bingham (Phillips Academy Class of 1894), not long after presenting Machu Picchu to the world, politely but firmly tells Moorehead to save his ideas for the meeting of the committee (Hiram Bingham III to Warren K. Moorehead, October 8, 1914, Robert S. Peabody Museum of Archaeology, Warren K. Moorehead records). The committee recommendations, accepted by the trustees in 1914, represent a critical turning point in the history of the Peabody, limiting Moorehead and Honorary Director Charles Peabody's aspirations for more exhibit space, while opening the door for Alfred V. Kidder and the southwestern expedition.

A long-term involvement with the archaeological community in New England demonstrates the deep-rootedness of the emerging profession in the late nineteenth and early twentieth centuries. Charles Peabody and Moorehead made an early connection with A. E. Marks of Yarmouth, Maine. The museum's catalog notes the purchase on August 24, 1899, of artifact collections made by Marks. Marks and his brother first excavated the well-known locations of Hollaway Farm, Orland, Passadumkeag, and Mason Farm (Moorehead 1922). The museum purchased the resulting collection of 1,065 specimens, listed in a hardbound catalog of 112 pages. By identifying other collectors from whom Marks purchased materials, the catalog demonstrates the importance of the social connection of educated elite in New England and elsewhere and how it influenced the early foundation of archaeology. The museum's acquisition of the Marks collection also alerted Moorehead to the location of several other "Red Paint" sites he would subsequently excavate in central Maine (Robert S. Peabody Museum of Archaeology, Collector records).

As if Moorehead's resume wasn't full enough, he also served on the federal Board of Indian Commissioners. In fact, beyond the field archaeology and museum operation, some of Moorehead's best and most meaningful work was perhaps that accomplished on behalf of Native peoples. Appointed by President Theodore Roosevelt at the end of 1908, Moorehead dedicated considerable time and resources to this committee, which was in frequent opposition to other federal forces regarding policies toward

American Indians and Indian lands. Henry Fritz (1985) notes that Moorehead's appointment corresponds with a considerable revival in the efforts of the commission to reform the Indian Service and Bureau of Indian Affairs, with a decidedly Christian humanitarian philosophy, rather than one grounded in social science. Interestingly, Fritz (1985, 155–57) notes that Moorehead's upbringing in the Presbyterian church significantly influenced his perspective on Indian policy and that his connections with anthropologists in Washington DC led to his investigation of the rampant fraud and poor conditions at the White Earth Ojibwa (Anishinaabeg) reservation in northern Minnesota (also see Meyer 1994). At great personal risk Moorehead collected affidavits from homeless Ojibwa to provide proof of fraud perpetrated by land speculators and timber companies. He received a number of gifts from the Anishinaabeg people at White Earth, including a feathered war flag, pipes, and several intricately beaded bandolier bags now preserved in the museum (Bacon 2009). Moorehead's 1914 book *The American Indian in the United States, Period 1850–1914* relates directly to the investigations into abuse, fraud, and poor health of American Indians and particularly cases of land and timber fraud perpetrated by neighboring non-Indians.

Apparently Moorehead's effective advocacy for Native peoples while he served on the Board of Indian Commissioners influenced other members, those in other advocacy groups, and Congress. According to Fritz (1985, 161), it was Moorehead who first outlined many of the projects associated with the Indian New Deal of Franklin Roosevelt's administration, including a proposal to create a Bureau of Indian Arts and Industries. The enactment of the Indian Reorganization Act of 1934 was another example of Moorehead's influence.

This positive relationship with American Indians led to many interesting acquisitions for the Peabody Museum, including a horn spoon signed by Sitting Bull and a rifle that had belonged to Plains Cree leader Pitikwahanapiwiyin, or Poundmaker. In the 1930s Jack Red Cloud, son of Lakota Chief Red Cloud, presented his father's peace medal to the Peabody Museum at Andover for "safe keeping." This medal, struck at the Philadelphia Mint, had been presented to Red Cloud on behalf of U.S.

President Ulysses S. Grant and was frequently worn by the Lakota leader (Goodyear 2003, 23, 47, 154, 188, fig. 23).

Despite Moorehead's stymied Maine survey, published as *A Report on the Archaeology of Maine* in 1922, and his foiled plans for expansion of the museum, he persisted in excavations well into the late 1920s as mounting concern about "states' rights" and local archaeological protections increased. (For example, Moorehead expressed apprehension that some states were considering limits to work by outsiders, as mentioned in his annual report to the academy trustees, August 20, 1924, and in a letter to James H. Ropes, October 31, 1923, Robert S. Peabody Museum of Archaeology, Warren K. Moorehead records). By 1930, however, Moorehead had announced that he was refocusing his efforts away from fieldwork and on "a study of type distributions in the United States during the next six years" (Moorehead 1931; Schnell 1999, 36). Prior to this shift Moorehead led excavations at the Etowah mounds, near Cartersville, Georgia, where he excavated a remarkable collection of embossed copper, shell, and stone artifacts, which were featured in the *Etowah Papers* publication in 1932 (fig. 5). Like other important sites that he dug, Etowah played a pivotal role in understanding of the Mississippian culture. A small news item in the *Lewiston Daily Sun* from October 1933 gives some hint of Moorehead's activities at the Peabody Museum following publication of the Etowah project. Titled "Pre-De Soto Murals at Andover," the article reports on the installation of watercolors by Boston artist and architect Woldemar Ritter depicting artifacts from Georgia, Ohio, and Alabama. Today the niches are still ornamented by Ritter's larger-than-life exploration of Hopewellian and Mississippian artwork, no doubt Moorehead's indelible stamp on the museum after Alfred V. Kidder joined the Carnegie Institution in 1929.

Moorehead, as far as we know, was the only representative of the Peabody at the organizational meeting of the Society for American Archaeology, held in Pittsburgh in December 1934 (Griffin 1985; Guthe 1967). His concerns at that meeting were recorded in a report published in the first volume of *American Antiquity* a few years later (Society for American Archaeology 1935, 143); Moorehead was keenly interested in the role that avocational archaeologists would have in this new organization, which seemed to give

FIG. 5. Archaeologist Neil M. Judd (left) with Warren K. Moorehead and Alfred Vincent Kidder (right) at the Etowah site near Cartersville, Georgia, March 1927. Photographic collection of the Robert S. Peabody Museum of Archaeology.

preference to the professional. The following year the first annual meeting of the SAA convened in Samuel Phillips Hall at Phillips Academy, Andover, in conjunction with the meetings of the American Anthropological Association. Doug Byers gave the first presentation, and despite Moorehead's concerns, the new guard of the Peabody would play a significant role in the SAA organization and in the professionalization of the discipline throughout coming decades.

Alfred Vincent Kidder and the American Southwest

Although his appointment was vigorously opposed by Moorehead, Alfred Vincent Kidder (1885–1963) is perhaps the best known archaeologist affiliated with the Robert S. Peabody Museum (Givens 1992; Greengo 1968; Woodbury 1973). As already noted, Moorehead and Charles Peabody were planning a significant expansion of the museum facilities. Moorehead was in touch with architect Guy Lowell and was visiting other institutions for ideas. One complaint was that the existing museum building had little wall space for exhibits; another was the need to display and store the burgeoning collection. Guy Lowell's lovely building was really not suited to exhibitions and displays, a fact that continued to bother curators and directors into the 1990s. Academy Headmaster Alfred Stearns wrote to the academy's archaeology committee chair, Dr. James H. Ropes, suggesting that "for Goodness's sake let's get out of the country before the completed plan arrives," referring to the extensive additions envisioned by Peabody and Moorehead for their scaled-back synoptic exhibit (Alfred E. Stearns to James Hardy Ropes, February 23, 1915, Robert S. Peabody Museum of Archaeology, Warren K. Moorehead records). The trustees of the academy agreed with Stearns and communicated to Moorehead their concern that the museum lacked a clear plan.

Despite Moorehead's alarm at the academy's idea of a governing board, such an oversight committee was created and ultimately recommended an expanded program in southwestern archaeology. In 1912 a "Panel of Eminent Experts" was convened to clarify the mission of the Department of Archaeology. These scholars included William Henry Holmes, chair of the Bureau of American Ethnology; Frederic Ward Putnam, chairman of the Peabody Museum of Archaeology and Ethnology, Harvard College; Franz Boas, Columbia University, and Hiram Bingham III, Yale University (Phillips Academy Class of 1894). The committee determined that research would be the museum's objective for the future (Boas et al., "Report of the Advisory Committee on Archaeology to the Trustees of Phillips Academy," January 1914, Robert S. Peabody Museum of Archaeology, Warren K. Moorehead records). Moorehead opposed this plan, stating that while his interests had largely been confined to the eastern United States, he had in fact made forays into Arizona and New Mexico in 1892 and 1897. The outcome, however, was that Kidder joined the museum as director of the Southwestern Expedition, and the academy used funds from the original Peabody endowment to construct Peabody House directly behind the museum on Phillips Street (Domingue 1990, 127). Peabody House was completed in October 1915 and was dedicated to student activities, and Kidder, based on a recommendation from Roland Dixon and Hiram Bingham ("Recommendations of the Advisory Committee of the Department of Archaeology" No. 3, November 9, 1914, Robert S. Peabody Museum of Archaeology, Warren K. Moorehead records), began his groundbreaking work at Pecos that same year. The panel specifically recommended an extensive scientific examination of a region or particular site. Kidder, having recently earned a doctorate from Harvard, selected Pecos Pueblo in the Pecos Valley, New Mexico, because he believed that its deep midden deposits represented a very lengthy occupation. From summer 1915 until 1929, excluding army service in World War I, Kidder worked at Pecos Pueblo (see Browman and Williams 2013, 323–27).

Kidder's work in New Mexico is well known to contemporary archaeologists and, despite Moorehead's reservations, has been a point of pride for the Peabody for the decades since 1929, when Kidder joined the Carnegie Institution and refocused his work on Mesoamerica (see Cordell, this volume). Browman and Williams (2013, 325) explain that Kidder was connected to both the Harvard and Andover Peabody museums during this period, which accounts for the split collections from Pecos and other sites (see Bradley, this volume). Kidder is often referred to as the "Father of American Archaeology" because he demonstrated the importance of stratigraphic excavation in the Americas (Greengo 1968; Woodbury 1973). He also formed important and lasting collaborations with other scholars, such as Carl Guthe and Anna O. Shepard, who worked together to build the first deep-time chronology for the American Southwest, while Harvard's Earnest Hooton studied the human remains. The large number of extant Native American communities in the American Southwest offered opportunities to work with living peoples to understand the past. Guthe and Elsie Clews Parsons designed ethnoarchaeological research projects at Jemez and San Ildefonso pueblos in New Mexico to test the efficacy of analogy as a tool to understanding the past. In 1921 Kidder enlisted Guthe to conduct a study of Pueblo pottery making early in the career of San Ildefonso virtuoso Maria Martinez and her husband Julian (Guthe 1925). One of the Peabody's most distinctive accessions is a Maria Martinez demonstration set, which includes nine pottery vessels, showing each stage of manufacture and decoration, two *puki* or base molds, samples of pigments, and two of Maria's potter's smoothing stones. Pecos still loomed large in the halls of the Peabody in the 1930s when Phillips Academy resident artist Stuart Travis created a diorama of the pueblo (see Seldin, this volume).

Kidder's multidisciplinary approach in the Southwest prefigured the later work done by Frederick Johnson, Douglas Byers, and Scotty MacNeish at the Peabody and also directly resulted in establishment of the Pecos Conference (Givens 1992; Woodbury 1983). First held in 1927 and sponsored by the Robert S. Peabody Museum, it was the earliest regional meeting to foster archeological research. To this day the Pecos Conference serves as a venue where archaeologists and others share their latest discoveries in Southwest prehistory.

Douglas Swain Byers and the Eastern Establishment

In 1938 Douglas S. Byers (1903–1978) became the third director of the museum (MacNeish 1979). Byers began his career with a separate trajectory. Oliver LaFarge, a southwestern anthropologist who went to Guatemala in 1927 to study Maya people, took as his assistant Harvard undergraduate Douglas Byers. Although Byers had initially aspired to become a banker, this field experience changed his life. Byers first joined the Peabody as assistant director in 1933 after work at Harvard's Peabody Museum (Browman and Williams 2013, 371–72). He and Frederick Johnson conducted excavations between 1936 and 1938 at the Nevin and Richards sites in Blue Hill Bay on the central Maine coast. At the conclusion of the field season in 1938 Byers was appointed director of the museum.

His succession marked a fundamental change from the field methodology practiced by Moorehead. Byers used the more appropriate "scientific," or stratigraphic, method in his investigations of shell heaps in Maine. With his close associate Frederick Johnson as curator, Byers published "Some Methods Used in Excavating Eastern Shell Heaps" (Byers and Johnson 1939). While Max Uhle, Nels Nelson, William Dall, and others had already worked out much of this methodology, Harris (1989, 9) notes that at this time articles on stratigraphy were still extremely rare, citing the Byers and Johnson piece as an exception. Their use of the new excavation technique reflected the growing professionalization of the field of archaeology. The authors' stated goal for the article also is interesting—specifically the education of avocational archaeologists in more rigorous methods.

Byers realized that his scientifically gathered data should be analyzed by specialists trained in specific fields, rather than just viewed from the more general environmental perspective employed by such nineteenth-century naturalist scholars as Louis Agassiz, Jeffries Wyman, and Edward Sylvester Morse. Associated with larger museums at Harvard and in Salem, Massachusetts, these earlier scholars began to focus aspects of their research on excavated animal remains to infer past marine and terrestrial landscape conditions. By the mid-twentieth century understanding and documenting the natural history of past and present environments was a customary focus of New England archaeologists. This method was further refined by Byers and Johnson in their development of an *interdisciplinary* paleoecological approach. At the Nevin and Richards sites in Blue Hill, Maine, they recovered large samples of animal bones identifiable to genus and species. Interest was further piqued as the excavations at Nevin uncovered rich Late Archaic deposits in association with numerous swordfish, moose, and bird remains. The abundance of specimens and their analysis strengthened scholarly interest in understanding past marine and coastal conditions in the Northeast (see Robinson, this volume). While Byers's publication record is less extensive than that of some of his colleagues, the quality and focus is notable; his particular interest was in early sites, and he brought scientific methods—especially environmental archaeology—and collegial attention to the Archaic, including a forward-thinking collection of papers by five scholars published in *American Antiquity* in 1959 (Byers 1959a, 1959b). Scotty MacNeish (1979), writing of his friend, shares the comment of one colleague, who noted that Byers's publications were "good, solid stuff, the sort you might expect of a New England gentleman."

Doug Byers (fig. 6) was a strong motivating force in the development of archaeological societies. In 1935 the Robert S. Peabody Museum hosted twenty-seven scholars for the first meeting of the Society for American Archaeology. As earlier noted, while Warren Moorehead had been in attendance at the organizational meeting of the society the previous year, in December 1935 Byers presented the first paper at the conference, which was held in Samuel Phillips Hall on the Andover campus (Cooper 1936, 312–13; Griffin 1985). Four years later the Massachusetts Archaeological Society was founded at the Peabody Museum, which was then named as its official repository.

Byers also played a significant role in the formation of the New Hampshire and Maine archaeological societies. These new national and regional organizations facilitated the professional and amateur interaction that continues to this day. Byers and Johnson promoted several new publications as well. From 1939 to 1946 Byers served as editor of *American Antiquity,* the publication of the Society for American Archaeology. The professional research quality of the publication grew under his guidance. However, he also emphasized making the journal readable by eliminating scientific jargon. For example, Byers's October 1941 *American Antiquity* editorial points out that the avocational archaeologists outnumber the professional members of the society and discourages authors from too much technical jargon, suggesting that there may be a need to start a "Waddayamean Department."

FIG. 6. Douglas S. Byers pointing out the stratigraphy at Bull Brook. Photographic collection of the Robert S. Peabody Museum of Archaeology.

Frederick Johnson and the Art of Archaeological Organizing

Frederick Johnson (1904–1994) got his first break in anthropology at the age of thirteen, when his father, a general contractor, did some work on Frank Speck's cabin in Gloucester, Massachusetts (Baich 2010, 18; MacNeish 1996) (fig. 7). Speck was impressed by Johnson's outdoor and paddling skills and included him on an ethnological field trip to northern Quebec. Johnson went on to study with Speck at the University of Pennsylvania, but did not excel there, ultimately doing some graduate work at Harvard before joining the Peabody as curator in 1936 (Browman and Williams 2013, 372).

Johnson had a gift for organization, as shown by the multidisciplinary work at the Boylston Street Fish Weir in Boston's Back Bay neighborhood. Johnson assembled geologists, malacologists, wood and plant specialists, and other scientists to collaborate in the study of the wattle structures that often turned up in Back Bay construction (Décima and Dincauze 1998; Johnson 1942, 1949). The Boylston Street Fish Weir site has a tremendous legacy in Boston, including an annual celebration and a

FIG. 7. Frederick Johnson with his supplies for excavation, in front of the Robert S. Peabody Museum of Archaeology, early in the 1950s. Photographic collection of the Robert S. Peabody Museum of Archaeology.

campaign to erect a permanent sculpture commemorating the weirs (see the website of the Ancient Fishweir Project, http://www.fishweir.org/). And despite having left academia, in 1941 Johnson organized an influential conference on northeastern archaeology, ultimately published as *Man in Northeastern North America* and dedicated to his friend and mentor Frank Speck (Johnson 1946). Marilyn Norcini, writing about Johnson's contributions to Americanist ethnography in Canada, describes his interests in ethnology, linguistics, physical anthropology, and archaeology as well as his ability to work across disciplines (Norcini 2008, 107). There is still interest in his skill as a visual anthropologist, particularly in the extensive archive of photographs taken by Johnson during his fieldwork in the early 1930s among First Nations groups in Canada—a small selection of these images have appeared in exhibits, documentaries, and in the exhibit catalog *Mikwite'lmanej Mikmaqi'k: Let Us Remember the Old Mi'kmaq* produced by the Confederacy of Mainland Mi'kmaq and the Robert S. Peabody Museum (Bernard et al. 2001). During the 1940s and 1950s he was a key member of the Committee for the Recovery of Archaeological Remains (CRAR), an interest group responsible for successfully lobbying Congress to require salvage archaeology during big federally funded projects, like hydroelectric dams built in the years following World War II (Wendorf and Thompson 2002, 319). The CRAR required considerable strategic planning and political acumen on Johnson's part, as he enlisted his most influential and pragmatic colleagues to lobby Congress, including Alfred V. Kidder, whom he knew through his Phillips Academy connections. In many ways the CRAR prefigures the development of contemporary federal historic preservation legislation and cultural resource management archaeology. In his master's thesis Keith Baich (2010) argues that Johnson positioned himself to lead the American Anthropological Association's scientific committee on radiocarbon dating.

In contrast to Byers's upper-class connections, Johnson's were decidedly non-establishment. Together they were able to attract professional and amateur archaeologists alike. In addition to serving in leadership roles in the Society for American Archaeology and the American Anthropological Association, Johnson in particular worked with many avocational individuals and groups. He maintained decades-long correspondence with avocational archaeologists, like artist Ross Moffett, who excavated sites on Cape Cod (Del Deo 1994, 236–37, 287–88, 377; Kirakosian 2015).

The tenures of Byers and Johnson asserted the museum's role in educating the public about archaeology, one of the fundamental objectives of Robert Singleton Peabody. They felt it especially important to work more closely with artifact collectors, in order to tap their knowledge of local sites and collections as well as to teach them proper methodologies for excavation and documenting their collection. Byers and Johnson also updated the old museum exhibits, replacing the cases organized by artifact type with those that showcased their multidisciplinary work. In 1939 they installed a diorama titled "A Pawtucket Village on the Merrimack River, 500 Years Ago," built by the Guernsey-Pitman Studios in Cambridge. The diorama—still present today—drew on Johnson's extensive ethnographic work in Canada and illustrated features of daily life of both northern and southern New England. Byers and Johnson envisioned a series of seven or eight such dioramas, but only the Pawtucket and Pecos models were actually built (Douglas Byers to Philip L. Reed, April 2, 1936, and enclosure "Estimates of the Cost of Remodeling the Museum of the Department of Archaeology of Phillips Academy," Robert S. Peabody Museum of Archaeology, Richard S. MacNeish records). Other exhibits featured objects from their projects at sites like Nevin, Maine, and the Boylston Street Fish Weir in Boston, while others drew on older collections like those from Hopewell and Etowah (Exhibit diagrams, Robert S. Peabody Museum of Archaeology, Exhibition records).

The Growth of the Collections

As earlier noted, Robert Peabody's original bequest included approximately 38,000 archaeological objects. Moorehead (1906, 167–78) reports that within a few years the number of specimens had grown to over 55,928 objects. He notes the source of these collections—some from expeditions, others acquired from individuals. A scant amount of information on each item was recorded in a series of large ledger books, including a catalog number; by 1929 there were over 78,000 specimens recorded in the ledgers. Acquisitions also included ethnographic items, often acquired from tribal members with whom Moorehead was in contact or from collectors and private individuals. The growing collection and limited storage and exhibition space quickly became a problem, and Moorehead received permission to deaccession objects that he deemed duplicative. The Peabody archives contain correspondence, flyers, and advertisements distributed by Moorehead advertising the availability of specimens. In many cases objects were gifted, traded, or sold to other institutions or collectors. Especially interesting transactions include Moorehead's exchange for French Paleolithic specimens in the 1920s (see Gallou, this volume). Byers and Johnson developed a new cataloging system in the 1930s and continued to add archaeological specimens to the collections. In many cases the older collections were recataloged to address inconsistencies or missing and unreadable catalog numbers. Collections continued to grow under Byers and Johnson, including materials from their numerous field projects as well as exchanges with other institutions and gifts from those connected with Phillips Academy. The Pecos collections, in particular, were numerous and formed the basis for many exchanges with other museums far and wide, adding to the breadth of the collection. For example, Byers and Johnson traded Pecos artifacts with Chicago's Field Museum, receiving in turn William Duncan Strong's Inuit artifacts from Labrador (Hood 2008).

While the archaeological collections are generally known to scholars, a small but significant ethnographic collection exists as well. The sources of this material vary wildly, but with few exceptions they represent gifts made to the museum rather than collections made by ethnographers. These collections range from historic Pueblo pottery collected during the Pecos expedition to American Indian baskets and a recent acquisition of the Copeland H. Marks collections of Guatemalan textiles. One example of a fascinating yet little studied collection is the baskets given to the Peabody by Gertrude "Cosie" Hutchings Mills and her son William Mills. Cosie Hutchings was born in 1867 in California's Yosemite, where her father was an early entrepreneur. Her basket collection from this area is notable as it is well documented and primarily pre-1900, a time before there was extensive contact between Yosemite's original inhabitants and the growing number of tourists. The total Peabody basket collection is relatively small, numbering about 350 pieces, but has broad geographic coverage and exhibits a wide range of styles and traditions that support classroom use.

Ripley P. Bullen and Adelaide Kendall Bullen

Interest in archaeology, indeed as in other academic disciplines, fluctuates according to the needs and dictates of the larger society. It is a reality that has affected the Peabody, at times profoundly, at several stages (see Blustain, ch. 7). The national economy, during and after the World War II, was one such instance, necessitating contraction of Peabody research projects to a localized New England scale. However, New England was still relatively unknown archaeologically, providing an opportunity for Peabody investigators to expand understanding of its regional dynamics throughout prehistory. One of the Peabody's most prolific investigators at this time was Ripley Bullen.

Ripley Pierce Bullen (1902–1976) joined the Peabody in 1940 as a "student and helper" (Byers 1941, 8; Wilkerson 1978). He had left a career in engineering research and sales with General Electric to pursue his interests in archaeology. A modest stipend of ten dollars a month was enough to begin graduate studies at Harvard with Gordon Willey, while his wife, physical anthropologist Adelaide Kendall Bullen (1908–1987), enrolled in Radcliffe College as an undergraduate. While Ripley split his time between helping at the Peabody and working with the newly formed Massachusetts Archaeological Society, Adelaide worked at the Harvard Fatigue Laboratory. In 1941 they both attended the University of New Mexico's archaeological field school at Chaco Canyon. There they excavated a cluster of pueblo rooms and kivas; afterward spent a week excavating a cave site; and then enjoyed some sightseeing. A color slide in the Peabody photo archive shows Ripley, Adelaide, and their two sons, Dana Ripley and Pierce Kendall, touring Aztec ruin near Farmington, New Mexico. The two boys graduated from Phillips Academy in 1949 and 1952, respectively, and are credited as helping with fieldwork for the Shawsheen Valley survey (Bullen 1949, vii), a local project that was organized as a consequence of short gasoline rations during World War II.

Despite its modest scale, the Shawsheen River Valley survey produced some significant fieldwork. One site of particular importance was "Black Lucy's Garden," now called the Lucy Foster site. Through careful excavation and recovery of very scant historical documentation, Ripley and Adelaide were able to reconstruct the life of the African American woman who lived on the plot from 1815 to her death in 1845. Published by the Bullens in 1945, the account is historically important as the first excavation of an African American site. The site continues to have sustained interest from scholars, for example Vernon G. Baker, who reanalyzed the ceramics in the late 1970s (1978, 1980). Others, including Mark Leone and his colleagues (2005), suggest that the site materials are now ripe for reanalysis through the lens of gender studies. Whitney Battle-Baptiste (2011) worked with historian Barbara Brown and archaeologist Gene Winter to refine and contextualize the Lucy Foster story in just that way, including correcting a misunderstanding that Lucy had an illegitimate child with Job Foster.

The Bullens produced what became an impressive legacy of publications. Prior to leaving for a post with the Florida Park Service archaeology program in 1948, Ripley wrote more than forty monographs, articles, and reviews on New England archaeology between 1939 and 1951. His Shawsheen Valley report stood for many years as one of the few publications on Massachusetts archaeology available to scholars and avocationalists.

After the Florida Park Service dissolved its archaeology program, Ripley began as the first curator of social sciences at the Florida State Museum (now the Florida Museum of Natural History). Rochelle Marrinan (1999, 152–53), in her biographical essay on Adelaide, suggests that the Bullens were not accepted by the Florida archaeological community, possibly due to class differences and lack of graduate degrees. Despite criticism from other professional archaeologists, like the University of Florida's John Goggin, who thought their research lacked innovation, Ripley and Adelaide developed an extensive network of friends and collaborators among avocational archaeologists in Florida and the Caribbean (Figueredo 1978). Perhaps most ironic is that, contrary to Thomas Patterson's (1986) argument about conflicts between the so-called eastern establishment and the American "core culture," the Bullens seem to have bridged the gap successfully between professional archaeologists and the avocational community, continuing a Peabody Museum tradition that began with Warren Moorehead.

In addition to extensive fieldwork and publication, Ripley Bullen had other achievements. He persuaded members of the Massachusetts Archaeological Society to build site survey data that included mapped locations on fifteen-inch topographic maps and to compile the site data. The mapped data included sites documented by Moorehead as well as previously unknown locations, and they helped form the initial survey basis for Massachusetts and Maine. Records for nearly two thousand sites in Massachusetts were transferred to the master site file now managed by the Massachusetts Historical Commission. Likewise in 1968, Dean Snow, the first archaeologist on the faculty at the University of Maine, used Peabody

Museum survey data to help establish the statewide survey managed by the Maine Historic Preservation Commission.

Richard Stockton "Scotty" MacNeish and the Origins of Civilization

After thirty years as director, Byers retired in 1968, and Frederick Johnson became the fourth director of the Robert S. Peabody Museum (1968–69). He and Byers had already worked together for decades. In the early 1960s, before he became the Peabody's director, Johnson's focus on interdisciplinary research collaborations set the stage for investigation of the origins of plant and animal domestication, a seminal issue in archaeology. Previous reconnaissance by Richard Stockton MacNeish in the Tehuacán Valley in central Mexico had indicated that it was a good area to look for the beginnings of corn agriculture. A variety of natural scientists including paleobotanists, botanists and palynologists, geologists, malacologists, and other specialists were brought to Tehuacán to work under the field direction of Richard S. "Scotty" MacNeish (MacNeish et al. 1967, 6). The archaeological team included curator Fred Johnson; Kent Flannery, a zooarchaeologist; Irmgard Johnson, a specialist in archaeological textiles; Ángel García Cook and Antoinette Nelken-Terner, two students from the Mexican Escuela Nacional de Antropología, who excavated and devised artifact classification systems; and MacNeish's colleague, Frederick A. Peterson. Excavations at sites such as Coxcatlán Cave revealed deep stratified archaeological sequences that could be used to document changes in technology, subsistence patterns, and occupational density over time. This analysis resulted in state-of-the-art environmental reconstructions for the Tehuacán Valley (see Eubanks, this volume).

The Tehuacán Archaeological-Botanical Project was internationally recognized at a time of significant growth in the number of postgraduate degree recipients in the field of archaeology. The project was conceived at a time often referred to as the dawn of "New Archaeology" or a "Processual Phase" in the history of American archaeology (Willey and Sabloff 1993, 237–38, 262–63; also see Flannery [2001, 153–54] on the significance of the Tehuacán project). Clearly the deep professional connections and engaged dialogue regarding the origins of domestication expanded opportunities to

FIG. 8. Richard S. "Scotty" MacNeish making a site map. Photographic collection of the Robert S. Peabody Museum of Archaeology.

understand the past. One of the catalysts for such projects was competitive funding available from the National Science Foundation.

In 1970 Richard "Scotty" MacNeish (1918–2001) was appointed the fifth director of the Robert S. Peabody Museum (fig. 8). His style of interdisciplinary team archaeology focused on the origins of agriculture in the New World and resulted in major excavations in Mexico, Peru, and Belize (Ferrie 2001; Flannery 2001). The projects in the Tehuacán Valley in Mexico and the Ayacucho Valley in Peru established deep cultural sequences and provided crucial insight into the process of plant and animal domestication. The resulting oft-cited works, published between 1967 and 1983, are considered some of the most important interdisciplinary studies of twentieth-century American archaeology. MacNeish's contributions to archaeology were acknowledged through more than a dozen medals and honors, including election to the National Academy of Sciences in 1974. The Robert S. Peabody Museum managed the National Science Foundation grants for the Tehuacán and Ayacucho projects. Today it curates the artifactual, faunal, and floral type collections published in the five Tehuacán volumes. MacNeish's professional papers, field notes, maps, photographs, publications, and library of archaeological reports also are part of the Peabody Museum collections.

In addition to his focus on fieldwork, MacNeish was responsible for installation of a number of exhibits throughout the building. Photographs supplied by Mary Ellen Conaway, who had worked with MacNeish on exhibits, indicate that contemporary themes in anthropology like race and urbanization were showcased along with archaeology. There was one exhibit on MacNeish's work in the Tehuacán Valley. Another intriguing exhibit called *New World Puzzle Pieces* included an outsized jigsaw puzzle, with each piece featuring an object from a different site. Another, designed to resemble a giant slot machine, demonstrated that racial characteristics like skin color, hair, and facial features were not linked to intelligence. The point was driven home by identical casts of human brains under the likeness of professional boxers of different ethnicities! Other photos show that many of the exhibits were fabricated by MacNeish's friend Fred Johnson in the basement of the museum.

MacNeish departed the museum after acrimony in 1983, primarily due to a dispute regarding the insurance money paid to the academy after Peabody House burned in 1981. Tension already existed between MacNeish and the school as early as 1978, when he placed several ads in the newsletter of the American Anthropological Association; in May and June 1978 the "positions wanted" section of *Anthropology Newsletter* included two lines, "Scotty MacNeish is looking for a job. Please call 617/475–1326 (h) or 617/475–0248 (o)." Donald W. McNemar, headmaster of Phillips Academy, assumed responsibilities as acting director of the Peabody Museum. The museum was relatively dormant between 1983 and 1990, but the exhibits were still open to the general public.

James Bradley—the Peabody and NAGPRA

In 1990 the trustees of Phillips Academy hired James W. Bradley from the Massachusetts Historical Commission as the sixth director of the Peabody Museum (fig. 9). Bradley faced two major challenges. First, to bring the

FIG. 9. Director James W. Bradley and Honorary Curator Eugene Winter, in front of a portion of the museum's ceramic collection. Photographic collection of the Robert S. Peabody Museum of Archaeology.

museum into compliance with the Native American Graves Protection and Repatriation Act, which was signed into law in 1990 by President George H. W. Bush (Phillips Academy Class of 1942); and second, to review the original objectives of Robert S. Peabody's bequest with a thought toward building consensus on a new statement of the museum's educational mission—particularly within the academy. NAGPRA required a new, more respectful approach to Native peoples and mandated active consultation with tribes (see Bradley, this volume). Compliance with NAGPRA, in which the museum took a leadership role, resulted in a national model of partnership with Native American tribes. Over the years Bradley consulted with more than two hundred federally recognized tribal groups. His endeavors resulted in major repatriation efforts. As an example, the Robert S. Peabody Museum partnered with Harvard's Peabody Museum of Archaeology and Ethnology in a combined repatriation of human remains and special objects recovered during Kidder's excavation of Pecos Pueblo. Among the largest repatriation efforts under NAGPRA, the burials and objects were returned to the people of the Pueblo of Jemez. Working closely with tribes on NAGPRA forged enduring partnerships. The museum's collections oversight committee now boasts among its membership representatives of both the Pueblo of Jemez and the Mashpee Wampanoag Tribe.

It was during Bradley's tenure as director that the word "museum" was added to the name, replacing the word "foundation." This signaled an interest in establishing the museum as a more traditional, exhibition-centered institution. The exhibition program began almost immediately, with a grand reopening in 1991. Many of the exhibitions were grant funded and mounted in collaboration with other institutions, ranging from the University of Maine's Hudson Museum to the Yale Peabody Museum of Natural History. Major exhibitions included:

> Warren K. Moorehead: The Man Behind the Museum (1991)
> Images of Native Americans from Phillips Academy Collections (1991–92)
> Maps and Dreams: Native Americans and European Discovery (1992)
> Ten Thousand Years in Tewksbury: Archaeological Investigations of the Heath Brook Site, Tewksbury, Massachusetts (1993)
> Corn Hills on Cape Cod: Archaeological Investigations at Sandy's Point, Yarmouth, Massachusetts (1994)
> Pecos Pueblo: Crossroads of Cultures (1995, reinstalled 2005)
> Opus Travi: Stuart Travis at Andover 1928–1942 (1998)
> Origins and Ancestors: Investigating New England's Paleo Indians (1998)
> Blanket Statements: A Brief History of American Indian Trade Blankets (1999)
> Peru: From Village to Empire (2000–2001)
> Mikwite'lmanej Mikmaqi'k: Let Us Remember the Old Mi'kmaq (2000–2001)

Some of the exhibitions were accompanied by books and catalogs, including *Mikwite'lmanej Mikmaqi'k: Let Us Remember the Old Mi'kmaq*, which featured Fred Johnson's photography from 1930 and 1931. The exhibition project involved serious collaborative work with the Mi'kmaq community in Canada—the curators tell us in the introduction to the catalog that between 1997 and 1999 seven community meetings were held with tribal elders who shared stories about the people and places in Johnson's photographs (Bernard et al. 2001). Press coverage indicates that the exhibitions were well received; for example, Hollis Walker (1999) wrote in the *Santa Fe New Mexican*, "Though the Peabody's exhibits are designed for educational purposes, there's nothing simplistic or patronizing about Blanket Statements, created by curator Malinda Stafford Blustain." He went on to describe the exhibition, which drew on object and photographic collections, concluding: "What's striking about the Peabody exhibit besides the wonderful old black-and-white photos and the blankets, old and new is that it serves as an analogy for the history of the relationship between the indigenous population and the European newcomers." However, the limitations of the building—namely about 2,000 square feet of accessible exhibit space—along with competition from larger institutions in Boston and other nearby towns made the exhibition program unsustainable (see Blustain, chapter 7).

Bradley also revived the museum's research and educational functions and built clear linkages with other scholars and students at Phillips Academy. A significant component of the integration and use of the museum's resources resulted in the inauguration of the first of the Peabody's highly successful expeditionary learning programs for students, Pecos Pathways (see Randall and Toya, this volume).

The revitalization of research and the assessment of existing collections to comply with NAGPRA resulted in a concerted effort at modern collections management. As collections manager (1992–97) and later curator (1997–2001), Malinda Stafford Blustain assumed this responsibility, which focused on proper curation standards and the building of a relational database for better access to and management of the collection of some 500,000 or more objects. As relations improved with the Native community, educators, avocational archaeologists, and other museum and archaeology professionals, new life was breathed into the museum. The staff increased and assumed well-defined roles. Contributing to the task of assessing the collection were grants from the National Science Foundation and from patrons of Phillips Academy and the museum.

Malinda Stafford Blustain—the Peabody and Phillips Academy, Reunited

After Bradley left the Peabody in 2001, Malinda Stafford Blustain became interim director. In this role her two primary tasks were to accelerate an inventory of the museum's collections and to participate in an internal review of the Peabody and its operations by Phillips Academy. After successful conclusion of the review in 2004, she was appointed the seventh director of the Robert S. Peabody Museum. As director, her focus was on deploying the wealth of information embedded within the museum's collections toward the curricula of Phillips Academy and other schools. This fit in particularly well with school initiatives to promote cultural diversity in a global, multicultural world. Under Blustain's aegis the museum's advisory committee drafted a Strategic Plan, FY 2009–2013, and a detailed Report of Progress for FY 2004–2008 that won approval from the Phillips Academy Board of Trustees.

In March 2010 the executive board of the Society for American Archaeology traveled to Andover to commemorate the seventy-fifth anniversary of the society's first meeting there. The SAA executive board also met with officials of Phillips Academy to reaffirm and sustain the opportunities and successes achieved under Bradley and Blustain since the 1990s. The following year, at the seventy-sixth annual meeting of the SAA, the symposium that was the genesis of the present volume was held.

The museum's eighth director, Ryan Wheeler, now continues to strengthen the academic connection between the museum and academy. Current strategic themes include collaborative learning, collections stewardship, decolonizing museum practices, and sustainable outreach programs.

Robert Singleton Peabody would be very happy with where his creation is today. It has had a long and illustrious run that took it from a gift meant to kindle interest in the sciences at an exclusive New England preparatory school to the vanguard of scientific investigation on a regional, then national, then international scale; to an exemplary repatriation program that emphasized institutional collaborations and fostering close ties with tribes; and to development of innovative, collections-based educational initiatives. It is a legacy that reflects deep commitment from its directors and staff, the archaeology and museum communities, tribes, students, teachers, volunteers, and all others within its singular sphere of influence.

NOTE

Gene Winter (1927–2014), co-author of this overview, worked with six of the eight Peabody directors and is a prime example of the interest and dedication found in the archaeology community. In recognition of his contributions the SAA awarded him the Crabtree Award for amateur work, and he was the first recipient of the Eugene C. Winter Award established by the Robert S. Peabody Museum.

REFERENCES

Bacon, Anabel. 2009. "Warren King Moorehead: The Peabody Museum's First Cura-tor, a Champion of Native American Rights." *Andover Bulletin* (Spring):22–23.

Baich, Keith D. 2010. "American Scientists, Americanist Archaeology: The Committee on Radioactive Carbon 14." Master's thesis, Portland State University.

Baker, Vernon G. 1978. *Historical Archaeology at Black Lucy's Garden, Andover, Massa-chusetts: Ceramics from the Site of a Nineteenth Century Afro-American.* Papers of the Robert S. Peabody Foundation for Archaeology 8. Andover MA: Phillips Academy.

———. 1980. "Archaeological Visibility of Afro-American Culture: An Example from Black Lucy's Garden, Andover, Massachusetts." In *Archaeological Perspec-tives on Ethnicity in America*, edited by Robert L. Schuyler, 29–37. Amityville NY: Baywood Publishing.

Battle-Baptiste, Whitney. 2011. *Black Feminist Archaeology*. Walnut Creek CA: Left Coast Press.

Bernard, Tim, Catherine Anne Martin, and Leah Rosenmeier. 2001. *Mikwite'lmanej Mikmaqi'k: Let Us Remember the Old Mi'kmaq*. Confederacy of Mainland Mi'kmaq and the Robert S. Peabody Museum of Archaeology. Halifax, Nova Scotia: Nimbus Publishing.

Bricker, Harvey M. 2002. "George Grant MacCurdy: An American Pioneer of Palaeo-anthropology." In *New Perspectives on the Origins of Americanist Archaeology*, edited by David L. Browman and Stephen Williams, 265–85. Tuscaloosa: University of Alabama Press.

Browman, David L. 2002. "Origins of Stratigraphic Excavation in North America: The Peabody Museum Method and the Chicago Method." In *New Perspectives on the Origins of Americanist Archaeology,* edited by David L. Browman and Stephen Williams, 242–64. Tuscaloosa: University of Alabama Press.

———. 2003 Origins of Americanist Stratigraphic Excavation Methods. In *Picking the Lock of Time: Developing Chronology in American Archaeology,* edited by James Truncer, 22–39. Gainesville: University Press of Florida.

Browman, David L., and Stephen Williams. 2013. *Anthropology at Harvard: A Biographical History, 1790–1940.* Monographs of the Peabody Museum of Archaeology and Ethnology, Harvard University 11. Cambridge MA: Peabody Museum Press.

Bullen, Ripley P. 1949. *Excavations in Northeastern Massachusetts.* Papers of the Robert S. Peabody Foundation for Archaeology 1, no. 3. Andover MA: Phillips Academy.

Byers, Douglas S. 1939. "Warren King Moorehead." *American Anthropologist* 41, no. 2:286–94.

———. 1941. "Annual Report, Department of Archaeology, 1940." Accessed October 20, 2016. https://archive.org/details/robertspeabodymu1940doug.

———. 1959a. "The Eastern Archaic: Some Problems and Hypotheses." *American Antiquity* 24, no. 3:233–56.

———. 1959b. "An Introduction to Five Papers on the Archaic Stage." *American Antiquity* 24, no. 3:229–33.

Byers, Douglas S., and Frederick Johnson. 1939. "Some Methods Used in Excavating Eastern Shell Heaps." *American Antiquity* 4, no. 3:189–212.

Christenson, Andrew L. 2011. "Who Were the Professional Archaeologists of 1900? Clues from the Work of Warren K. Moorehead." *Bulletin of the History of Archaeology* 21, no. 1:4–23.

Cooper, John M. 1936. "Program, Joint Meeting of the American Anthropological Association, American Folk-Lore Society, and Society for American Archaeology, Held at Phillips Academy, Andover, Massachusetts." *American Anthropologist* 38, no. 2:311–13.

Décima, Elena B., and Dena F. Dincauze. 1998. "The Boston Back Bay Fish Weirs." In *Hidden Dimensions: The Cultural Significance of Wetland Archaeology,* edited by Kathryn N. Bernick, 157–72. Vancouver: University of British Columbia Press.

Del Deo, Josephine C. 1994. *Figures in a Landscape: The Life and Times of the American Painter, Ross Moffett, 1888–1971.* Virginia Beach VA: Donning Company.

Domingue, Robert A. 1990. *Phillips Academy, Andover, Massachusetts: An Illustrated History of the Property.* Wilmington MA: RAD Publishing.

Faxon, Susan C. 2000. "Forces of Change: The Transformation of the Campus, 1900–1932." In *Academy Hill: The Andover Campus, 1778 to the Present,* 101–43. New York: Princeton Architectural Press.

Ferrie, Helke. 2001. "An Interview with Richard S. MacNeish." *Current Anthropology* 42, no. 5:715–35.

Figueredo, Alfredo E. 1978. "Ripley Pierce Bullen, 1902–1976: A Memoir." *Journal of the Virgin Islands Archaeological Society* 5:3–5.

Flannery, Kent V. 2001. "In Memoriam, 'There Were Giants in those Days,' Richard Stockton MacNeish, 1918–2001." *Ancient Mesoamerica* 12:149–57.

Fritz, Henry E. 1985. "The Last Hurrah of Christian Humanitarian Indian Reform: The Board of Indian Commissioners, 1909–1918." *Western Historical Quarterly* 16, no. 2:147–62.

Givens, Douglas R. 1992. *Alfred Vincent Kidder and the Development of Americanist Archaeology*. Albuquerque: University of New Mexico Press.

Goodyear, Frank H., III. 2003. *Red Cloud: Photographs of a Lakota Chief*. Lincoln: University of Nebraska Press.

Greengo, Robert E. 1968. "Alfred Vincent Kidder 1885–1963." *American Anthropologist* 70, no. 2:3210–325.

Griffin, James B. 1985. "The Formation of the Society for American Archaeology." *American Antiquity* 50, no. 2:261–71.

Guthe, Carl. 1925. *Pueblo Pottery Making: A Study at the Village of San Ildefonso*. New Haven: Yale University Press.

———. 1967. "Reflections on the Founding of the Society for American Archaeology." *American Antiquity* 32, no. 4:433–40.

Harris, Edward. 1989. *Principles of Archaeological Stratigraphy*. New York: Academic Press.

Hood, Bryan C. 2008. *Towards an Archaeology of the Nain Region, Labrador*. Contributions to Circumpolar Anthropology 7, edited by William W. Fitzhugh. Washington DC: Arctic Studies Center, National Museum of Natural History, Smithsonian Institution.

Johnson, Frederick, ed. 1942. *The Boylston Street Fishweir: A Study of the Archaeology, Biology, and Geology of a Site on Boylston Street in the Back Bay District of Boston, Massachusetts*. Papers of the Robert S. Peabody Foundation for Archaeology 2. Andover MA: Phillips Academy.

———. 1946. *Man in Northeastern North America*. Papers of the Robert S. Peabody Foundation for Archaeology 3. Andover MA: Phillips Academy.

———. 1949. *The Boylston Street Fishweir II: A Study of the Geology, Palaeobotany, and Biology of a Site on Stuart Street in the Back Bay District of Boston, Massachusetts*. Papers of the Robert S. Peabody Foundation for Archaeology 4, no. 1. Andover MA: Phillips Academy.

Kidder, Alfred V. 1958. *Pecos, New Mexico: Archaeological Notes*. Papers of the Robert S. Peabody Foundation for Archaeology 5. Andover MA: Phillips Academy.

Kirakosian, Katie. 2015. "Mapping the Social Worlds of Shell Midden Archaeology in Massachusetts." *Bulletin of the History of Archaeology* 25, no. 2. Accessed October 20, 2016. http://doi.org/10.5334/bha.260.

Knipmeyer, James. 2006. *In Search of a Lost Race: The Illustrated American Exploring Expedition of 1892*. Bloomington IN: Xlibris.

Leone, Mark P., Cheryl Janifer LaRoche, and Jennifer J. Babiarz. 2005. "The Archaeology of Black Americans in Recent Times." *Annual Review of Anthropology* 34:575–98.

MacCurdy, George G. 1948. "Charles Peabody 1867–1939." *Bulletin of the American School of Prehistoric Research* 16:xxiii–xxiv.

MacNeish, Richard S. 1979. "Douglas Swain Byers 1903–1978." *American Antiquity* 44, no. 4:708–10.

———. 1996. "Frederick Johnson 1904–1994." *American Antiquity* 61, no. 2:269–73.

MacNeish, Richard S., Antoinette Nelken-Terner, and Irmgard W. Johnson. 1967. *The Prehistory of the Tehuacán Valley*, vol. 2: *The Non-Ceramic Artifacts*. Austin: University of Texas Press.

Marrinan, Rochelle A. 1999. "Best Supporting Actress? The Contributions of Adelaide K. Bullen." In *Grit-Tempered: Early Women Archaeologists in the Southeastern United States*, edited by Nancy Marie White, Lynne P. Sullivan, and Rochelle A. Marrinan, 148–63. Gainesville: University Press of Florida.

Meyer, Melissa L. 1994 *The White Earth Tragedy: Ethnicity and Dispossession at a Minnesota Anishinaabe Reservation*. Lincoln: University of Nebraska Press.

Moorehead, Warren King. 1902. *The Field Diary of an Archaeological Collector*. Andover MA.

———. 1906. "A Sketch of Mr. Robert Singleton Peabody." In *A Narrative of Explorations in New Mexico, Arizona, Indiana, Etc., Together with a Brief History of the Department*, edited by Warren K. Moorehead, 26–29. Bulletin of the Department of Archaeology 3. Andover MA: Phillips Academy.

———. 1910. *The Stone Age in North America*. 2 vols. Boston: Houghton Mifflin.

———. 1914. *The American Indian in the United States, Period 1850–1914: The Present Condition of the American Indian; His Political History and Other Topics; A Plea for Justice*. Andover MA: Andover Press.

———. 1922. *Report on the Archaeology of Maine: Being a Narrative of Explorations in That State, 1912–1920, Together with Work at Lake Champlain, 1917*. Andover MA: Andover Press.

———. 1931. "Phillips Academy," in Anthropological News and Notes, *American Anthropologist* 33, no 2:299.

———. 1938. "The Archaeology Department of Phillips Academy: A Brief History." *Phillips Bulletin* 32, no. 3:6–11. Andover MA: Phillips Academy.

———. 2000a. *The Cahokia Mounds*. Edited and with an introduction by John E. Kelly. Tuscaloosa: University of Alabama Press.

———. 2000b. *Exploration of the Etowah Site in Georgia: The Etowah Papers*, reprint edition. Gainesville: University Press of Florida.

Norcini, Marilyn. 2008. "Frederick Johnson's Canadian Ethnology in the Americanist Tradition." *Histories of Anthropology Annual* 4:106–34.

O'Brien, Michael J., and R. Lee Lyman, eds. 2001. *Setting the Agenda for American Archaeology: The National Research Council Archaeological Conferences of 1929, 1932, and 1935.* Tuscaloosa: University of Alabama Press.

Parker, Franklin. 1971. *George Peabody: A Biography.* Nashville: Vanderbilt University Press.

Patterson, Thomas C. 1986. "The Last Sixty Years: Toward a Social History of Americanist Archeology in the United States." *American Anthropologist* 88, no. 1:7–26.

Petraglia, Michael, and Richard Potts. 2004. *The Old World Paleolithic and the Development of a National Collection.* Smithsonian Contributions to Anthropology 48. Washington DC: Smithsonian Institution.

"Pre-De Soto Murals at Andover." *Lewiston Daily Sun* (Lewiston ME), October 13, 1933, 4.

Robert S. Peabody Museum of Archaeology. Collector records (1922–1990) 101.04. Andover: Phillips Academy.

———. Exhibition records 04.01 Andover: Phillips Academy.

———. Founder records (1898–1903) 00.00. Andover: Phillips Academy.

———. Richard S. MacNeish records (1950s–early 1980s) 01.04. Andover: Phillips Academy.

———. Robert S. Peabody correspondence and other materials (1863–1904) 101.14 Andover: Phillips Academy.

———. Warren K. Moorehead records (1890s–1930s) 01.02 Andover: Phillips Academy.

Schnell, Frank T., Jr. 1999. "Margaret E. Ashley: Georgia's First Professional Archaeologist." In *Grit-Tempered: Early Women Archaeologists in the Southeastern United States*, edited by Nancy Marie White, Lynne P. Sullivan, and Rochelle A. Marrinan, 25–41. Gainesville: University Press of Florida.

Snead, James E. 2016. "Relic Hunters in the White City: Artifacts, Authority, and Ambition at the World's Columbian Exposition." In *Coming of Age in Chicago: The 1893 World's Fair and the Coalescence of American Anthropology*, edited by Curtis M. Hinsley and David R. Wilcox, 337–61. Lincoln: University of Nebraska Press.

Society for American Archaeology. 1935. "The Society for American Archaeology Organization Meeting." *American Antiquity* 1, no 2:141–51.

Walker, Hollis. 1999. "Out of Context: Indian Trade Blankets Are Back in Vogue." *Santa Fe New Mexican*, June 4, p. 8.

Wendorf, Fred, and Raymond H. Thompson. 2002. "The Committee for the Recovery of Archaeological Remains: Three Decades of Service to the Archaeological Profession." *American Antiquity* 67, no. 2:317–30.

Wilkerson, S. Jeffrey K. 1978. "Ripley Pierce Bullen, 1902–1976." *American Antiquity* 43, no. 4:622–31.

Williams, Stephen. 1999. "A Tribute to Charles Peabody." Typescript on file, Robert S. Peabody Museum of Archaeology, Phillips Academy, Andover MA.

Willey, Gordon R., and Jeremy A. Sabloff. 1993. *A History of American Archaeology*, 3rd edition. New York: W. H. Freeman.

Woodbury, Richard B. 1973. *Alfred V. Kidder*. Leaders of Modern Anthropology Series. New York: Columbia University Press.

———. 1983. "Looking Back at the Pecos Conference." *Kiva* 48, no. 4:251–66.

Chapter 2

A History of Research

FOCUSING ON THE PEOPLING OF THE AMERICAS

James B. Richardson III and James M. Adovasio

Maintaining only a relatively small research staff throughout its 112 years of operation, the Robert S. Peabody Museum of Archaeology has nonetheless played a central role in the highly contentious avenue of research into the peopling of the Americas. Its significant research accomplishments have earned both national and international acclaim.[1] Intertwined throughout this chapter are accounts of the Peabody's staff and of their achievements, especially the stratigraphic and dating revolutions that proved so crucial in analyzing the manner and timing of the arrival of the First Americans.

The American Paleolithic, 1860–1900

The search for the First Americans began in earnest after 1860, when stone tools and human remains were found in association with Paleolithic-age mammals in Europe—a breakthrough that ran directly counter to the accounts of human antiquity in biblical and existing historical sources. This development spurred American archaeologists to "discover" an American Paleolithic contemporary with that of Europe, based on the assumption that the geological strata where Pleistocene artifacts were found in Europe were of equal age to their counterparts in eastern North America. This bandwagon approach yielded apparent results when physician Charles Conrad Abbott investigated the Trenton Gravels in New Jersey in the 1870s and found crude tools similar to their presumed European counterparts.

FIG. 10.Warren K. Moorehead and crew doing a survey along the Merrimack River. Photographic collection of the Robert S. Peabody Museum of Archaeology.

Abbott, however, argued that they were not made by ancestors of the American Indians but by a glacial age population and were of similar antiquity and technology to those of the European Paleolithic (Abbott 1881; Putnam et al. 1888).

Frederic Ward Putnam, a major figure in North American archaeology, entered the fray in support of Abbott. Putnam was the first director of the Peabody Museum at Salem, and at Harvard he served both as a curator and as a director (1874–1909; Mark 1980; Tozzer 1933). Subsequent investigators found crude bifacial tools throughout the Mid-Atlantic and the Midwest, and by the late 1880s most investigators accepted the notion of an American Paleolithic.

As David Meltzer (2015) has discussed in detail, the debate on the purported ancient stone tools is a complicated story. The acceptance of the American Paleolithic was the last straw for John Wesley Powell, the head of the Bureau of American Ethnology (1879–1902) and director of the United States Geological Survey (1880–94), who felt that the scientific approach of the claimants was invalid. In the interest of restoring scientific rigor to the discipline, Powell transferred William Henry Holmes from the Geological Survey to the Bureau of American Ethnology in 1889, changing Holmes's title to archaeologist, and directing him to investigate the claims for Paleolithic-like tools in North America. Holmes insisted that conclusive proof of the age of Paleolithic tools must come from secure geological contexts in order to provide their geological age. When Holmes entered the debate, the Great Paleolithic War broke out (Adovasio and Page 2002; Meltzer 2005, 2009, 2015). At Piney Branch Creek near Washington DC, Holmes recovered crude bifacial tools that superficially resembled French Acheulean hand axes. He also visited other sites of purported Paleolithic age, such as Abbott Farm, in an effort to discredit the notion of an American Paleolithic (Mark 1980, 149–50). By 1893 he claimed, "The fact is that a large part of the literature relating to the Paleolithic and Ice Age questions is so hopelessly embarrassed with the blunders and misconceptions that it is but little more than a stumbling-block to science" (Holmes 1893, 30). Holmes concluded that the crude bifacial tools he had excavated were in fact blanks reflecting the initial stages in the manufacture of more sophisticated tools. Rather than ancient tools, claimed Holmes, these tools merely represented manufacturing debris from quarry sites that were visited by more recent American Indians (Holmes 1890; Mark 1980).

Moorehead and the American Paleolithic Debate

Warren King Moorehead (1866–1939) had become interested in artifact collecting in Ohio (fig. 10). By the age of twenty, with self-financed crews, he had amassed a large collection from excavating numerous sites, including Fort Ancient, a huge Hopewell earthwork in Warren County (Moorehead 1890). He further enhanced his reputation as a professional archaeologist by publishing extensively on his work throughout his career (Burns 2008, 15–17; Byers 1939; Christenson 2011; Kelly in Moorehead 2000; Weatherford 1956).

When Putnam was appointed chief of the Ethnological Section

responsible for assembling archaeological displays for the Columbian Exposition, the World's Fair held in Chicago in 1893, he hired Moorehead to provide artifacts for the Ohio displays. For the exposition Moorehead selected a mound complex at Captain M. C. Hopewell's farm in the Scioto Valley of Ohio, earning him fame for identifying what would ultimately be known as the Hopewell tradition (Moorehead 1922a). The display of the elaborate Hopewell funerary artifacts of copper, obsidian, mica, and stone at the Columbian Exposition brought heightened attention to his work, as did the publication of *Primitive Man in Ohio* (Moorehead 1892), which summarized all his previous fieldwork in that state. In 1894 Moorehead was hired as the first curator of the Ohio Archaeological and Historical Society and curator of the Museum of Ohio State University in Columbus, where he stayed until 1897.

Moorehead's November 1895 article on mound exploration in the *Philadelphia Press* (Moorehead 1906a, 17) alerted Robert Singleton Peabody to Moorehead's archaeological and collecting skills (Moorehead 1906b; Williams 1999). Between 1897 and 1901 Moorehead supplied Peabody with artifacts from sites throughout the United States (Moorehead 1902a). Moorehead appears to have been held in high esteem by Peabody, who not only supported Moorehead's research but paid for his two-year recovery from tuberculosis at a sanitarium in Saranac Lake, New York, after spending time in Arizona seeking a cure. Ever diligent, while in the sanitarium Moorehead continued to carry out his artifact collecting via mail. In gratitude and friendship, Moorehead named his second son Singleton Peabody Moorehead.[2]

His association with Peabody paid great dividends, for in 1901 Peabody and his wife, Margaret, provided the funds to establish a Department of Archaeology at Phillips Academy in Andover. On May 1, 1901, Peabody donated 38,000 artifacts, now known as the Founder's Collection, to the department. Many of these artifacts had been sold to Peabody by none other than Moorehead, who was subsequently hired as the museum's first curator.[3] Phillips Academy Principal Cecil F.P. Bancroft was to have been the museum's first director but died before he could assume the post, so Peabody's son Charles was selected as honorary director. Charles

Peabody held this post through the early 1920s and was succeeded in 1924 by Moorehead, who served until his retirement in 1938 (Barss 1934, 14; Moorehead 1901).

Moorehead spent the years 1888–90 as an assistant to Thomas Wilson in the Department of Prehistoric Archaeology of the United States National Museum, Smithsonian Institution. Wilson was a French specialist who had spent five years at the famous Paleolithic sites at Abbeville and in the Dordogne Valley. Wilson advocated that there was a New World Paleolithic, asked for collectors to send to the Smithsonian the quantities of crude (i.e., Paleolithic) stone tools they had in their collections, and wrote up the results (Wilson 1890, 680). The 209 responding collectors reported more than 6,000 supposed Paleolithic tools, which Wilson felt were similar to Paleolithic tools in Europe (Wilson 1889, 1890). Moorehead devoted his first chapter of *Primitive Man in Ohio* (1892) to Paleolithic man, noting such items as a Paleolithic tool found eight feet deep in the gravels near Madisonville in 1885, authenticated by Putnam. Another Paleolithic artifact, verified by George Frederick Wright, professor of geology at Oberlin College, was recovered from a terrace gravel deposit near New Comerstown in 1889 (Moorehead 1892, 1–9). Yet Moorehead remained unconvinced that an American Paleolithic actually existed. Only a year after the publication of *Primitive Man in Ohio*, writing in *Science*, Moorehead (1893, 192) noted that despite extensive survey of Ohio gravel deposits for Paleolithic finds:

> My men, all good specimen hunters, quick to see an artificial object, could never find them in any kind of stratified gravel. I lay no claim to a knowledge of the gravels, but had implements been found in them by geologists from Columbus or Cincinnati they would have examined and named the deposits after me. During the coming summer, I will spend as much time as possible in a further search for [Paleolithic] implements. . . . Any number can be found on the surface, but as yet I have not been able to find one in gravel layers. Probably my eyes are not sharp enough.

It appears that even though Moorehead was closely associated with Putnam and Wilson, leading proponents of an American Paleolithic, he clearly preferred to take a wait-and-see approach in his subsequent publications

(Moorehead 1900, 188–89; 1910, 2:350–51; 1917, 46). At one point he declared, "It is not my purpose to attempt to decide this question—as to the age of man on the American continent" (Moorehead 1910, 1:34).

In later years Alfred V. Kidder, who investigated Pecos Pueblo, New Mexico, for the Peabody, lamented that the period of the American Paleolithic debate deterred further investigation into the timing of the arrival of humans into the Americas, noting (Kidder 1936, 143–44):

> As everyone knows, the discovery of the European Paleolithic was followed by attempts to identify, in America, the traces of an occupation, equally remote. The often ill-founded and sometimes preposterous claims for the great age of man in the New World brought about the then very salutary reactions of Holmes and Hrdlička.[4] But these gentlemen eventually swung very far to the right. Indeed, they became so ultraconservative that their attacks upon any find even of respectable age were so merciless, that further purposeful search for early remains was most harmfully discouraged. Paleontologists and geologists, with whom for the past forty years archaeologists should be working upon the problem of man's arrival in America, were actually frightened away from participating in the investigation.

The Stratigraphic and Dating Revolutions

Kidder (1936, 143) commented further upon the question of dating:

> All through the years that we excavated at Pecos we were bombarded with questions. Tourists visited our work in shoals, for the highway passes close to the ruin. We had people of every sort, and their queries ran the entire gamut of human curiosity. But there was one that we always knew would, sooner or later, be asked by every visitor. From ranchman, movie director, hitch-hiker, plutocrat, we had the inevitable "How old!" And our modest guesses that a thousand or, in moments of exaltation, fifteen hundred years would carry back to the founding of Pecos. . . . We were often told that Pompeii (we got awfully sick of Pompeii) was older than that.

The key to determining the age of specific archaeological phenomena is rigorous excavation technique, as it permits the recognition and accurate delineation of stratigraphy and facilitates the use of dating techniques to determine the age of associated cultural assemblages. In this regard, the Peabody Museum made significant contributions. Its director Charles Peabody (1867–1939) was among the first to recognize that the different depositional levels of sites reflect different time periods. Charles Peabody was an accomplished archaeologist who had received a bachelor's degree from the University of Pennsylvania in 1889 and a PhD in philology from Harvard in 1893. At Harvard he was trained by Putnam and served as instructor/assistant in European archaeology, and later (1913–39) as curator of European archaeology at the Peabody Museum of Harvard University.[5] He also co-founded the American School of Prehistoric Research in 1920 (Bricker 2002; MacCurdy 1948; Williams 1999) and conducted extensive archaeological research in Europe (Bricker 2002, 277–80).

Charles Peabody used a grid system to provide horizontal and vertical control in the excavation of cultural deposits, techniques he learned from Putnam, his mentor at Harvard. This protocol became known as the Putnam or Peabody Museum method of stratigraphic excavation (Browman 2002). Although the stratigraphic revolution is said to have begun after 1910 (Browman and Givens 1996, 80; Willey and Sabloff 1993, 96), the identification of discrete cultural strata reflecting time depth and chronological differences actually began in the last quarter of the nineteenth century (Lyman et al. 1997, 20–31).

Peabody exemplified the use of precise field methodology in the excavation of archaeological sites in the eastern United States. Among the earliest stratigraphic excavations was Peabody's 1901–2 research at Dorr and Edward's Mound (also known as the Oliver Mounds) in Coahoma County, Mississippi, where he employed a grid system and metric measurements in the identification of two cultural strata (Peabody 1904).[6] In 1903, working with Moorehead at Jacob's Cavern in Missouri, Peabody further refined his excavation methods to record accurate artifact provenience and identified three discrete cultural strata (O'Brien and Lyman 1999, 154–57; Peabody and Moorehead 1904) (fig. 11). At Bushey Cavern in

FIG. 11. Jacob's Cavern with grid stakes. Photographic collection of the Robert S. Peabody Museum of Archaeology.

Cavetown, Maryland, in 1905, Peabody and Moorehead not only gridded the site but recorded the artifacts by depth and the stratigraphic layers by depth and color (Peabody 1908).

Peabody conducted additional systematic mound excavations in North Carolina. In 1918 he returned to Mississippi to excavate the Spendthrift and Alligator sites (Peabody 1910; Williams 1999). Later excavations of Jacob's Cavern by amateur archaeologist L. B. Taylor (the site's owner) produced what was said to be a carving on bone of a mammoth or mastodon. When Moorehead was unable to excavate the site further, he suggested that Taylor contact Clark Wissler of the American Museum of Natural History. Wissler in turn encouraged his colleague Nels C. Nelson to excavate the site for evidence of early man. The 16-meter trench Nelson excavated failed to produce any early cultural deposits (O'Brien 1996, 158–69). The elephant carving was pronounced a fake, but as it has not been located since the excavations by the American Museum of Natural History, it is not possible to authenticate the carving. The recent discovery of a Pleistocene extinct animal bone with a mammoth image at Vero Beach, Florida, has undergone intensive analysis, and Barbara Purdy (2012) has concluded that this carving may well be genuine, thus the importance of locating the Jacobs Cavern specimen for reanalysis.

Kidder and the Stratigraphic and Dating Revolution

The Advisory Committee on Archaeology of Phillips Academy proposed a major excavation program in the Southwest (Fowler 2000, 286; Givens 1992, 38; Kidder 1924, 1; Schwartz 2000; Willey 1967, 297; Woodbury 1973). Chairman of the committee was James Hardy Ropes, a graduate of Phillips Academy and the Andover Theological Seminary, a member of the Phillips Academy Board of Trustees, and the Bussey Professor of New Testament Criticisms and Interpretation at Harvard. The other committee members were Roland Dixon of Harvard, one of Kidder's professors, and Hiram Bingham of Yale University, a graduate of Phillips Academy and a Harvard PhD who in 1911 achieved fame for discovering Machu Picchu in Peru. In 1915 they selected Alfred Vincent Kidder (1885–1963) to head up the research program. Kidder had a doctorate in anthropology from Harvard (1914) and had already spent eight seasons of fieldwork in the Southwest.

He selected Pecos Pueblo for his research. After the first field season, when he excavated by arbitrary levels, he recognized the stratigraphic relationships between ceramic types and began to excavate by stratigraphic levels. He noted that ceramic types in lower levels were different from those in the upper levels and diagramed the relative changes of ceramic types against their stratigraphic position, creating a ceramic stratigraphy that reflected time depth (Cordell, this volume; Kidder 1924, 1925, 3–4, 1958; O'Brien and Lyman 1999, 167–72). In *An Introduction to Southwest Archaeology* Kidder indicates that the "ideal form of chronological evidence is provided by stratigraphy, i.e., when remains of one type [of pottery] are found underlying below those of another" (Kidder 1924, 45–46). His research at Pecos refined approaches and provided new techniques of analysis to identify cultural stratigraphy based on changes in artifacts within natural strata. These methods included attempts to date the artifact assemblages.

In summer 1921, the only year he did not go to Pecos (due to the illness of his mother), Kidder applied his stratigraphic techniques to the Andover town dump. He examined a sewer trench dug through the garbage that had been dumped over the bank since the eighteenth century. He developed a stratigraphy-based chronology using lighting devices (ranging from candles to light bulbs) very much in the way he seriated style changes in ceramics in the Pecos middens (Thompson 2002).

Despite its support of Kidder's work at Pecos, the Robert S. Peabody Museum faced a conflict of purpose. Moorehead, then its curator, proposed reorganizing the Department of Archaeology. Apparently he was upset that his research in the Southwest was not fully recognized and his title was not comparable to Kidder's (director of southwestern expeditions). Moorehead wanted to be named either director in charge of field work and explorations, or director of New England archaeology. He complained that his fieldwork had been unnecessarily curtailed because substantial funds were diverted to Kidder's Pecos project (1916–20) and to the hiring of Carl E. Guthe as the project's full-time assistant director (Brief outline of a conversation between Principal Alfred E. Stearns and Curator Warren K. Moorehead, February 6, 1919, Robert S. Peabody Museum of Archaeology, Warren K. Moorehead records).

Woodbury (1973, 30) states that the selection of Kidder for the Peabody position was "a vigorous expression of support to the new kind of archaeology he represented, in contrast to the traditional excavation for the sake of collection." Moorehead, on the other hand, exemplified the collector tradition of archaeology that was followed by many museum scholars of his generation (Burns 2008; Christenson 2011; Kelly in Moorehead 2000). Moreover, as David Browman (2002, 251–53) notes, "Although Moorehead worked with Charles Peabody, and with other Harvard students trained in the Peabody Museum Method as early as 1892, [he] did not employ this strategy on his own until 1919 or 1920." Indeed, Moorehead noted in various venues that artifacts should be the main focus of study, and that not much could be gained through excavation (Moorehead 1902b; 1904; 1910, 1:23–24). In *The Stone Age of North America*, for example, he states, "It has been the purpose of this volume to emphasize differences in the arts and crafts among prehistoric tribes. A man who does not love to hunt specimens for the sake of hunting them has not his heart in his work. . . . If some of our students would, for a few years, lay aside cameras, ground-plans, tape-lines, and get to real fieldwork, much more progress would ensue" (Moorehead 1910, 2:365–66).

Moorehead's attitude toward professional archaeology is further reflected in his view of the 1913 excavations at the Calf Island shell midden in Frenchman's Bay, Maine, where he was joined by Director Peabody, who "proposed that one shell heap should be carefully hand-troweled out in order to ascertain all possible facts" (Moorhead 1922b, 158). Moorehead, however, considered such features as "refuse piles, quite different from cemeteries" and believed that "not much more could be learned from intensive digging by means of larger tools" (Moorehead 1922b, 158). He was criticized for this attitude; for example, Kidder (1932, 6–7) insisted that museums were primarily—and perhaps unduly—interested in artifact collecting as opposed to understanding the lifeways of the people who produced the artifacts. Nevertheless, Moorehead became director of the Peabody Museum in early 1924 and held the position until his retirement in 1938. Thus Moorehead had persevered through the transition from the focus on digging to accrue collections to a more scientific approach toward archaeological excavation methods and problem-oriented research.

The scientific approach gained further support in 1919 when Andrew Ellicott Douglass perfected the use of tree rings (dendrochronology) to date archaeological sites in the American Southwest. Douglass took samples from wood preserved at archaeological sites and counted the tree rings, ultimately noting correlations with living trees and other archaeological specimens. This process marked the first development and application of

FIG. 12. Douglas S. Byers (left) and Frederick Johnson at Nevin site. Photographic collection of the Robert S. Peabody Museum of Archaeology.

an "absolute" dating technique. Kidder extolled dendrochronology and its tremendous value in the dating of southwestern sites (Kidder 1924, 106, 280–84). The ninety-nine tree ring dates from Pecos ranged from AD 1299 to 1539 (Linda Cordell, pers. comm., 2011).

Kidder left the Peabody in 1929 for the Carnegie Institution in Washington DC, where he directed the Division of Historical Research and became a major figure in Maya archaeology. He continued to publish about the Pecos site and maintained an office at the Peabody Museum. He also maintained an office at Harvard when the Carnegie's Division of Historical Research moved there in 1938 (Givens 1992, 111–12).

Byers, Johnson, and Bullen: The Stratigraphic and Dating Revolution

Kidder was instrumental in the appointment of Douglas Swain Byers in 1933 as the Peabody's assistant to the director. Byers succeeded Moorehead

FIG. 13. Ripley Bullen (standing, front center), Adelaide Kendall Bullen (standing, far left) and members of the Massachusetts Archaeological Society in the 1940s. Photo courtesy Bulletin of the Massachusetts Archaeological Society.

as director, serving from 1938 to 1968 (MacNeish 1979a, 709). With bachelor's and master's degrees from Harvard, Byers had served as an assistant dean at Harvard (1929–31) and assistant to the director of the Peabody Museum at Harvard (1931–33). He had field experience with Kidder in the Southwest in 1926–27 and in Guatemala in 1930. He also worked with Samuel K. Lothrop of Harvard at Sitio Conte in Panama, where he met Frederick Johnson (Hearne and Sharer 1992).

In 1936 Byers hired Johnson as curator (fig. 12). Johnson had received a bachelor's degree from Tufts, a master's degree from Harvard, and was ABD (all but dissertation) for his doctorate. He had conducted extensive ethnological research among the Canadian Mi'kmaq from 1925 to 1931 (Bernard et al. 2001; MacNeish 1996; Norcini 2008).

Byers and Johnson worked as an efficient team and fostered a vigorous and focused program in northeastern archaeology. The museum building was renovated and the resources of the Peabody Foundation "were committed for an indefinite number of years, to the analysis of anthropological problems in northern and northeastern North America" (Johnson 1946, viii; MacNeish 1996, 270). In 1940 Ripley Pierce Bullen (1902–76) became an integral part of the northeastern archaeological program at the Peabody Museum while attending graduate school at Harvard (Wilkerson 1978) (fig. 13). As part of the new program, Byers and Johnson excavated the Hornblower and Squibnocket sites in Chilmark, Massachusetts, in 1936 using, for the first time in New England, a classification of projectile points based on their shapes (Byers and Johnson 1940, 34). Bullen's research at Foster's Cove, Clarke Pond, and other sites in Massachusetts fully exploited stratigraphy for developing the first cultural chronology of eastern Massachusetts (Bullen 1949; Wilkerson 1978, 622). To facilitate the research program, a symposium on the current state of northeastern anthropology was presented at the 1941 annual meeting of the American Anthropological Association in Andover. It resulted in the landmark volume *Man in Northeastern North America* (Johnson 1946).

At that time the earliest evidence for the arrival of humans in the Northeast was thought to date to the Late Archaic, as reflected in the work by William A. Ritchie at Lamoka Lake in New York (Ritchie 1932). Additionally, the Red Paint tradition of Maine (now known as the Moorehead tradition), researched by Moorehead from 1912 to 1920, was then the earliest known cultural manifestation in far northeastern North America (Moorehead 1922b; Richardson 2006b; Robinson 1996).

In 1936 Byers (1979) excavated at the Nevin site in Maine; in 1939 Johnson (1942, 1949) excavated at the Boylston Street Fish Weir in Boston (fig. 14). His project was one of the first interdisciplinary research projects in the Northeast. As Petersen (1995, 207) notes, there was no radiocarbon dating of Archaic sites at the time, but Byers (1946, 8) proposed a date range of 2000–1000 BCE (Before Common Era) for the Nevin site, and Johnson (1942, 190–92) suggested 1700–1400 BCE for the Boylston Street Fish Weir. In 1958 Johnson received two radiocarbon dates for the fish weir dating to 4450 RCYBP (Radiocarbon Years Before Present; Byers

FIG. 14. Some of the preserved stakes at the Boylston Street Fish Weir. Photographic collection of the Robert S. Peabody Museum of Archaeology.

1959, 242–43). At the time, there was wild speculation on the temporal placement of the archaeological sites that were under investigation (see Hamilton and Winter, this volume). Johnson (1946, 2) stated:

> The realization of the antiquity of the fishweir has, from the point of view of North American archaeology, a number of engaging, if not important, implications. It may well be asked, is the fishweir evidence of the first occupation of the region? If this is so, is it not possible to stimulate one's curiosity with the questions: was the fishweir made by immigrants who were related to those who succeeded Folsom man [see below]; were these successors descended in a direct line? Or, are we dealing with a completely different group of immigrants who arrived in New England without previous contact with Folsom?

Décima and Dincauze (1998) ultimately dated the weir to between 5300 and 3700 RCYBP, further suggesting that the fish weirs encountered in Boston's Back Bay represented successive generations of weir building, rather than one massive weir.

Antiquity of Folsom and Clovis

In 1927 speculation about the peopling of the Americas intensified. In that year Jesse D. Figgins of the Colorado Museum of Natural History (now the Denver Museum of Nature and Science) excavated the Folsom site in New Mexico (fig. 15). The momentous find of a fluted spear point in the rib cage of an extinct bison was the first indisputable evidence that hunters and gatherers lived in North America during the last Ice Age, at the same time as now extinct Pleistocene animals.

In late August, after attending the first Pecos Conference (August 21–29, 1927), Frank H. H. Roberts of the Smithsonian Institution visited Figgins's excavations at Folsom and immediately called Kidder, who was then at Pecos, to join him in verifying the direct association of spear points with extinct bison remains (Meltzer 1991, 25, 1994, 16; 2009, 86). In a letter to Figgins on October 13, 1927, Kidder wrote:

FIG. 15. Folsom point in matrix with bison bones. © Denver Museum of Nature & Science.

As an archaeologist, I am of course not competent to pass either upon the paleontological or geological evidences of antiquity, but I have paid special attention for many years to questions of deposition and association. On these points I am able to judge, and I was entirely convinced of the contemporaneous association of the artifact which you so wisely had left "in situ" and the bones of the bison. (Cited in Meltzer 2009, 89)

Meltzer (2009, 89) says Kidder's acceptance of this association "carried enormous weight, for in the 1920s, he was at the height of his considerable power and influence." Soon after visiting the Folsom site Kidder delivered a lecture at the Southwest Museum in Los Angeles in October 1927, stating that the " first journey into the New World took place at least 15 or 20 thousand years ago" (Kidder 1927, 5; Meltzer 2005).

In 1932 Figgins excavated the Dent site in Colorado and uncovered fluted points (now known as Clovis) with butchered mammoths. The next year Edgar Howard excavated at Blackwater Draw near Clovis, New Mexico, and also recovered Clovis points in association with mammoth (*Mammuthus columbi*) remains from strata underlying the site's Folsom level. Clearly Clovis was the earlier of the two fluted point traditions (Adovasio and Page 2002, 104; Andrews et al. 2008; Meltzer 2009, 82–87; Richardson 2006a, 20). Kidder (1936, 144) noted, "It can no longer be questioned that human beings were here at the very least ten thousand years ago." Unknown to Charles Peabody and Moorehead at the Peabody Museum, the Founder's Collection contained a number of Paleoindian points, including Gainey, Simpson, and Clovis points (D. Clark Wernecke and Michael R. Waters, pers. comm. to Ryan Wheeler, February 2013) that held a clue to the antiquity of the First Americans now known to date ca. 11,500–11,000 RCYBP (fig. 16).

The Folsom and Clovis discoveries signaled the final demise of the American Paleolithic and, albeit unwittingly, the creation of the so-called Clovis Barrier of 11,500 RCYBP. Indeed, this barrier remained an almost insurmountable conceptual obstacle for the next half century.

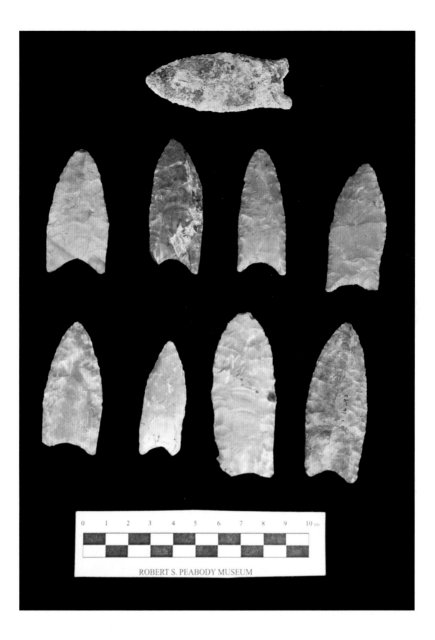

FIG. 16. Clovis points from the Founder's Collection at the Robert S. Peabody Museum. Photographic collection of the Robert S. Peabody Museum of Archaeology.

FIG. 17. The extensive Debert excavation site used an elaborate grid system. Photographic collection of the Robert S. Peabody Museum of Archaeology.

The Peabody, Radiocarbon Dating, and Paleoindians

In 1949, some thirty years after Douglass developed the tree-ring dating method in the Southwest, Willard Libby and his research team at the University of Chicago developed radiocarbon dating, ultimately earning Libby a Nobel Prize in chemistry (1960). The Peabody's Frederick Johnson became a leader in disseminating this revolutionary new dating technique (see Baich 2010 for an in-depth discussion of Johnson's role in the radiocarbon dating revolution). At the Viking Fund Conference in 1948 the American Anthropological Association was urged to appoint a committee to work with Libby to secure samples from the archaeological community for obtaining dates using the new technique. In February 1948 Johnson was appointed chair of the committee to facilitate the dissemination and application of radiocarbon dating (Johnson 1951, 2; 1967; Marlowe 1999) and went on to chair the First International Conference on Radiocarbon Dating, held at the Peabody in 1956. MacNeish (1996, 271) relates, "Fred's little office on the second floor of the Peabody Foundation in Andover became the hub of an important advance in American archaeology."

The earliest radiocarbon dated Paleoindian sites in northeastern North America were Bull Brook and Debert. The Bull Brook site in Ipswich, Massachusetts, discovered in 1951 by avocational archaeologists, was the first Clovis site identified in the Northeast (Eldridge and Vaccaro 1952; Robinson 2006; Robinson et al. 2009; Robinson and Winter 2011). Bull Brook was excavated through 1958 with the aid of Douglas Jordan (1960) and Douglas Byers (1954), and data from the site revolutionized thinking on Paleoindians in the Northeast, for it evinced both a dense occupation and evidence interpreted as possible Paleoindian shelters forming a village. Although structures were radiocarbon dated, the dates were considered too late for a Paleoindian occupation.

Debert, a fluted point site in Nova Scotia, became the best dated Paleoindian site in far northeastern North America at that time (Rosenmeier et al. 2012; Stuckenrath 1966). The site was discovered in 1948 and in 1955 was reported to Richard S. MacNeish, then senior archaeologist with the National Museum of Canada (MacDonald 1968, 1–2). A note on the site in *American Antiquity* (Cotter 1962, 456) prompted John S. Erskine, the Nova Scotia provincial archaeologist, to visit it. Soon Byers contacted Erskine, visited the site, and returned to Debert with MacNeish to conduct test excavations and formulate a plan for full excavation (MacDonald 1968, 3; Stuckenrath 1964, 21) (fig. 17). The project was supported by partial funding from the Robert S. Peabody Foundation for Archaeology (MacDonald 1968, iii, 3; 1971). George F. MacDonald, Atlantic archaeologist for the National Museum of Canada and a Yale University graduate student who later served as founding director of the Canadian Museum of Civilization, was selected as co-director of the excavations along with Byers. Some twenty radiocarbon determinations from the excavations, which commenced in 1963, dated the Debert occupation to 10,600 RCYBP.

MacNeish and the Pre-Clovis Debate

After the discovery of Folsom (1927) and Clovis (1932, 1933), Paleoindian points were found from Alaska and southern Canada to northern Venezuela, with the densest concentrations in the southeastern United States (Haynes 2002; Meltzer 2009). Although many sites were found that were thought to be older than Clovis, most—due to dating problems, poor stratigraphy, or stone tools of dubious human manufacture and/or provenance—were rapidly weeded out (Adovasio and Page 2002; Dillehay 2000; Meltzer 2009). Each time one of the purportedly ancient sites fell by the scholarly wayside, the Clovis Barrier was reinforced. As with the American Paleolithic, the battle lines were drawn once again, this time pitting those for human occupation of the Americas before Clovis against those who believed Clovis was the earliest occupation.

Alex Krieger (1952, 239), then of the University of Washington, lamented the fact that since the discovery of Folsom and Clovis, a great skepticism existed about the possibility that any earlier populations had migrated into the Western Hemisphere before Clovis. The makers of Clovis literally became the "First Americans" (Krieger 1952, 239; Meltzer 2009), and 10,000–11,500 RCYBP became the new "allowed Antiquity" for the hemisphere's first colonization. Krieger (1964, 42, 68) coined the term Pre-Projectile Stage, for cultural levels without spear points. He believed this stage preceded Clovis in the Americas and cited fifty sites as examples.

The search for pre-Clovis sites soon became synonymous with breaking the Clovis Barrier. In the 1950s a number of purportedly early sites harkened back to the fatal flaw of the American Paleolithic, wherein crude tools were either equated with great antiquity or reflected a pre-projectile occupation of an early age. One of these sites was the Smith Farm Site on Wasp Island, located near Ellsworth Falls, Maine. Excavated from 1947 to 1950 by Byers and Wendell S. Hadlock of the Robert Abbe Museum, it held evidence of four levels of occupation (Byers 1959, 243–50). The interface of Strata 2 and 3 yielded a date of 3975 RCYBP (Byers 1959, 244), the first for the Archaic of New England. The undated Stratum 1, designated the Kelly Phase, had an assemblage of crude percussion flaked cores, sinuous edged knives, and scrapers. Byers noted, "The Kelly Phase should not be properly be assigned to the Archaic Stage. It appears to belong to the remains of one of the older occupations of the Northeast, but its temporal position is unknown" (Byers 1959, 247–48). He believed that although undated, the Kelly Phase might date to just before or after the fluted point traditions.

The hunt was on for pre-Clovis sites, and Richard Stockton "Scotty" MacNeish became one of its most ardent chasers. MacNeish (1918–2001) became involved with the Peabody early in his career. He had been fascinated with the Maya since eighth grade, when his grandfather, an avocational archaeologist, had returned from visiting Alfred V. Kidder at Chichén Itzá in the Yucatán and had shown him photos of the excavations. The thirteen-year-old grandson wrote to Kidder asking to be hired as a water boy. As MacNeish recounts, Kidder replied saying that "he had lots of water boys, but he encouraged me to keep studying hard so I would become an archaeologist someday" (Ferrie 2001, 715). In 1937 while Scotty was a participant in the Rainbow Bridge Monument Valley Expedition in Arizona, Kidder visited the excavations and, upon being introduced to Scotty, Kidder exclaimed, "Don't I know you?" He remembered the letter MacNeish had sent him. Kidder added, "Looks like you are moving in the right direction" (Ferrie 2001, 716). Thus began his lifelong friendship with Doc Kidder, as Scotty called him. Forty years later the American Anthropological Association awarded MacNeish the Alfred Vincent Kidder Medal for eminence in the field of archaeology.

MacNeish attended the University of Chicago, receiving a bachelor's degree in 1940 and a doctorate in 1949, supporting himself by boxing; he earned a Golden Gloves Championship in 1938 (Ferrie 2001, 716). By the end of his student career he had gained extensive field experience at archaeological sites in the Midwest and Southwest (Flannery and Marcus 2001, 4–5). Upon graduation with a doctorate, he accepted a position as senior archaeologist at the National Museum of Canada (1949–62).

While fully employed at the National Museum, MacNeish worked in northern Canada for Canada's Geological Survey and in Mexico. Scotty explains how he managed to accrue vacation time for his months of field research in Mexico: "For every Saturday and Sunday I worked north of 60°, I got an extra day added to my three-week vacation time and wound up with ten weeks for Mexico" (Ferrie 2001, 719). Through the early 1950s he worked in Tamaulipas, having discovered in 1949 the first cobs of early maize there (MacNeish 1958). This discovery initiated a quest that would engage his efforts for the rest of his life (see Eubanks, this volume).

Sometime in the early 1950s MacNeish contacted the Peabody's Frederick Johnson, who had worked in the Yukon in 1944 and 1948 (Johnson and Raup 1964). They talked about MacNeish's plans for fieldwork in the Yukon, which he subsequently conducted between 1957 and 1962 (MacNeish 1964a). Their acquaintance developed into a long-term association that ultimately aided MacNeish's quest for an institution with a venerable tradition of interdisciplinary research that would support his search for the earliest maize agriculture in the Americas.

In 1960 he met with Byers and Johnson at the Society for American Archaeology meetings to ask the Peabody to administer his newly granted funds from the National Science Foundation, which sponsored the Tehuacán Archaeological-Botanical Project. John Kemper, headmaster of Phillips Academy, appointed MacNeish a research associate of the Peabody, and he moved to Andover for two years (1963–64), after which he accepted a position at the University of Calgary (MacNeish 1974, 224). The Trustee Committee overseeing the Robert S. Peabody Foundation for Archaeology allocated additional Peabody Museum funds for the Tehuacán project (MacNeish 1974). Not only did the Peabody administer National Science Foundation grants for the Tehuacán project from 1960 to 1964, but Byers and Johnson became an integral part of the Tehuacán research team, ultimately contributing to and editing the five volumes of *The Prehistory of the Tehuacan Valley* (1967–75). Here, as in Tamaulipas, the occupation dated back to over 9000 RCYBP. MacNeish and his colleagues developed the best record not only of agricultural origins but also of the entire Archaic time period and the rise of sedentary life in Mexico (see Eubanks, this volume; Flannery and Marcus 2001, 15; MacNeish 1964b; Mangelsdorf et al. 1964).

Johnson retired in 1969 but was instrumental in hiring MacNeish to replace him as director of the Peabody Museum (MacNeish 1996, 271).[7] In 1969, after an extensive survey of the southern Peruvian Andes for suitable

FIG. 18. Excavations inside Pikimachay Cave, Ayacucho Valley, Peru. Photographic collection of the Robert S. Peabody Museum of Archaeology.

rockshelters, MacNeish selected the Ayacucho Basin as the prime area for investigation into agricultural origins. From 1969 to 1975 MacNeish directed the Ayacucho Archaeological-Botanical Project (fig. 18). At Pikimachay Cave (Flea Cave) his excavations uncovered evidence of the association of extinct animals with stone tools dating to 25,000 RCYBP (MacNeish 1971, 1979b, 1983). The oldest complexes, Paccaicasa and Ayacucho, produced crude stone tools made of volcanic tuff and were putatively associated with extinct sloth remains. Most reviewers (Adovasio and Page 2002, 201–2; Dillehay 2000; Lavallée 2000, 48–49; Lynch 1974, 1990, 25; Richardson 1994, 32–33; Rick 1988, 13–16) questioned the human origin of the tools in the earliest levels, believing they were spalls from the walls and roof of the cave produced by freezing and thawing. They argued that the 25,000 RCYBP dates applied to the extinct sloth remains but not to human habitation. MacNeish (see MacNeish and Libby 2003, 476) reaffirmed his steadfast interpretation that the Paccaicasa level had valid human evidence dating to 30,000–16,000 RCYBP based on the few identifiable tools that he was sure were not intrusive from upper levels. His dates of the succeeding Ayacucho phase (16,000–13,000 RCYBP) also were met with skepticism. Recent restudy of the assemblage, however, supports MacNeish's conclusions that the Ayacucho phase may well be pre-Clovis (Canales and Yataco Capcha 2008; Lavalleé 2000, 48–49). Because there is but a single radiocarbon date of 14,000 RCYBP, more dates are needed to confirm the age of the Ayacucho phase. Despite the challenges to the date, Dillehay (2000, 176) stresses the importance of MacNeish's research at Pikimachay Cave, stating that "MacNeish's interpretations are a valuable picture of how early highland social and technological changes might have occurred."

Unrest in Peru caused MacNeish to look elsewhere in his continuing search for the origins of agriculture. From 1979 to 1982, he directed the Belize Archaic Archaeological Reconnaissance (Zeitlin 1984). He defined six phases ranging in age from 11,000 RCYBP through to the appearance of pottery. MacNeish's provisional Archaic chronology and artifact assemblages (Lohse et al. 2006, 212) were based mainly on surface collections and disturbed sites, but his research was the first to point out the long Archaic sequence for Belize.[8]

MacNeish left the Peabody Museum in 1983 after disagreements with Phillips Academy administrators. He and Johnson established the Andover Foundation for Archaeological Research (AFAR), which operated out of Johnson's boathouse. This enterprise is currently directed by Phillips Academy alumnus and MacNeish colleague Barry V. Rolett at the University of Hawai'i Manoa. AFAR continued MacNeish's research on the origins of agriculture and the search for pre-Clovis sites. MacNeish never gave up and, in the mode of his 1938 Golden Gloves championship, he kept slugging against the notion that Clovis represented the first peoples in the Americas. His last foray into the first Americans debate was in 1989 at Pendejo Cave in New Mexico, where he claimed to have discovered pre-Clovis levels dating to 50,000 years ago, which again reached a skeptical archaeological audience (Hyland et al. 2003; MacNeish and Libby 2003). His last major research venue was in China, where he conducted excavations to determine the origins of rice domestication (Flannery and Marcus 2001, 21). He spent twenty-three years of his life doing fieldwork

FIG. 19. Jim Bradley (right) and geologist Stephen Pollock at the Mount Jasper lithic site, New Hampshire, 1996. Photographic collection of the Robert S. Peabody Museum of Archaeology.

in the Americas and China, publishing extensively on the results of his research, an achievement that few other archaeologists have attained.

The Peabody Museum continued to support archaeological research, but after MacNeish retired, the museum had a much diminished program. In the 1990s its major focus shifted. The museum today is the product of the program pursued by its subsequent directors. In 1990 James W. Bradley, a former member of the Massachusetts Historical Commission, became the sixth director of the Robert S. Peabody Museum (fig. 19). Bradley received a doctorate from Syracuse University in 1979 and is well known for his research on New York Iroquois (Bradley 1987) and on the archaeology of New England (Bradley 1998; McManamon and Bradley 1988). At the Peabody Museum he published extensively on the Paleoindian period in New England, and in 1998 he and his colleagues (Spiess et al. 1998) used data from all known fluted point sites and isolated fluted points in New England to reconstruct Paleoindian colonization, settlement, and subsistence patterns within the context of the late Pleistocene environment. This research resulted in *Origins and Ancestors: Investigating New England Paleo Indians* (Bradley 1998), an educational booklet. It accompanied an exhibit at the Peabody Museum and was awarded first place for educational materials from the New England Museum Association.

Conclusions

The Robert S. Peabody Museum today is a vibrant outgrowth of its directors' programs and of close ties with Phillips Academy and its scholastic community. Over the decades the curators and directors of the Peabody Museum have made substantial contributions to the development of archaeological methodology, the stratigraphic and dating revolutions, and the elucidation of the complex issues of the initial peopling of the Americas. Using data gathered from a broad swath of the Americas, scholars employed by or connected with the Peabody have addressed a series of interrelated topics about Paleoindians—their homeland(s), their ethnic identity, their mode(s) of arrival and lifestyle(s), and most vexing, the chronology of their arrival(s). Meadowcroft Rockshelter (Adovasio and Page 2002; Adovasio and Pedler 2016) in southwestern Pennsylvania and Monte Verde in southern Chile (Dillehay 2000; Dillehay et al. 2015) are the "bookends" that have been crucial to proving to most archaeologists' satisfaction that there is a Pre-Clovis occupation of the Americas dating to as early as 15,000 or more years ago. In the past fifteen years there have been many more sites excavated, strongly supporting the evidence from these two famous sites of an earlier population of hunters and gatherers that precedes Clovis (Adovasio and Pedler 2016; Bonnichsen et al. 2005; Dillehay et al. 2012; Goebel et al. 2008; Graf et al. 2014; Richardson 2006a; Stanford and Stenger 2014). Thanks to discoveries made by the museum's scholars, among others, in the melodramatic words of one recent synopsis, "*Clovis ist todt*" (Clovis is dead!; Karge 2011, 60). After eighty years of bitter and often vitriolic debate, the Clovis first/pre-Clovis war is over due in part to the tenacity and research of Peabody-affiliated scholars as well as many other investigators.

Acknowledgments

The authors would like to thank Malinda Blustain, James W. Bradley, Harvey Bricker, Mary Ellen Conaway, Linda Cordell, Robert D. Drennan, David H. Evans, Mark McConaughy, Michael O'Brien, Brian Robinson, Barry V. Rolett, Edward Sisson, Bonnie Sousa, Marla Taylor, D. Clark Wernecke, Gene Winter, Jane Wheeler, and Ryan Wheeler. We also wish to acknowledge with gratitude the many contributions from David Pedler, who edited our original manuscript, and thanks go to Malinda Blustain and Jane G. Libby for their editorial comments, all of which greatly improved this essay.

NOTES

1. The prominence and stature of the curators and directors of the Robert S. Peabody Museum of Archaeology is reflected in their professional affiliations.

   Charles Peabody was a co-founder of the American School of Prehistoric Research in Europe in 1921.

   Moorehead was elected Fellow of the American Association for the Advancement of Science in 1890 and secretary of Section H (Anthropology) in 1893. He was appointed to the Board of Indian Commissioners in 1908 by President Theodore Roosevelt. Moorehead was also elected first vice president of the American Anthropological Association (AAA) in 1932 (Byers 1939). He received an honorary doctorate from Dartmouth College, an institution his benefactor Robert Singleton Peabody supported.

   Kidder was chairman of the Division of Anthropology and Psychology of the National Research Council (1926–27), elected a member of the National Academy of Sciences in 1936, served as president of SAA in 1937–38 and as president of the AAA in 1942–43 (Givens 1992; Willey 1967; Woodbury 1973); and founded the Institute of Andean Research in 1947 (see Willey 1967, 306–7 for awards and honorary degrees).

   Byers was the second editor of *American Antiquity* (1938–47) and president of SAA (1947–48) (MacNeish 1979a).

   Johnson was SAA treasurer and president (1946–47), and secretary and guiding force of the Committee for the Recovery of Archaeological Remains (CRAR), established in 1945 to salvage archaeological resources before they were inundated by dams and reservoirs (Banks and Czaplick 2014; Johnson 1966). Wendorf and Thompson (2002, 327–28) state that "there is no doubt that Johnson, with his clear vision, political acumen, sense of responsibility, and incredible energy, created the CRAR." Johnson was also executive secretary of the AAA (1948–54), chairman of the Joint Committee on Radioactive Carbon 14 of the AAA and the Geological Society of America (1949), and was elected fellow of the American Geological Society in 1952 for his interdisciplinary research (MacNeish 1996).

MacNeish was elected to the American Academy of Arts and Sciences in 1967, served as president of the SAA (1971–72), was elected to the British Academy (1973) and to the National Academy of Sciences in 1974 (Flannery and Marcus 2001, 23–24).

Bradley was a member of the NAGPRA Review Committee (1998–2003) and was responsible for Peabody Museum's exemplary role in consultation with American Indian communities on repatriation issues. He was also editor of the *Bulletin of the Massachusetts Archaeological Society* (2002–8).

Eugene C. Winter Jr., honorary curator at the museum, received the Society for American Archaeology's Crabtree Award as an outstanding avocational archaeologist in 2005 for his lifelong contributions to archaeology.

2. Singleton Peabody Moorehead (1900–64) was in the class of 1918 at Phillips Academy and received a degree in architecture from Harvard University. He is well known as the director of architecture during the restoration of Colonial Williamsburg and is buried in the Bruton Parish Church on the grounds of Colonial Williamsburg. Singleton also acted as a field assistant for Kidder at Pecos (1922), where he drew a reconstruction of Pecos church (Givens 1992, 64).

3. Robert S. Peabody (Moorehead 1906b) had first entered discussions with Frederic Ward Putnam at the Peabody Museum at Harvard, established by his uncle George Peabody, to determine if Harvard would entertain an endowment for a building in which to teach students about American Indian cultures. Moorehead relates the outcome of the visit between Robert Peabody and Putnam: "It is sufficient to record that he [Peabody] was not pleased with the reception accorded him by the distinguished professor." There has been speculation that Peabody had asked Putnam to hire Moorehead as a condition of the gift, but was refused, thus he established the Department of Archaeology at Phillips Academy, through the largest donation it had ever received (Moorehead 1938, 6, 9; see also Barss 1934, 14). In his bequest to the trustees of Phillips Academy (Robert S. Peabody to Trustees of Phillips Academy, March 6, 1901, Robert S. Peabody Museum of Archaeology, Founder records), Peabody includes a statement about who the first curator should be: "I have consulted Dr. Bancroft as to the propriety of asking

that Professor Moorehead be appointed the first curator, or incumbent, if this department should be established, and received his approval of doing so."

4. Aleš Hrdlička was hired by Holmes in 1903 and was the first curator of physical anthropology at the U.S. National Museum (now the Smithsonian Institution's National Museum of Natural History). He joined Holmes in critically evaluating evidence for an American Paleolithic, declaring that most human skeletal remains, thought to date to the Ice Age, were intrusive into earlier geological strata or poorly collected by non-professionals.

5. Charles Peabody had a close personal association with Frederic Ward Putnam, the leading archaeologist of his day. Peabody invited Putnam to inaugurate the new museum building for the Department of Archaeology in 1903. In his 1915 address on the dedication of Peabody House, Peabody acknowledged Putnam's role in the development of the Peabody Museum. (Peabody 1915a, 16–17). Peabody (1909) also contributed an essay in a volume honoring Putnam on the occasion of his seventieth birthday, as did Moorehead (1909). At the groundbreaking ceremony for the third addition to the Peabody Museum at Harvard in 1913, Putnam was too ill to give the dedicatory speech and asked his friend Charles Peabody to read his presentation (Putnam 1913, 25; Williams 1999, 18). Two years later Peabody wrote Putnam's obituary (Peabody 1915b).

6. Charles Peabody is known not only for his archaeological research but for being the first academic to discover the blues, now known as the "Delta Blues," developed in the Yazoo region of Mississippi by African slaves. In his 1901 and 1902 field seasons in Coahoma County, Mississippi, he excavated at the Dorr and Edwards mounds, where most of his workers were African Americans who sang while working. Peabody's publication "Notes on Negro Music" in 1903 forms the basis for all later histories of Delta Blues as a major folk song style (Evans 1982, 33–34; Gioia 2008, 20–22; Hamilton 2007; Peabody 1903). He also published about songs from the southern Appalachians (Peabody and Rawn 1916) and about a musical instrument from Pecos, excavated by Kidder (Peabody 1917).

7. While director, MacNeish hired three curators, Sisson (1970–73); Drennan (1974–77); and Wheeler (1977–82) who carried out research in Mexico and Peru. Edward Sisson (PhD, Harvard, University of Mississippi) worked on the Late Postclassic Period in the Tehuacán Valley. Foreshadowing an important goal of the modern museum, he took Phillips Academy students on educational trips to Mexico and included a number in his excavations (Sisson, pers. comm., 2011). Robert D. Drennan (PhD, University of Michigan, University of Pittsburgh, and member of the National Academy of Sciences) developed the Palo Blanco Project in the Tehuacán Valley, focusing on the Late Formative and Classic Periods. Drennan also ran a

Peabody field school at the Andover town dump (Drennan, pers. comm., 2011). Jane C. Wheeler (PhD, Michigan, president of CONOPA—Instituto de Investigación y Desarrollo de Camélidos Sudamericanos, Lima, Peru) conducted research and analysis of the fauna from the Early Preceramic cave of Telarmachay in Peru and at Pucara in Bolivia with Elias Mujica. She became the leading researcher on the domestication of camelids and on modern camelids. She also ran a field school at the Andover town dump for Phillips students (Wheeler, pers. comm., 2011). All the curators also taught courses at Phillips Academy. MacNeish hired Mary Ellen Conaway (PhD, University of Pittsburgh, former director of the Carson Valley Museum and Culture Center) to design and implement new exhibits in the museum (1970–74). She also participated in the Ayacucho research.

8. MacNeish was not the only Peabody curator or director to conduct research in Latin America. Byers and Johnson both participated in the Sitio Conte excavations in Panama under Samuel K. Lothrop of Harvard in 1931 and were involved in the Tehaucán project. As a graduate student at Harvard, Johnson conducted research in ethnology and archaeology in Mesoamerica (1931–36). His publications include articles in *The Maya and Their Neighbors* and in the circum-Caribbean volume of the *Handbook of South American Indians*. Bullen became an eminent Florida and Caribbean archaeologist (Wilkerson 1978). Curators Drennan and Sisson worked in the Tehuacán Valley, while Jane Wheeler worked in Peru. Blustain, who became collections manager in 1992, worked at El Cajón in Honduras. In 2001 she developed the R. S. Peabody Museum exhibition titled Peru: From Village to Empire, which traveled to the Hudson Museum at the University of Maine and to the Peabody Museum at Yale University. Donald Slater, museum educator (2002–14) and instructor of history and social science, continues the Peabody's Latin American research venue in Belize and Mexico (see Slater and Hamilton, this volume).

REFERENCES

Abbott, Charles C. 1881. *Primitive Industry: Illustrations of the Handiwork in Stone, Bone, and Clay of the Native Races, Atlantic Seaboard of America.* Salem MA: George A. Bates.

Adovasio, J. M., and Jake Page. 2002. *The First Americans: In Pursuit of Archaeology's Greatest Mystery.* New York: Random House.

Adovasio, J. M., and David Pedler. 2016. *Strangers in a New Land: What Archaeology Reveals About the First Americans.* Richmond Hill, Ontario: Firefly Books.

Andrews, Brian N., Jason M. LaBelle, and John D. Seebach. 2008 "Spatial Variability in the Folsom Archaeological Record: A Multi-Scalar Approach." *American Antiquity* 73, no. 3:464–90.

Baich, Keith D. 2010. "American Scientists, Americanist Archaeology: The Committee on Radioactive Carbon 14." Master's thesis, Portland State University.

Banks, Kimball, and Jon S. Czaplick. 2014. *Dam Projects and the Growth of American Archaeology: The River Basin Surveys and the Interagency Archaeological Salvage Program*. Walnut Creek CA: Left Coast Press.

Barss, John S. 1934. "Archaeology at Phillips Academy." *Phillips Bulletin* 28, no. 4:13–15. Andover MA: Phillips Academy.

Bernard, Tim, Catherine Anne Martin, and Leah Rosenmeier. 2001. *Mikwite'lmanej Mikmaqi'k: Let Us Remember the Old Mi'kmaq*. Confederacy of Mainland Mi'kmaq and the Robert S. Peabody Museum of Archaeology. Halifax, Nova Scotia: Nimbus Publishing.

Bonnichsen, Robson, Bradley Lepper, Dennis Stanford, and Michael Waters, eds. 2005. *Paleoamerican Origins: Beyond Clovis*. Center for the Study of the First Americans. College Station: Texas A&M University Press.

Bradley, James W. 1987. *Evolution of the Onondaga Iroquois: Accommodating Change, 1500–1655*. Syracuse NY: Syracuse University Press.

———. 1998. *Origins and Ancestors: Investigating New England's Paleo Indians*. Andover MA: Robert S. Peabody Museum of Archaeology, Phillips Academy.

Bricker, Harvey M. 2002. "George Grant MacCurdy: An American Pioneer of American Paleoanthropology." In *New Perspectives in Americanist Archaeology*, edited by David L. Browman and Stephen Williams, 265–86. Tuscaloosa: University of Alabama Press.

Browman, David L. 2002. "Origins of Stratigraphic Excavation in North America: The Peabody Museum Method and the Chicago Method." In *New Perspectives in Americanist Archaeology*, edited by David L. Browman and Stephen Williams, 242–64. Tuscaloosa: University of Alabama Press.

Browman, David L., and Douglas R. Givens. 1996. "Stratigraphic Excavation: The 'First' New Archaeology." *American Anthropologist* 98, no. 1:80–95.

Bullen, Ripley P. 1949. *Excavations in Northeastern Massachusetts*. Papers of the Robert S. Peabody Foundation for Archaeology 1, no. 3. Andover MA: Phillips Academy.

Burns, J. Conor. 2008. "Networking Ohio Valley Archaeology in the 1880s: The Social Dynamics of Peabody and Smithsonian Centralization." *Histories of Anthropology Annual* 24, no. 3:1–33.

Byers, Douglas S. 1939. "Warren K. Moorehead." *American Anthropologist* 41, no. 2:286–94.

———. 1946. "The Environment of the Northeast." In *Man in Northeastern North America*, edited by Frederick Johnson, Papers of the Robert S. Peabody Foundation for Archaeology 3, 3–32. Andover MA: Phillips Academy.

———. 1954. "Bull Brook: A Fluted Point Site in Ipswich, Massachusetts." *American Antiquity* 19, no. 4:343–51.

———. 1959. "The Eastern Archaic: Some Problems and Hypotheses." *American Antiquity* 24, no. 3:233–56.

———. 1979. *The Nevin Shellheap: Burials and Observations.* Papers of the Robert S. Peabody Foundation for Archaeology 9. Andover MA: Phillips Academy.

Byers, Douglas S., and Frederick Johnson. 1940. *Two Sites on Martha's Vineyard.* Papers of the Robert S. Peabody Foundation for Archaeology 1, no. 1. Andover MA: Phillips Academy.

Canales, Elmo León, and Juan Yataco Capcha. 2008. "New Analysis of Lithic Artifacts from the Ayacucho Complex, Peru." *Current Research in the Pleistocene* 25:34–37.

Christenson, Andrew L. 2011. "Who Were the Professional Archaeologists of 1900? Clues from the Work of Warren K. Moorehead." *Bulletin of the History of Archaeology* 21, no. 1:4–23.

Cotter, John. 1962. "Notes and News: Northeast." *American Antiquity* 27, no. 3:456.

Décima, Elena B., and Dena F. Dincauze. 1998. "The Boston Back Bay Fish Weirs." In *Hidden Dimensions: The Cultural Significance of Wetland Archaeology,* edited by Kathryn Bernick, 157–72. Vancouver: University of British Columbia Press.

Dillehay, Tom D. 2000. *The Settlement of the Americas: A New Prehistory.* New York: Basic Books.

Dillehay, Tom D., Duccio Bonavia, Steven Goodbred, and Teresa Rosales. 2012. "A Late Pleistocene Human Presence at Huaca Prieta, Peru, and Early Pacific Coastal Adaptations." *Quaternary Research* 77:418–23.

Dillehay, Tom D., Carlos Ocampo, José Saavedra, Andre Oliveira Sawakuchi, Rodrigo M. Vega, Mario Pino, Michael B. Collins, Linda Scott Cummings, Iván Arregui, Ximena S. Villagran, Gelvam A. Hartmann, Mauricio Mella, Andrea González, and George Dix. 2015. "New Archaeological Evidence for an Early Human Presence at Monte Verde, Chile." *PLOS ONE* 10(11). Accessed October 17, 2016. http://dx.doi .org/10.1371/journal.pone.0141923.

Eldridge, William, and Joseph Vaccaro. 1952. "The Bull Brook Site, Ipswich, Mass." *Bulletin of the Massachusetts Archaeological Society* 13, no. 4:39–43.

Evans, David. 1982. *Big Road Blues: Tradition and Creativity in the Folk Blues.* Berkeley: University of California Press.

Ferrie, Helke. 2001. "An Interview with Richard S. MacNeish." *Current Anthropology* 42, no. 5:715–35.

Flannery, Kent V., and Joyce Marcus. 2001. "Richard Stockton MacNeish, 1918–2001." In *Biographical Memoirs of the National Academy of Sciences* 80, 3–27. Washington DC: National Academy of Sciences.

Fowler, Don D. 2000. *A Laboratory for Archaeology: Science and Romanticism in the American Southwest 1846–1930*. Albuquerque: University of New Mexico Press.

Gioia, Ted. 2008. *Delta Blues: The Life and Times of the Mississippi Masters Who Revolutionized American Music*. New York: W. W. Norton.

Givens, Douglas R. 1992. *Alfred Vincent Kidder and the Development of American Archaeology*. Albuquerque: University of New Mexico Press.

Goebel, Ted, Michael R. Waters, and Dennis H. O'Rourke. 2008. "The Late Pleistocene Dispersal of Modern Humans in the Americas." *Science* 319:1497–1502.

Graf, Kelly E., Caroline V. Ketron, and Michael R. Waters, eds. 2014. *Paleoamerican Odyssey*. College Station: Texas A&M University Press.

Hamilton, Marybeth. 2007. *In Search of the Blues: Black Voices, White Visions*. London: Jonathan Cape.

Haynes, Gary. 2002. *The Early Settlement of North America: The Clovis Era*. New York: Cambridge University Press.

Hearne, Pamela, and Robert J. Sharer. 1992. *Rivers of Gold: Precolumbian Treasures from Sitio Conte*. Philadelphia: University of Pennsylvania Museum.

Holmes, William H. 1890. "A Quarry Workshop of the Flaked Stone Implement Makers in the District of Columbia." *American Anthropologist* 3, no. 1:1–26.

———. 1893. "Gravel Man and Palaeolithic Culture: A Preliminary Word." *Science* 21:29–30.

Hyland, David C., J. M. Adovasio, and H. Ervin Taylor. 2003. "The Perishable Artifacts." In *Pendejo Cave*, edited by Richard S. MacNeish and Jane G. Libby, 297–416. Albuquerque: University of New Mexico Press.

Johnson, Frederick. 1966. "Archaeology in an Emergency: The Federal Government's Inter-Agency Archaeological Salvage Program Is 20 Years Old." *Science* 152:1592–97.

———. 1967. "Radiocarbon Dating and Archaeology in North America." *Science* 155(3759):165–69.

Johnson, Frederick, ed. 1942. *The Boylston Street Fishweir*. Papers of the Robert S. Peabody Foundation for Archaeology 2. Andover MA: Phillips Academy.

———. 1946. *Man in Northeastern North America*. Papers of the Robert S. Peabody Foundation for Archaeology 3. Andover MA: Phillips Academy.

———. 1949. *The Boylston Street Fishweir II*. Papers of the Robert S. Peabody Foundation for Archaeology 4, no. 1. Andover MA: Phillips Academy.

———. 1951. *Radiocarbon Dating: A Report on the Program to Aid in the Development of the Method of Dating*. Memoirs of the Society for American Archaeology 8. Salt Lake City: Society for American Archaeology.

Johnson, Frederick, and Hugh Raup. 1964. *Investigations in Southwest Yukon*. Papers of the Robert S. Peabody Foundation for Archaeology 6, no. 1. Andover MA: Phillips Academy.

Jordan, Douglas F. 1960. "The Bull Brook Site in Relation to 'Fluted Point' Manifestations in Eastern North America." PhD diss., Harvard University.

Karge, Désirée. 2011. "Im Fellboot Nach Amerika." *Bild der Wissenschaft* 6:60–67.

Kidder, Alfred V. 1924. *An Introduction to the Study of Southwestern Archaeology with a Preliminary Account of the Excavations at Pecos*. Papers of the Southwest Expedition 1. Department of Archaeology, Phillips Academy. New Haven: Yale University Press.

———. 1925. Introduction. *Pueblo Pottery Making: A Study at the Village of San Ildefonso*, by Carl E. Guthe, 1–15. Papers of the Southwestern Expedition 2. Department of Archaeology, Phillips Academy. New Haven: Yale University Press.

———. 1927. "Early Man in America: Lecture by Dr. A. V. Kidder at the Southwest Museum, October 2, 1927." *Masterkey* 1, no. 5:5–13.

———. 1932. *The Artifacts of Pecos*. Papers of the Southwestern Expedition 6. Department of Archaeology, Phillips Academy. New Haven: Yale University Press.

———. 1936. "Speculations on New World Prehistory." In *Essays in Anthropology, Presented to A. L. Kroeber in Celebration of His Sixtieth Birthday, June 11, 1936*, edited by Ralph Lowie, 143–52. Berkeley: University of California Press.

———. 1958. *Pecos, New Mexico: Archaeological Notes*. Papers of the Robert S. Peabody Foundation for Archaeology 5. Andover MA: Phillips Academy.

Krieger, Alex D. 1952. "New World Cultural History: Anglo-America." In *Anthropology Today: An Encyclopedic Inventory*, edited by Alfred A. Kroeber, 239–64. Chicago: University of Chicago Press.

———. 1964. "Early Man in the New World." In *Prehistoric Man in the New World*, edited by Jesse D. Jennings and Edward Norbeck, 23–84. Chicago: University of Chicago Press.

Lavallée, Danièle. 2000. *The First South Americans: The Peopling of a Continent from the Earlier Evidence to High Culture*. Salt Lake City: University of Utah Press.

Lohse, Jon C., Jaime Awe, Cameron Griffith, Robert M. Rosenswig, and Fred Valdez Jr. 2006. "Preceramic Occupations in Belize: Updating the Paleoindian and Archaic Record of Belize." *Latin American Antiquity* 17, no. 2:209–26.

Lyman, R. Lee, Michael J. O'Brien, and Robert C. Dunnell. 1997. *The Rise and Fall of Cultural History*. New York: Plenum Press.

Lynch, Thomas. 1974. "The Antiquity of Man in South America." *Quaternary Research* 4:356–77.

———. 1990. "Glacial-Age Man in South America." *American Antiquity* 55, no. 1:12–36.

MacCurdy, George Grant. 1948. "Charles Peabody 1867–1939." *American School of Prehistoric Research Bulletin* 16:xxiii–xxiv.

MacDonald, F. George. 1968. *Debert: A Paleo-Indian Site in Central Nova Scotia*. Anthropology Papers 16. Ottawa: National Museum of Canada.

————. 1971. "A Review of Research on Paleo-Indian in Eastern North America, 1960–1970." *Arctic Anthropology* 8, no. 2:32–41.

MacNeish, Richard S. 1958. "Preliminary Archaeological Investigations in the Sierra de Tamaulipas, Mexico." *Transactions of the American Philosophical Society* 48(6).

————. 1964a. *Investigations in Southwest Yukon.* Papers of the Robert S. Peabody Foundation for Archaeology 6, no. 2. Andover MA: Phillips Academy.

————. 1964b. "Ancient Mesoamerican Civilization." *Science* 143(3606):531–37.

————. 1971. "Early Man in the Andes." *Scientific American* 224:36–46.

————. 1974. "Reflections on My Search for the Beginnings of Agriculture in Mexico." In *Archaeological Researches in Retrospect*, edited by Gordon Willey, 207–36. Cambridge MA: Winthrop.

————. 1979a. "Douglas Swain Byers 1903–1978." *American Antiquity* 44, no. 4:708–10.

————. 1979b. "The Early Remains from Pikimachay Cave, Ayacucho Basin, Highland Peru." In *Pre-Llano Cultures of the Americas: Paradoxes and Possibilities*, edited by Robert L. Humphrey and Dennis Stanford, 1–47. Washington DC: Anthropological Society of Washington.

————. 1983. "Early Man or Early Man in the New World: A Controversy." *Anthro-Quest, the L.S.B. Leakey Foundation News* 26:26–18.

————. 1996. "Frederick Johnson 1904–1994." *American Antiquity* 61, no. 2:269–71.

MacNeish, Richard S., and Jane G. Libby, eds. 2003. *Pendejo Cave.* Albuquerque: University of New Mexico Press.

Mangelsdorf, Paul C., Richard S. MacNeish, and Walton C. Galinat. 1964. "Domestication of Corn." *Science* 143(3606):538–45.

Mark, Joan. 1980. *Four Anthropologists: An American Science in Its Early Years.* New York: Science History Publications.

Marlowe, Greg. 1999. "Year One: Radiocarbon Dating and American Archaeology, 1947–1948." *American Antiquity* 64, no. 1:9–32.

McManamon, Francis P., and James W. Bradley. 1988. "The Indian Neck Ossuary." *Scientific American* 258, no. 5:98–104.

Meltzer, David J. 1991. "'On the Paradigms' and the 'Paradigm Bias' in Controversies over Human Antiquity in America." In *The First Americans: Search and Research*, edited by Tom D. Dillehay and David J. Meltzer, 13–52. Boca Raton FL: CRC Press.

————. 1994. "The Discovery of Deep Time: A History of the Views on the Peopling of the Americas." In *Method and Theory for Investigating the Peopling of the Americas*, edited by Robson Bonnichsen and D. Gentry Steele, 7–26. Center for the Study of the First Americans. Corvallis: Oregon State University.

————. 2005. "The Seventy-Year Itch: Controversies over Human Antiquity and Their Resolution." *Journal of Anthropological Research* 61, no. 4:433–68.

———. 2009. *First Peoples in a New World: Colonizing Ice Age America*. Berkeley: University of California Press.

———. 2015. *The Great Paleolithic War: How Science Forged an Understanding of America's Ice Age Past*. Chicago: University of Chicago Press.

Moorehead, Warren K. 1890. *Fort Ancient, the Great Prehistoric Earthwork of Warren County, Ohio, Compiled from a Careful Survey, with an Account of Its Mounds and Graves*. Cincinnati: Robert Clarke.

———. 1892. *Primitive Man in Ohio*. New York: G. P. Putnam and Sons.

———. 1893. "The Results of Search for Paleolithic Implements in the Ohio Valley." *Science* 21(531):192.

———. 1900. *Prehistoric Implements: A Reference Book*. Cincinnati: Robert Clarke Company.

———. 1901. "Notes and News [Phillips Academy]." *American Anthropologist* 3, no. 3:590–91.

———. 1902a. *Field Diary of an Archaeological Collector*. Andover MA.

———. 1902b. "Anthropologic Miscellanea [Archaeology at Phillips Academy]." *American Anthropologist* 4, no. 1:196–97.

———. 1904. "Commercial vs. Scientific Collection: A Plea for 'Art for Art's' Sake." *Ohio Archaeological and Historical Society Publications* 12, no. 1:112–17.

———. 1906a. "A Brief History of the Department of Archaeology at Phillips Academy." In *A Narrative of Explorations in New Mexico, Arizona, Indiana, Etc., Together with a Brief History of the Department*, edited by Warren K. Moorehead, 17–25. Department of Archaeology Bulletin 3. Andover MA: Phillips Academy.

———. 1906b. "Sketch of Mr. Robert Singleton Peabody." In *A Narrative of Explorations in New Mexico, Arizona, Indiana, Etc., Together with a Brief History of the Department*, edited by Warren K. Moorehead, 26–29. Department of Archaeology Bulletin 3. Andover MA: Phillips Academy.

———. 1909. "A Study of Primitive Culture in Ohio." In *Putnam Anniversary Volume: Anthropological Essays Presented to Frederic Ward Putnam in Honor of his Seventieth Birthday, April 16, 1909, by his Friends and Associates*, 137–50. New York: G. E. Stechert.

———. 1910. *The Stone Age in North America*. 2 vols. Boston: Houghton Mifflin.

———. 1917. *Stone Ornaments Used by Indians in the United States and Canada*. Andover MA: Andover Press.

———. 1922a. *The Hopewell Mound Group of Ohio*. Field Museum of Natural History Publication 211, Anthropological Series 6, no. 5. Chicago: Field Museum of Natural History.

————. 1922b. *Report on the Archaeology of Maine: Being a Narrative of Explorations in that State, 1912–1920, Together with Work at Lake Champlain, 1917.* Andover MA: Andover Press.

————. 1938. "The Archaeology Department of Phillips Academy: A Brief History." *Phillips Bulletin* (Andover MA: Phillips Academy) 33(3):6–12.

————. 2000. *The Cahokia Mounds.* Edited and with an introduction by John E. Kelly. Tuscaloosa: University of Alabama Press.

Norcini, Marilyn. 2008. "Frederick Johnson's Canadian Ethnology in the Americanist Tradition." *Histories of Anthropology Annual* 4:106–34.

O'Brien, Michael J. 1996. *Paradigms of the Past: The Story of Missouri Archaeology.* Columbia: University of Missouri Press.

O'Brien, Michael, and R. Lee Lyman. 1999. *Seriation, Stratigraphy and Index Fossils: The Backbone of Archaeological Dating.* New York: Kluwer Academic/Plenum Publishers.

Peabody, Charles. 1903. "Notes on Negro Music." *Journal of American Folk-Lore* 16, no. 62:148–52.

————. 1904. *Exploration of Mounds, Coahoma County, Mississippi.* Papers of the Peabody Museum of American Archaeology and Ethnology 3, no. 2. Cambridge MA: Harvard University.

————. 1908. *The Exploration of Bushey Cavern, near Cavetown, Maryland.* Bulletin of the Department of Archaeology 4, no. 1:5–25. Andover MA: Phillips Academy.

————. 1909 "Certain Quests and Doles." In *Putnam Anniversary Volume, Anthropological Essays Presented to Frederic Ward Putnam in Honor of His Seventieth Birthday, April 16, 1909, by his Friends and Associates,* 344–67. New York: G. E. Stechert.

————. 1910. "The Explorations of Mounds in North Carolina." *American Anthropologist* 12, no. 3:425–33.

————. 1915a. "Dedication of Peabody House, Address of Dr. Charles Peabody." *Phillips Bulletin* (Andover MA: Phillips Academy) 10, no. 1:16–17.

————. 1915b. "Frederic Ward Putnam." *Journal of American Folklore* 28, no. 109:302–6.

————. 1917. "Prehistoric Wind-Instrument from Pecos, New Mexico." *American Anthropologist* 19, no. 1:130–33.

Peabody, Charles, and Warren K. Moorehead. 1904. *The Explorations of Jacob's Cavern, McDonald County, Missouri.* Bulletin of the Department of Archaeology 1:1–29. Andover MA: Phillips Academy.

Peabody, Charles, and Elizabeth Manton Rawn. 1916. "More Songs and Ballads from the Southern Appalachians." *Journal of American Folk-Lore* 29:198–202.

Petersen, James B. 1995. "Preceramic Archaeological Manifestations in the Far Northeast: A Review of Recent Research." *Archaeology of Eastern North America* 23:207–30.

Purdy, Barbara A. 2012. "A Mammoth Engraving from Vero Beach, Florida: Ancient or Recent?" *Florida Anthropologist* 65, no. 4:205–17.

Putnam, Frederic Ward. 1913. "The Completion of the Great Museum." *Harvard Graduate's Magazine* 22, no. 83:25–28.

Putnam, Frederic Ward, Charles Conrad Abbott, George Frederick Wright, Warren Upham, Henry Williamson Haynes, and Edward Sylvester Moore. 1888. "Paleolithic Man in Eastern and Central North America." Reprinted from *Proceedings of the Boston Society of Natural History* 23. Cambridge MA: Peabody Museum of American Archaeology and Ethnology, Harvard University.

Richardson, James B., III. 1994. *People of the Andes.* Washington DC: Smithsonian Institution Press.

———. 2006a. "Peopling the New World: The View from South America." *Western Pennsylvania History* 89, no. 2:18–25.

———. 2006b. "Looking in the Right Places: Maritime Adaptations in Northeastern North America and the Central Andes." In *From the Arctic to Avalon: Papers in Honour of Jim Tuck,* edited by Lisa Rankin and Peter Ramsden, 83–98. British Archaeological Reports (BAR) International Series 1507.

Rick, John. 1988. "The Character and Context of Highland Preceramic Society." In *Peruvian Archaeology: An Overview of Pre-Inca and Inca Society,* edited by Richard W. Keatinge, 3–40. London: Cambridge University Press.

Ritchie, William A. 1932. "The Lamoka Lake Site." *Researches and Transactions of the New York State Archaeological Association* 7, no. 4:79–134.

Robert S. Peabody Museum of Archaeology. Founder records (1898–1903) 00.00. Andover: Phillips Academy.

———. Warren K. Moorehead records (1890s–1930s) 01.02 Andover: Phillips Academy.

Robinson, Brian S. 1996. "Regional Analysis of the Moorehead Burial Tradition." *Archaeology of Eastern North America* 24:95–148.

———. 2006. "Bull Brook and Debert: The Original Large Paleoindian Sites in Northeast North America." Paper presented at the Debert Workshop Conference, sponsored by the Confederacy of Mainland Mi'kmaq, Debert, Nova Scotia, October 20, 2005.

Robinson, Brian S., Jennifer C. Ort, William A. Eldridge, Adrian L. Burke, and Bertrand G. Pellier. 2009. "Paleoindian Aggregation and Social Context at Bull Brook." *American Antiquity* 74, no. 3:423–47.

Robinson, Brian S., and Eugene Winter. 2011. "A Wonderful Piece of Cooperative Work: Douglas F. Jordan's Contributions to Bull Brook." *Archaeology of the Eastern United States* 39:169–90.

Rosenmeier, Leah M., Scott Buchanan, Ralph Stea, and Gordon Brewster. 2012. "New Sites and Lingering Questions at the Debert and Belmont Sites, Nova Scotia." In *Late Pleistocene Archaeology and Ecology in the Far Northeast*, edited by Claude Chapdelaine, 113–34. College Station: Texas A&M University Press.

Schwartz, Douglas W. 2000. "Kidder and the Synthesis of Southwestern Archaeology." In *An Introduction to the Study of Southwestern Archaeology* by Alfred Vincent Kidder, 1–55, reprint of the 1924 edition. New Haven: Yale University Press.

Spiess, Arthur, Deborah Wilson, and James W. Bradley. 1998. "Paleoindian Occupation in the New England Maritimes Region: Beyond Cultural Ecology." *Archaeology of Eastern North America* 26:189–99.

Stanford, Dennis Joe, and Alison T. Stenger, eds. 2014. *Pre-Clovis in the Americas*. International Science Conference Proceedings. CreateSpace Independent Publishing Platform, Smithsonian Edition.

Stuckenrath, Robert, Jr. 1964. "The Debert Site: Early Man in the Northeast." *Bulletin of the University Museum* (Philadelphia: University of Pennsylvania), 7:20–9.

———. 1966. "The Debert Archaeological Project, Nova Scotia: Radiocarbon Dates." *Quaternaria* 8:75–80.

Thompson, Raymond H. 2002. "A. V. Kidder and the Andover Dump." *Kiva* 68, no. 2:129–33.

Tozzer, Alfred M. 1933. "Frederic Ward Putnam 1839–1915." In *Biographical Memoirs of the National Academy of Sciences* 16:125–53. Washington DC: National Academy of Sciences.

Weatherford, John W. 1956. "Warren King Moorehead and His Papers." *Ohio Historical Quarterly* 65, no. 2:179–90.

Wendorf, Fred, and Raymond H. Thompson. 2002. "The Committee for the Recovery of Archaeological Remains: Three Decades of Service to the Archaeological Profession." *American Antiquity* 67, no. 2:317–30.

Wilkerson, Jeffrey K. 1978. "Ripley Pierce Bullen, 1902–1976." *American Antiquity* 43, no. 4:622–30.

Willey, Gordon R. 1967. "Alfred Vincent Kidder 1885–1963." In *Biographical Memoirs of the National Academy of Sciences* 39: 293–322. Washington DC: National Academy of Sciences.

Willey, Gordon R., and Jeremy A. Sabloff. 1993. *A History of American Archaeology*, 3rd ed. New York: W. H. Freeman.

Williams, Stephen. 1999. "A Tribute to Charles Peabody." Typescript on file, Robert S. Peabody Museum of Archaeology, Phillips Academy, Andover MA.

Wilson, Thomas. 1889. "The Paleolithic Period in the District of Columbia." *American Anthropologist* 2:235–40.

————. 1890. "Results of an Inquiry as to the Existence of Man in North America during the Paleolithic Period of the Stone Age." In *Report of the National Museum 1887–1888*, 677–702.

Woodbury, Richard B. 1973. *Alfred V. Kidder*. New York: Columbia University Press.

Zeitlin, Robert N. 1984. "A Summary Report on Three Seasons of Field Investigations into the Archaic Period Prehistory of Lowland Belize." *American Anthropologist* 86, no. 2: 358–69.

Chapter 3

A. V. Kidder, Pecos Pueblo, and the Robert S. Peabody Museum

A CONTINUING LEGACY

Linda S. Cordell

The Robert S. Peabody Museum of Archaeology sponsored A. V. Kidder's multiyear excavations at Pecos Pueblo in New Mexico. This research established the standards for twentieth-century American archaeology. At Pecos, Kidder demonstrated the importance of stratigraphic excavation, produced the first synthesis of southwestern archaeology, and introduced a system of nomenclature that southwestern archaeologists still use today. Kidder engaged archaeologists, ethnologists, scholars from other disciplines, and students in his work. His vision and approach remain models for today and are reflected in the policies and programs of the museum and Phillips Academy.

The Robert S. Peabody Museum of Archaeology at Andover is rightfully credited with being of fundamental importance to the development of American archaeology in the early twentieth century. The intellectual legacy of the research sponsored by the R. S. Peabody Foundation for the museum and directed by Alfred Vincent Kidder (1885–1963) at Pecos Pueblo was and continues to be of singular importance to American archaeology in general and particularly to archaeology in the American Southwest.

Becoming an Archaeologist

A. V. Kidder (called "Ted" by his family), who was to become the preeminent American archaeologist of the twentieth century, was born in

Marquette, Michigan, on October 29, 1885, the son Alfred Kidder of Boston and Kate Dalliba of Chicago. When the family moved to Massachusetts Kidder went to school in Cambridge and Boston, and then was sent for two years of study to Ouchy, Switzerland, before entering Harvard in 1904 (Willey 1967). Kidder intended to study medicine, though in his own words (cited in Woodbury 1973, 4), he "abominated" his courses in chemistry. He did enjoy his anthropology classes, especially one on the archaeology and ethnology of American Indians, taught by the renowned and dynamic lecturer Roland B. Dixon (with Vilhjamur Stefansson, the future famed ethnographer of the Arctic, as teaching assistant), and those courses offered by F. W. Putnam, curator of the Harvard Peabody Museum and a friend of Kidder's father (Willey 1988, 305; Woodbury 1973, 5).

The turning point in Kidder's decision to change from a career in medicine to one in anthropology came at breakfast one morning in his junior year when he noticed "an announcement in the [Harvard] *Crimson* for three men who had specialized in anthropology who might be accepted as volunteers on an expedition to the cliff-dwelling country under the auspices of the Archaeological Institute of America" (Woodbury 1973, 5). The ad had been placed at the behest of Edgar L. Hewett, who that summer was leading a group from the University of Utah (Fowler 2000, 267). Because Kidder, Sylvanus Morley, and John Gould Fletcher were the only three to respond, all were accepted. The three young men arrived at Bluff City, Utah, in 1907. After instructing them to survey, map, and test ruins in the area, a task described as similar to being pushed off the pier, Hewett pretty much abandoned them (Givens 1992, 11).

Edgar Lee Hewett was a powerful, though controversial, figure in southwestern archaeology throughout his life (Fowler 2000, 26, 262–63). Although he did not have an Ivy League education and was not trained in archaeology, he was director of the Museum of New Mexico and of the School of American Archaeology in Santa Fe. Founded at Hewett's behest by the Archaeological Institute of America, this institution later became the School for American Research and now is the School of Advanced Research on the Human Experience (Fowler 2000, 267). In California,

Hewett was director of the San Diego Museum of Man and was professor of anthropology at San Diego State Teachers College. Later he became professor of anthropology at the University of New Mexico and assisted in founding the Anthropology Department at the University of Southern California. Hewett was instrumental in crafting and seeing to the passage of the Antiquities Act of 1906. He played an important part in Kidder's selection of Pecos Pueblo as the site of the R. S. Peabody Museum's expedition to the Southwest.

In summer 1907 Kidder wrote he was "dazed" by the vast desolation of "naked red rock below and all about, mesas, pinnacles, ragged canyon walls, sheer cliff [and] a bit overcome by what Mr. Hewett so casually told us we were to do. He [Hewett] waved an arm, taking in, it seemed, about half the world, 'I want you boys to make an archaeological survey of this country. I'll be back in three weeks'" (cited in Fowler 2000, 265–66). The three young men wasted no time. Kidder noted that Morley was the "sparkplug" of their expedition (Givens 1992, 133–34).[1] Having just completed a field season doing Maya archaeology in the Yucatán, Morley knew what an archaeological survey was, including writing descriptions, taking notes and photographs, and drawing plans of archaeological sites without excavation.

Kidder seems to have been enchanted by the Southwest, especially the Mesa Verde country, where, having saddled his horse and "had a splendid gallop in the cool of the early hours," he found himself above a canyon. He wrote:

Desolation, these ruined settlements of a lost people are its typification. Flat tops of the mesas with their dusty sage brush and dried-up, tortured cedars; the rock upper stretches of the canyons; and between stand the broken brown walls. Rabbits dodge above the towers, lizards whisk in and out of the gaping windows; the only sound is the far-off coo of a wild dove, and upon all the sun beats down out of the cloudless sky. (Cited in Givens 1992, 136–37)

That fall Kidder returned to Harvard and earned a bachelor's degree in 1908, an MA in 1912, and a PhD in 1914, all in anthropology. Among his teachers and mentors were Dixon, Putnam, and perhaps most significant, Egyptologist George A. Reisner, who was curator at the Museum of Fine Arts in Boston as well a professor at Harvard. Kidder also took a class from Franz Boas, often considered the founder of American anthropology, who did a term as guest professor at Harvard and who had been Dixon's major professor (Willey 1967, 295–96). Boas was not particularly interested in archaeology, but he was determined to remake anthropology as a science. Those of his students who were archaeologists brought scientific techniques and perspectives to the study of remains from the past. Under the influence of Boas and most especially his students, museums began to mount scientific expeditions and to become repositories for knowledge about the past, rather than simply settings in which to display exotic objects. Archaeologists undertook fieldwork to increase knowledge about past societies and cultures, not to find treasures for exhibit or sale.

In Egypt Sir Flinders Petrie was revolutionizing archaeology through the detailed study of pottery, especially changes in design styles over time. He classified designs on pottery found in graves that could be dated to a particular time period, such as the reign of a pharaoh. Petrie was then able to use the pottery design style to give chronological order not only to the pottery but to other objects found with it in the grave, because he assumed that pottery and other objects were placed in the grave at the same time with the deceased. Petrie's technique is referred to as grave-lot seriation or sequencing in time. Reisner devised his own method of documenting stylistic change in Egyptian pottery and texts that was more detailed than Petrie's. This seriation and his work on the royal tombs of Giza brought well-deserved recognition (Dunham 1942). Kidder's fascination with pottery was reflected in his master's and doctoral work. He saw the systematic study of southwestern pottery as a key to the culture history and development of Pueblo Indian peoples, a topic that remains of major and continuing interest in Southwest archaeology. Kidder's recognition that pottery was an important tool for scientific archaeology was something he would have learned from Reisner or one of the other early practitioners of stratigraphic excavation (Browman 2003, 36–37; Browman and Givens 1996; Wauchope 1965, 151).

Kidder's (1914) doctoral dissertation, "Southwestern Ceramics: Their Value in Reconstructing the History of the Ancient Cliff Dwellings and Pueblo Tribes: An Exposition from the View of Type Distinctions," drew heavily on Reisner's methods. Kidder viewed the study of pottery technology and design not as an end in itself but as a means to gaining information and serving as a yardstick of cultural development in the Americas. Comparing the rich archaeological resources of the American Southwest with those of Egypt and Ancient Greece, and using the same scholarly approach to unraveling cultural developments in the two hemispheres, was an intellectual activity close to Hewett's heart. Hewett's School for American Archaeology in Santa Fe was founded to be the equivalent to the Archaeological Institute of America's schools in Rome and Athens (Snead 2001, 83). Hewett frequently compared archaeological sites in the American Southwest with well-known classical antiquities. For example, the tenth-century site called Chetro Ketl, in Chaco Canyon, New Mexico, "almost exactly equals in extent that of the palace site of Knossos in Crete" (Hewett 1930, 295). Of New World cultures in general, Hewett (1930, 51) wrote, "In esthetic attainments they rivaled the ancient Egyptians; they were fairly comparable to the Orientals." Kidder applied the most advanced methods used to study Ancient Egypt to his research in the American Southwest.

To understand Kidder's unique contributions, we need to recall that in 1914 (the year of his PhD), there were no techniques for giving calendar dates to archaeological sites—no tree-ring dates, no radiocarbon determinations, no obsidian hydration, no thermoluminescence dating, and so on. Moreover, while field techniques were fairly advanced in Europe, the same was not true for the Americas. Stratigraphic excavation was known to be of importance for European Paleolithic caves, but it was generally thought that stratigraphy did not apply in the Americas, where shorter periods of time are represented in the archaeological record. Stratigraphy—or the ordering of layers of earth and cultural deposits in the ground—is a key to understanding change over time, a conceptual cornerstone in paleontology and archaeology. The intellectual basis of stratigraphic ordering depends upon the geological principle of superposition. In essence, it is the inference that in a stack of things (such as papers and books on a desk), the items on the bottom were placed there before those above. The relevance of this observation and its implications are enormous.

In the early twentieth century the importance of careful, stratigraphically controlled excavations was underdeveloped and poorly understood in the Americas. In the Southwest credit for introducing stratigraphic excavation is usually given to Nels C. Nelson (1916) for his work in the Galisteo Basin of New Mexico (Willey and Sabloff 1980, 17). Kidder's work expanded upon this concept of stratigraphy. He systematically and scientifically traced cultural development by studying pottery with the same detail as did Reisner for Egypt, and he associated materials over time as revealed by their occurrences in stratigraphic sequences. Kidder's intellectual approach, learned at Harvard, provided the method archaeologists needed to begin to unravel the ancient histories of American Indian cultures. Further, having been in the field and trained by his peers and colleagues to record archaeological data carefully (to "read dirt"), Kidder had the ability actually to demonstrate the value of his technique. Kidder's approach was not armchair speculation. It was the first new, explicitly scientific archaeology in the Americas (Snead 2001), and through this work, the R. S. Peabody Museum became an exemplar of scientific archaeology in the Southwest.

Pecos Pueblo

After his initiation into the joys of southwestern fieldwork in 1907, Kidder continued working in the area during the summers while he pursued his graduate studies. He worked primarily in the Four Corners region, in southeastern Utah in 1908, and with Samuel Guernsey in northeastern Arizona (Kidder and Guernsey 1919). He continued to publish papers on his early work in the Mesa Verde region (Kidder 1917). Phillips Academy, "although a boys' preparatory school rather than a college or university, had developed an important museum and archaeological research program under W. K. Moorehead" (Willey 1967, 297). According to Kidder (1962 [1924], 1), in

1915 the trustees of Phillips Academy, at the suggestion of Dixon and Hiram Bingham, who were acting as Advisory Committee to the Trustees for the academy's Department of Archaeology, decided to undertake excavations in the Southwest. They wanted to select a place of sufficient size and scientific importance to justify work over several years. The new archaeological initiative seems to have come about through a confluence of otherwise dissimilar political agendas among Hewett and Kenneth Chapman in Santa Fe, Dixon at Harvard, and Hiram Bingham at Yale.

The selection of Kidder, forwarded by Bingham and Dixon, was a strong statement of support by the eastern establishment for the new, scientific archaeology (Woodbury 1973, 30). Kidder, however, had been thinking about working at Aztec Ruins on the San Juan River south of Mesa Verde, in the country he knew well and loved (cited in Givens 1992, 39). Hewett favored Pecos Pueblo over Aztec for at least two reasons. Pecos was closer to Santa Fe than was Aztec and therefore would be a splendid showcase for visitors, especially East Coast philanthropists and scholars. As Kidder wrote (cited in Givens 1992, 47), "Hewett was very anxious to make a tourist attraction out of Pecos." Second, Hewett had done a reconnaissance survey of the Upper Pecos valley in 1904 and had conducted ethnographic interviews among the descendants of Pecos Pueblo who were living at Jemez Pueblo. He realized that Pecos offered one of those relatively rare situations in which a combined ethnographic, archaeological, and historical study of a people would be possible. Such a study would be comparable to those done among the classical cultures of the Old World and to studies of the Hopi (Fewkes 1900) that attempted to link migrations to archaeological sites (Cordell 1998, 13). Still, it is unlikely that Kidder would have agreed to Pecos had he not visited the pueblo one day with Kenneth Chapman, who was just beginning his scholarly and artistic explorations of Pueblo pottery (Munson 2007). At Pecos Kidder said he "happened to find two or three sherds of Little Colorado Pottery as well as one or two Hopi sherds, plus every known form of pottery of the upper Rio Grande" (Kidder, in Givens 1992, 39). In his characteristically gracious way, Kidder remarked that his not taking Aztec was a good choice, because Earl Morris, who did excavate Aztec (Morris 1939), did a better job than he (Kidder) could have done (Kidder, in Givens 1992, 39). Certainly the history of Southwest archaeology, and likely American archaeology as a whole, would have been very different had Kidder not chosen Pecos.

Kidder began work at Pecos Pueblo in 1915 and continued there in 1916. His work was interrupted by his service in World War I (1917–18), but he returned to Pecos in 1919 and continued to work there until 1929, when he left Phillips Academy to do Maya research for the Carnegie Institution of Washington (see Givens 1992, 57–61 and Thompson 2002 on Kidder's war service and Carl Guthe's continuation of the Pecos expedition). Nevertheless, Kidder continued publishing on his Southwest research into the 1950s.

Kidder's excavations at Pecos Pueblo, financed by the Robert S. Peabody Foundation for Archaeology, "were the first large-scale systematic stratigraphic excavations in New World archaeology," wherein Kidder "made explicit the methodological differences between the stratigraphic placement of cultural materials and their geological physical stratigraphy and the implications of these differences for archaeology" (Willey 1988, 307). The materials Kidder recovered from Pecos, rather than being used for exhibition on dusty museum shelves or displays in then popular "Indian rooms," became part of continuing research. Because they came from documented systematic excavations, the Pecos collections were (and are) used by generations of archaeologists to study broad anthropological topics, such as how and why technology changes and the culture history of Pueblo Indian peoples. With his work at Pecos, Kidder became—and still is—the most respected Southwest archaeologist of all time (Willey 1988, 307).

Legacies of Kidder's Work at Pecos

Kidder made lasting achievements at Pecos. To begin with, his publication of *An Introduction to the Study of Southwestern Archaeology with a Preliminary Account of the Excavations at Pecos* (1924) was the first systematic organization of southwestern archaeological data. The book is described as "a vitally alive, un-pedantic account of what archaeologists do in the field and why" (Willey 1988, 309). Those who work in Southwest archaeology refer to this book frequently. Kidder's prose is always "lucid, simple and thoughtful" (Woodbury 1973, x). Kidder's clear and thoughtful writing is one reason southwestern archaeologists have spent a lot of time with Kidder's book in our tents and later at our computers.

Second, Kidder demonstrated the value of using scientific methods. The work at Pecos showed that stratigraphic excavations of cultural material did yield valuable information about change over time. There could be no excuse *not* to excavate in careful, stratigraphic levels. As a concomitant to stratigraphic excavation at Pecos, Kidder developed the ceramic chronology that is still used in the Rio Grande region. His ceramic analysis also provided a forum for other kinds of scientific study of pottery, such as the optical petrography of Anna O. Shepard, whose work continues to guide and inspire research today (see Cordell and Habicht-Mauche 2012; Habicht-Mauche et al. 2006).

Further, Kidder's work at Pecos initiated a framework for archaeological investigations that became a model not only in the American Southwest but in Maya studies as well. Kidder demonstrated the value of what is sometimes termed the direct historical approach. This method of investigation basically "works back from the known." In the case of Pecos, it meant studying both historic (Spanish) records of the Pecos people and also their modern descendants in the Pueblo of Jemez. In what is surely one of the first examples of ethnoarchaeology—or the use of ethnographic observation to understand past behavior better, especially technology—Kidder encouraged research by ethnologist Elsie Clews Parsons and archaeologist Carl Guthe. Parsons studied Jemez Pueblo for insights about Pecos, and Guthe studied San Ildefonso Pueblo for additional insights into pottery making. These studies also established the value of interdisciplinary, collaborative efforts in archaeology. While they were not always welcomed by the descendant communities (Toya 2006), they had the beneficial result of firmly tying American Indians to their ancestral homes.

Third, Kidder established the Pecos Conference, a forum for the discussion of problems in regional archaeology (Woodbury 1983). Out of the Pecos Conference came a classificatory system for Ancestral Pueblo material culture and development that—while it has acknowledged faults—is still in use by southwestern archaeologists today. The Pecos Conference is a model for the inclusion of the diverse perspectives from academic and professional archaeologists, students, avocational archaeologists, and those who contribute to archaeology from other disciplines. For example, it was at a Pecos Conference that tree-ring dating was encouraged. At another Pecos Conference the finds at Folsom, New Mexico, were announced, providing incontrovertible evidence of the great antiquity of American Indians on this continent. It was also at these annual meetings that Charles Lindbergh demonstrated the archaeological value of aerial photography. The Pecos Conference continues today, convening in a different location in the Southwest each year but returning to Pecos every five years.

After Kidder carried out systematic excavations in the American Southwest he went on to a spectacular career in Maya archaeology (Givens 1992; Greengo 1968; Willey 1988; Woodbury 1973). But it was the Southwest that drew him into the profession, and it is his work in the Southwest that professionalized all of American archaeology.

Knowing how inspirational the Pecos Pathways program is for young people, (see Randall and Toya, this volume), I wondered how Kidder was as a teacher and mentor of students and how he was with kids—his own and others—in general. During his career Kidder did no teaching except while he was a graduate student teaching fellow at Harvard and, late in his life, one semester as a visiting professor at the University of California at Berkeley. Yet he is credited with encouraging young scholars, especially Carl Guthe, Samuel Lothrop, George Vaillant, Earl Morris, and Anna O. Shepard. In interviewing Kidder's grandson, Rudy Busé, and Carol Decker, who knew Kidder when she was a child, I learned that he was not "particularly cuddly with kids." Richard Woodbury (1993, 44, 73) notes that Kidder's three youngest children were "banished" from the inaugural Pecos Conference and that Kidder lamented the presence of Leslie Spier's two small children. From his children's perspectives Madeleine Kidder dominated the household and organized the kids (Kidder Aldana 1983). On the other hand, Kidder acknowledged that he stayed a long time excavating Pecos Pueblo, because "it was a grand place to be with the kids" (quoted in Givens 1992, 145–46). Rudy Busé shared another bit of Kidder memorabilia that I am pleased to include here (fig. 20). Kidder's stick figure drawings are as legendary as the man himself. The one in

FIG. 20. Drawing by Alfred V. Kidder, showing different perspectives of archaeological fieldwork. Drawing provided to the author by Rudy Busé.

figure 20, presented to his colleague Joe Brew and to his grandchildren, was done for grandchildren and shared in bed on a Sunday morning. It is particularly charming—and revealing—as it humorously contrasts the changing perspectives of archaeological fieldwork.

Finally, Kidder's work at Pecos continues to be relevant to twenty-first-century concerns in American archaeology. As noted, basic questions about pottery and about technological and social change were raised at Pecos and continue to be a focus of research today. Kidder's collaborative view of how archaeology should be conducted remains a model for the field. The relationships Kidder established with descendant communities, although sometimes one-sided (with archaeologists and anthropologists on the taking side), did acknowledge the legitimacy of descendant community knowledge and oral history. This respect served as a model for the NAGPRA repatriations (see Bradley, this volume) and for the thoughtful, collaborative, educational sharing of knowledge that is the core of the Pecos Pathways program to this day (see Randall and Toya, this volume). It is a tribute to the Robert S. Peabody Museum and to Phillips Academy that all the work at Pecos—the science, the well-documented collections, the history of American archaeology—is shared with "youth from every quarter," including the students at Phillips Academy, the young people from the Pueblo of Jemez, and the youth from the village of Pecos.

Kidder's legacy is not obsolete. Dedicated Peabody and Phillips Academy advisors, staff, and trustees have helped maintain Kidder's high standards for scholarship. Kidder's dedication to science and his interest in increasing and sharing knowledge about humankind's achievements remain relevant today. The legacy he has left can serve as a model applicable to other institutions of learning and, in fact, to our twenty-first-century society.

Acknowledgments

I thank Malinda Blustain for the invitation to participate in the session devoted to the Robert S. Peabody Museum of Archaeology at the Society for American Archaeology annual meeting in Sacramento and for her asking my willingness to serve on the R. S. Peabody Museum's Advisory

Committee. I am grateful to Rudy Busé for providing his grandfather's stick-figure drawing for inclusion in this volume and for his time and commitment to all things Pecos. I appreciate the time Rudy and Carol Decker made available for interviews and the assistance of the R. S. Peabody staff in locating images.

NOTES

Editors' Note: This chapter was prepared prior to Linda Cordell's untimely passing in March 2013. Linda did not have an opportunity to address peer review comments, so the chapter is published as it was received from her in 2011.

1. The biographical treatments by Givens (1992) and Willey (1967) contain material from recorded interviews with Kidder and from Kidder's diaries and personal papers. Woodbury's (1973) book contains extensive excerpts from Kidder's writings.

REFERENCES

Browman, David L. 2003. "Origins of Americanist Stratigraphic Excavation Methods." In *Picking the Lock of Time: Developing Chronology in American Archaeology*, edited by James Truncer, 22–39. Gainesville: University Press of Florida.

Browman, David L., and Douglas R. Givens. 1996. "Stratigraphic Excavation: The First New Archaeology." *American Anthropologist* 98, no. 1:80–95.

Cordell, Linda S. 1998. *Before Pecos: Settlement Aggregation at Rowe, New Mexico*. Maxwell Museum of Anthropology, Anthropological Papers 6. Albuquerque NM: Maxwell Museum of Anthropology.

Cordell, Linda S., and Judith A. Habicht-Mauche, eds. 2012. *Potters and Communities of Practice: Glaze Paint and Polychrome Pottery in the American Southwest, A.D. 1250–1700*, Anthropological Papers of the University of Arizona 75. Tucson: University of Arizona Press.

Dunham, Dows. 1942. "George Andrew Reisner." *American Journal of Archaeology* 46, no. 3:410–12.

Fewkes, Jesse W. 1900. "Tusayan Migration Traditions." In *Nineteenth Annual Report of the Bureau of American Ethnology, 1897–98, Pt. 2*. Washington DC: Government Printing Office.

Fowler, Don D. 2000. *A Laboratory for Anthropology: Science and Romanticism in the American Southwest, 1846–1930*. Albuquerque: University of New Mexico Press.

Givens, Douglas R. 1992. *Alfred Vincent Kidder and the Development of Americanist Archaeology*. Albuquerque: University of New Mexico Press.

Greengo, Robert E. 1968. "Alfred Vincent Kidder 1885–1963." *American Anthropologist* 70, no. 2:320–25.

Habicht-Mauche, Judith A., Suzanne L. Eckert, and Deborah L. Huntley, eds. 2006. *The Social Life of Pots: Glaze Wares and Cultural Dynamics in the Southwest, A.D. 1250–1680*. Tucson: University of Arizona Press.

Hewett, Edgar L. 1904. "Studies on the Extinct Pueblo of Pecos." *American Anthropologist* 6, no. 4:426–39.

———. 1930. *Ancient Life in the American Southwest*. Bridgeport CT: Bobbs-Merrill.

Kidder, Alfred Vincent. 1914. "Southwestern Ceramics: Their Value in Reconstructing the History of the Ancient Cliff Dwellings and Pueblo Tribes: An Exposition from the View of Type Distinction." PhD diss., Harvard University.

———. 1917. "Prehistoric Cultures of the San Juan Drainage." In *Proceedings of the 19th International Congress of Americanists*, 108–13. Washington DC.

———. 1962 [1924]. *An Introduction to the Study of Southwestern Archaeology with a Preliminary Account of the Excavations at Pecos*, reprint edition, with an introduction by Irving Rouse. New Haven: Yale University Press.

Kidder, Alfred Vincent, and Samuel J. Guernsey. 1919. *Archaeological Explorations in Northeastern Arizona*. Bulletin of the Bureau of American Ethnology 65. Washington DC: Government Printing Office.

Kidder Aldana, Barbara. 1983. "The Kidder Pecos Expedition, 1924–1929: A Personal Memoir." *Kiva* 48, no. 4:243–50.

Morris, Earl H. 1939. *Archaeological Studies in the La Plata District, Southwestern Colorado, and Northwestern New Mexico*. Publications of the Carnegie Institution of Washington 519. Washington DC: Carnegie Institution.

Munson, Marit K. 2007. *Kenneth Chapman's Santa Fe, Artists and Archaeologists, 1907–1931: The Memoirs of Kenneth Chapman*. Santa Fe: SAR Press.

Nelson, Nels C. 1916. "Chronology of the Tano Ruins, New Mexico." *American Anthropologist* 18, no. 2:150–80.

Snead, James E. 2001. *Ruins and Rivals: The Making of Southwest Archaeology*. Tucson: University of Arizona Press.

Toya, Chris. 2006. "The View from Walatowa: A Jemez Pueblo Perspective on Archaeology and Traditional Cultural Properties." Paper presented at the 71st Annual Meeting of the Society for American Archaeology, San Juan, Puerto Rico.

Thompson, Raymond H. 2002. "Archaeological Innocence at Pecos in 1917–1918." *Kiva* 68, no. 2:123–27.

Wauchope, Robert. 1965. "Alfred Vincent Kidder, 1885–1963." *American Antiquity* 31, no. 2, pt 1:149–71.

Willey, Gordon R. 1967. "Alfred Vincent Kidder." In *Biographical Memoirs of the National Academy of Sciences* 39, 292–322. New York: Columbia University Press.

———. 1988. *Portraits in American Archaeology*. Albuquerque: University of New Mexico Press.

Willey, Gordon R., and Jeremy A. Sabloff. 1980. *A History of American Archaeology*. San Francisco: W. H. Freeman.

Woodbury, Richard B. 1973. *Alfred V. Kidder*. Leaders in Modern Anthropology Series. New York: Columbia University Press.

———. 1983. "Looking Back at the Pecos Conference." *Kiva* 48, no. 4:251–66.

———. 1993. *Sixty Years of Southwestern Archaeology: A History of the Pecos Conference*. Albuquerque: University of New Mexico Press.

Chapter 4

Laying the Foundations for Northeastern North American Archaeology

Brian S. Robinson

When the Department of Archaeology was established at Phillips Academy in Andover in 1901, it was the purpose of Robert S. Peabody "to give young men a means of knowing something of Indian history, manners, customs and character" (Moorehead 1938, 52). There was no particular focus on New England, but that is where Phillips Academy happened to be. This happenstance resulted in one of the most persistent and integrated investigations of Northeast archaeology that has ever been conducted, spanning all the major theoretical and ethical developments of Native American archaeology of the twentieth century. Among the Peabody Museum's achievements were both unique discoveries and "groundbreaking" methodologies that, taken together, continue to lead so many researchers back to the museum. This essay is focused on the early contributions of Warren K. Moorehead—since my dissertation was on the Moorehead burial tradition in Maine (Robinson 2001; Sanger 1973)—and spans the decades through the 1950s when the Robert S. Peabody Museum was the major center of northeastern archaeological research.

Neither the first director, Charles Peabody, nor the first curator, Warren K. Moorehead, was focused on the Northeast in 1901. Moorehead's earlier excavations at various Hopewell mound sites in Ohio yielded spectacular discoveries using what are now hair-raising methods (Moorehead 1922a, 102; Christenson 2011). Douglas Byers (1939, 288) would later call

Moorehead "a member of Old School of thought . . . forever occupied with the problems of surveys." It has also been said, "Although Moorehead understood the concepts of stratigraphy, his interest, as with many others before him, was the artifacts" (Kelly in Moorehead 2000, 2). He was intensely focused on the distribution and groupings of different classes of artifacts and their relation to major culture groups. Little was known about the relationship of artifacts, culture, and time when the Department of Archaeology at Andover was founded. Long before radiocarbon dating and the discovery of Folsom (see Richardson and Adovasio, this volume), there were sustained arguments about whether major archaeological patterns represented historically known Indian tribes or whether the patterns were older, and what that meant. In the Northeast the major prehistoric cultural periods were the "Pre-Algonquian," referring to the time shortly before European contact for the Algonquian-speaking groups, and the "Old Algonquian" of undefined earlier relationship (Willoughby 1935, 3). Culture areas in North America as a whole were broad and relatively few, based on the most visible kinds of traits, such as mounds, burial goods, and architecture. Moorehead's interests were spread across much of the continent, in both archaeology and modern Native issues.

When Moorehead (1922b, 12) came to New England, he noted that archaeology had been singularly neglected compared to other areas, due to the fact that there were no "conspicuous archaeological monuments, no mounds or earthworks, cliff houses or ruined buildings." He chose Maine as a starting place in 1912, largely based on the "splendid exhibits" of the "so-called Red Paint People" assembled by Charles Willoughby (1898). These artifact assemblages "opened the question of the extent of territory occupied by these people and the possibility of correlating their peculiar culture and others" (Moorehead 1922b, 13) (fig. 21). It was relationships, not just splendid finds, that motivated Moorehead. His survey of Maine was directed toward the Red Paint People, the coastal shell heaps, and the interior village sites. He and his crews traversed 5,400 miles of rivers and coastline, mostly by canoe, in nine years. They consulted local knowledge sources extensively, including Walter B. Smith (1926) and Ernest Sugden, who worked closely with Moorehead. In multiple publications Moorehead

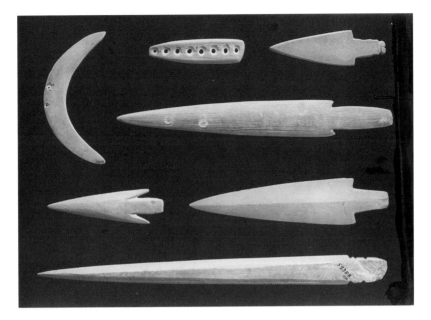

FIG. 21. Ground slate artifacts from the Red Paint burials of Maine (in Moorehead 1922b). Photographic collection of the Robert S. Peabody Museum of Archaeology.

(1914; 1922b, 150) presented and defended his interpretation of the "Red Paint People" as an ancient culture group in Maine, a conclusion largely borne out by radiocarbon dates of between 3,700 and 5,200 years ago and with origins up to 8500 BP (Before Present; Robinson 2006).

Moorehead did not try to refine the chronology of the "Red Paint People," as he was sufficiently absorbed by establishing regional boundaries and relationships. Benjamin Smith (1948) compiled a more extensive catalog of cemeteries and artifact types to address these problems. Chronological analysis was left until radiocarbon dating was introduced, combined with efforts to seriate assemblages reported by Moorehead and Smith (Bourque 1992, 2012; Sanger 1973; Snow 1975). My dissertation research at Brown University built on all these efforts in the 1980s and 1990s, further emphasizing the many research paths leading back to the Peabody Museum (Robinson 2001, 2006).

In the copious correspondence and papers left by Moorehead and his colleagues, one finds descriptive reporting, enthusiasm for various interests, constant need for fundraising, pleading, promoting, defending, and lively debates on seemingly timeless issues. From the changing perspectives of the 1920s to 1950s, Moorehead was an archaeologist of the old school. At the same time, the old school often produced the irreplaceable descriptive reports that are needed to address problems of modern culture history and changing theoretical interests. Moorehead was well aware of changing disciplines and varied interests. In a 1931 presentation to the Explorers Club in New York, he summarized his own profession through a conversation that he had had in Bar Harbor, Maine, with a prominent fiction writer:

> The author, on shaking hands, remarked, "So you're an anthropologist." "Not at all," I replied, "merely an archaeologist. . . . The anthropologists take themselves very seriously. Your true anthropologist stands before the altar of science within the inner court, where as the humble archaeologist is without, somewhat removed from the shrine and is engaged in contemplation of the foundations." (Moorehead 1931a, 1, 2)

Eighty years later there are archaeologists who would consider this to be precisely the case, others who would agree with the separation but describe it in opposite terms, and those of us who are happily convinced that good science depends on what we hold dear, just as history and humanism depend on good science. Moorehead's comments are from a different time, however, when precise dating of the past was only rarely accomplished. He considered that archaeology, taken literally, "means prehistory and therefore, when we are able to establish dates, we pass from the realm of archaeology into the more exact science, history" (Moorehead 1931a, 9). Detailed chronology was often a topic beyond reach and therefore of secondary interest.

Although Moorehead insisted that he was "merely an archaeologist," this did not conflict with his advocacy for modern Indian studies and the plight of living Native Americans, likely inspired in part by his attendance at the Ghost Dance at the Lakota Pine Ridge Indian Reservation shortly before the Massacre at Wounded Knee in 1890 (Moorehead 1891). His active role on the U.S. Board of Indian Commissioners (Bacon 2009), to which he was appointed in 1908 by Theodore Roosevelt, is representative of Moorehead's and the Robert S. Peabody Foundation's dedication to Native American issues as a whole, past and present (Bacon 2009). Moorehead's dedication to the whole of American archaeology manifested itself in what now appear to be eyebrow-raising goals, which in turn are reflected in his approach to New England. Moorehead viewed Native American archaeology—that is, prehistory—in terms of the distribution of differing artifact types that were in jeopardy of being lost to pot hunters and, sometimes equally urgent, of being discovered by other archaeologists.

Moorehead first and foremost was a researcher, and that is what he considered to be the mission of the Robert S. Peabody Museum. On October 17, 1919, Moorehead (Ohio History Connection, Moorehead papers, box 59) wrote in his "Report to the Archaeological Committee of Trustees of Phillips Academy":

> Your Curator desires to enter a protest against the setting aside yearly of a large sum for a new building. We do not have visitors here, and from indications [of] the past nineteen years, we will never have a large number of persons who desire to see our collections. Our Department should be for research. All the scientists I have talked with agree on this point. The American field is rapidly diminishing. I estimated that in twelve to fifteen years all the major archaeological problems will be solved.

If we chide Moorehead for his lack of foresight in terms of the problems of archaeology, we should realize he wrote at a time when the basic identification of archaeological culture areas across America was little known, even in terms of a nonchronological tally of artifact patterns and their boundaries. Moorehead took on this responsibility and crusade on a national scale, not always within the limits or vision of Phillips Academy. Charles Peabody (Ohio History Connection, Moorehead papers, box 59) responded with prescience to this ongoing debate in a letter to Moorehead from France, dated October 20, 1920:

> I do not think that the Department should become a research institution pure and simple; that side of it is becoming more and more emphasized

as time goes on, but there is still good reason for the Museum and its competent Curator, in spite of the fact that we have not very many visitors; when we take up our teaching work again the Museum will have a considerable role to play.

One can imagine the frustrations of the trustees at Phillips Academy when Moorehead made his requests. In a letter to Charles Peabody dated October 31, 1919, Moorehead (Ohio History Connection, Moorehead papers, box 57; the referenced Arkansas research was published in Moorehead 1931b) wrote:

> I have asked Professor Ropes [a trustee] for three or four months leave of absence this winter, and he has granted it. The reason for such request is that the Pan Handle of Texas has developed into a very important sector. I have sent another man through that region and he has found groups of ruins for three hundred miles south of Pecos over the mountains and in an entirely different river valley—the Arkansas. I notified Professor Ropes of the importance of this discovery twice but he was not interested. I told him that it was the dominant problem in the southwest and there the cultures mingle. Since he has declined to have me explore it for Phillips Academy it is proper for me to take up the matter of exploration elsewhere.

Indeed, the effort to have the academy enter the Texas and Arkansas sectors was recounted in the same letter as requests for further research on the Red Paint cemeteries in Maine. Moorehead (Ohio History Connection, Moorehead papers, box 57, referring to the Lancaster Cemetery in Winslow, Maine, reported in Moorehead 1922b, 95 and Wellman 1984) wrote in the very next paragraph:

> On my way home from Springfield, Mass., we stopped at Waterville, Maine, from whence I had been telegraphed of the discovery of a Red Paint cemetery and asked to take charge. I telephoned Professor Ropes that the place was farther west than we had found burials of this culture and that he should take it for Andover. He declined, but said for me to excavate it for others. I did so in the interests of the Bangor Historical Society, they paying the expenses.

FIG. 22. Warren K. Moorehead with Phillips Academy students at the Shattuck Farm site in Andover. Photographic collection of the Robert S. Peabody Museum of Archaeology.

Archaeology was changing. If Moorehead was comparatively disinterested in stratigraphy and chronology, the work of Alfred V. Kidder at Pecos, New Mexico, sponsored by Phillips Academy, is among the founding studies of cultural chronology in North America (see Richardson and Adovasio, and Cordell, this volume). Moorehead recognized the benefits of these new methods but remained focused on his unfinished tasks. But he was also in competition with the work at Pecos. He found himself scrambling for field and publication funds (Moorehead 1931a, 2) at the same time that he was pursuing his Archaeological Survey of New England with surveys or cooperative work in most New England states. Moorehead conducted excavations with students from Phillips Academy (fig. 22). For emergency excavations he frequently sought outside funding from wealthy associates, including Dr. John Wilson of Castine, Henry Parsons of Kennebunk, and William Sumner Appleton at the Society for

FIG. 23. Parsons family records in 1993 including files of archaeological correspondence. Photo by Brian Robinson.

the Preservation of New England Antiquities. Much of this effort was not directed toward amassing more artifacts for the Peabody Museum, but rather to gathering records on sites in danger of being lost to unsystematic digging, with artifacts retained by landowners or sponsors. In a letter to Appleton dated April 25, 1926, Moorehead laid out the budget for salvaging a portion of a cemetery in a gravel pit:

> That cemetery should be saved and I think we can dig out what remains for a total of not exceeding $500 hand hire and about $300 damages.... I would rather explore it in your interest, getting just the facts and photographs, etc. for Andover and giving you all the specimens.

Although less well known than some of the formal expeditions, these activities constitute a significant contribution with a network of research

FIG. 24. Lawrence Dwight uncovers the Warren K. Moorehead file in Crate 26, covered with a page from the *New York Times*, March 28, 1932. Photo by Brian Robinson.

avenues. Researching the Moorehead burial tradition in Maine yielded records from a widespread network of researchers and supporters. The book *A Report on the Archaeology of Maine* (1922b), was Moorehead's last substantive publication on the Red Paint burials of that state, but he continued to search for evidence regarding the extent and boundaries of the culture pattern. An example follows.

In Moorehead's correspondence at the Ohio History Connection in Columbus, I found a reference to a previously unpublished Red Paint cemetery in Maine. The Overlock Cemetery was excavated in 1929 by Gerald Towle, sponsored by Henry Parsons and arranged through Moorehead. After a lengthy and circuitous history, the Henry Parsons Collection made it intact to the Maine State Museum in 1982. Remarkably, original field labels often still remained with the artifacts, but there were virtually no other field records. Bruce Bourque suggested that there might be more records at Parsons's home in Kennebunk, Maine. The home had become the central repository for records of diverse family businesses from Georgia to New York as well as personal correspondence and research interests in Maine. The records dated from before the American Civil War until Henry Parsons's death in 1954. The accumulated records were stored in 54 wooden crates in a basement of what was then a summer home (fig. 23). Upon enquiry, Henry Parsons's 89-year-old niece-in-law, Mrs. Dwight, consulted the index to the family records and reported there was a Warren K. Moorehead file in crate 26, which was located with the assistance of Lawrence Dwight. After removing the 1932 newspaper that covered it, the Moorehead file was found with 158 pages of correspondence (fig. 24). After checking the index further and with considerable family assistance, a total of 322 pages of archaeological correspondence covering 25 years was retrieved from the 54 crates of family records. (All 54 crates were later donated to the Fogler Library at the University of Maine.) Correspondence included 1929 letters from the field by Gerald Towle and Margaret Ashley during excavation of the Overlock site, and letters from Frederick Johnson and Douglas Byers, in addition to many Moorehead letters. Margaret Ashley married Gerald Towle and went on to write the "bible" for Peruvian paleoethnobotany and ethnobotany, which is still used today.

Combined with the records and correspondence at the R. S. Peabody Museum, the Maine State Museum, and the University of Maine and other sources, a decade of unpublished excavations was discerned, coordinated but not sponsored by Moorehead. Including those from 1918 (the Lancaster Farm site, cited earlier in a letter to Charles Peabody) to 1929, the last six Red Paint cemeteries documented by Moorehead were excavated on behalf of others, with records kept or produced for the Peabody Museum, while the collections were retained by other institutions or individuals (see also Spiess 1985, 116). In all cases these sites were discovered by others and would have been less well documented and likely destroyed had Moorehead not intervened. Three of the sites were published in Moorehead's *A Report on the Archaeology of Maine*. The Overlock and Sunkhaze Ridge sites, excavated after the book was published, remained unpublished until recently (Robinson 1996, 2001). The collections from all five sites survived and have been reunited with the field records. In one case, the 1926 re-excavation of the Stevens site, in Warren, Maine, records were retained by the Peabody, but the collection was apparently deaccessioned. Important records also were found for the Erkilla site in Warren, Maine, for which permission to excavate was denied, although a flurry of letters and phone messages outlined important aspects of the site. The systematic effort to document sites without adding to the museum's collection represents one way in which the Peabody Museum became a repository for New England archaeological documents.

The persistent effort of the "Old School of thought . . . forever occupied by the problems of survey" laid an irreplaceable foundation of field records and excavation reports for my recent reinterpretation of the Moorehead burial tradition in terms of structured changes in land use and the social groups associated with them (e.g., Robinson 2001, 2006). The result is knowledge of an ancient monumental and sacred landscape that otherwise very likely would have been lost. The continuity through changing times and responsibilities makes these records of the past a unique resource from a variety of perspectives.

Certainly one of the great changes in perspective for New England archaeology occurred when Douglas Byers and Frederick Johnson arrived at the Robert S. Peabody Foundation in the 1930s. Building upon the pioneering stratigraphic developments by A. V. Kidder (see Cordell, this volume), Byers and Johnson brought original and critical chronological methods to the Northeast. While Moorehead was focused on culture in terms of the distribution of artifacts across the region, Byers and Johnson were interested in culture, environment, and chronology. Their efforts were pioneering at the national level.

Methodological developments, described by Hamilton and Winter in this volume, were applied to the Nevin shell heap (Byers 1979) in the context of ongoing research in Maine and the Northeast. At present four known Archaic period shell middens in the state of Maine have survived rising sea levels to provide a window on the maritime lifestyle associated with the so-called Red Paint People, hereafter referred to as the Moorehead

Phase, dating to 4,000 years ago (Bourque 1992, 2012). Three of these shell middens were excavated between 1936 and 1938. Only seven years earlier Moorehead had excavated the Jones Cove shell heap for the Abbe Museum. The presence of a clam fork in an excavation photograph, a probable excavation tool used by Moorehead's crew, suggests there was no stratigraphic or horizontal control. In 1936, in contrast, Byers and Johnson pioneered precise stratigraphic work on the Nevin shell heap, one of the unique sites in the Gulf of Maine. They described the methodology of shell midden archaeology at Nevin in 1939 (Byers and Johnson 1939). The excavators of both the other Archaic shell midden sites, at Tafts Point (Hadlock 1939) and Waterside shell heap (Rowe 1940), worked at Nevin with Byers and Johnson. Swordfish remains occurred commonly in the deepest levels of all three sites. What is the probability that, from hundreds of shell middens in the state of Maine, 75 percent of the Archaic period middens would be excavated within four years, and would be among the first stratified excavations in the state of Maine? Excavations that would have been a great loss using methods of only a few years before instead established another methodological foundation and contributed to recognition of early maritime adaptations in the Northeast.

Byers and Johnson, like Moorehead, worked in widely dispersed areas of North America, but their contribution to Northeast archaeology constitutes a dedicated research program. In one of the Peabody Museum's periodic reorganizations in the early 1940s, "the major part of the resources of the institution were committed, for an indefinite number of years, to the analysis of Anthropological problems in northern and northeastern North America" (Johnson 1946, viii). The outline of this proposal was discussed at a meeting of the American Anthropological Association in Andover in December 1941. Publication of the proceedings after the meeting was delayed until after World War II (Johnson 1946). It is a remarkable summary by a formidable group of anthropologists. The separation of anthropology and archaeology perceived by Moorehead late in his career is nowhere to be found in this volume, which is "affectionately and humbly" dedicated to Frank Speck, a prolific ethnographer and student of Franz Boas, and Frederick Johnson's mentor at the University of Pennsylvania (Norcini

2008). In addition to the role played in the formation of the Society for American Archaeology, the Massachusetts Archaeological Society was founded at the Peabody Museum in April 1939, with Doug Byers as the first editor of the society's *Bulletin*. The Massachusetts society "budded off" into other state societies. Ripley Bullen from the Robert S. Peabody Foundation was appointed to carry out a survey of the Indian sites in Massachusetts. Adelaide and Ripley Bullen (1945) undertook landmark research in historical archaeology at the Lucy Foster site in Andover (Battle-Baptiste 2011, 30; Hamilton and Winter, this volume). These activities were influential in communicating archaeological interests and methods within newly developing archaeology societies before most academic departments included Northeast archaeology.

In 1949 Fred Johnson gave a talk to the Massachusetts Archaeological Society on Paleoindian occupations and artifacts. In 1951 Joe Vaccaro picked up the first fluted point at the Bull Brook site in Ipswich, Massachusetts. Bill Eldridge, who had attended Johnson's talk, recognized its importance immediately and reported it to the Peabody Museum (Eldridge and Vaccaro 1952). The Bull Brook site would later be recognized as the largest settlement known from the Pleistocene epoch in North America (Robinson et al. 2009; Robinson 2012). Bull Brook excavators Bill Eldridge and Nick Vaccaro had previously trained under Rip Bullen at the Johnson's Spring site (Bullen 1950). Eldridge credited Bullen with solid training and constant admonishment to keep copious notes. Shortly after excavations at Bull Brook began in 1952, Bullen responded to a letter from Eldridge and Vaccaro, saying: "Incidentally, if you find a fireplace or charcoal that is definitely from the lower level, make copious notes and rush as much charcoal as possible into Fred Johnson in Andover for a possible Carbon-14 date. It should come out at least 5,000 B.C.!" (Bull Brook Records 258). The site is now dated to 10,000 calendar years BCE (Before Common Era). Byers (1954; 1955) brought the site to national attention, and the Peabody Museum continued to be a major source of information on this unique site, along with the Peabody Essex Museum in Salem (see Richardson and Adovasio, this volume).

Byers and Johnson promoted explicit problem orientations in their research, which became a hallmark of Peabody Museum publications. The excavation described in *Two Sites on Martha's Vineyard* (Byers and Johnson 1940) was not only part of a program to explore the character of shell middens but also a move to bring New England archaeology into a more modern anthropological framework.

The well-watered Northeast lacked the environmental conditions (such as widespread drought) that facilitate use of tree-ring dating (dendrochronology), the most precise of the chronological tools available at the time (Douglass 1924). But under the streets of Boston, the Boylston Street Fish Weir was developed into one of the premier interdisciplinary studies of archaeology (Johnson 1942, 1949). Previously discussed in Hamilton and Winter (this volume), the work is a masterful combination of stratigraphic excavation, pollen analysis, climate change, and sea level studies, resulting in an estimated date range of 1400 BCE to 1500 BCE for the Upper and Lower Wattle levels of the weir (Knox 1942, 126), placing it in a warmer climate period during the Sub-Boreal or early Sub-Atlantic climate phase (Johnson 1949, 127). Although absolute dating remained a problem, the fish weir remained one of the oldest cultural sites in the Northeast until the discovery of radiocarbon dating, providing direct evidence of climate change and speculations on changing subsistence patterns. "We may even point out that during and [before] 'Fishweir Time' conditions were more favorable for agriculture than they are now. However, we are not yet prepared to defend a statement that our early fishermen may have raised crops!" (Johnson 1949, 125). Fish weirs would become a major economic focus in archaeology and anthropology (Décima and Dincauze 1998).

Much has been written about the impact of radiocarbon dating in archaeology. Frederick Johnson's central role in the development of radiocarbon dating in archaeology brought a critical approach to this new (in 1949) means of absolute dating. Previously, aside from the environmentally restricted method of dendrochronology, sophisticated stratigraphic correlations were the major means of relative dating, while absolute dating was often beyond hope. The need for chronological understanding in anthropological interpretation of culture change made chronology a driving force, a clever quest to integrate diverse sources of evidence. We can sympathize with James B. Griffin's ironic comment in a 1947 letter to Johnson that radiocarbon dating "from one viewpoint would take much of the fun out of archaeology" (Marlowe 1999, 23). Similarly, Moorehead bemoaned the fact that the new methods of younger archaeologists, however useful, might distract from the love of artifacts, which from Moorehead's perspective involved the quest for understanding their distribution and relationships. Of course, radiocarbon dating does not replace the need for sophisticated stratigraphic correlations, and new methods of chronology do not replace the need for ever more precise spatial relationships among artifacts and assemblages. Whole careers have been justifiably focused on one trajectory more than another, in the struggle to overcome the extraordinary hurdles of deciphering the past from sparse bits and pieces.

Referring to the state of Maine, Spiess (1985, 102) notes, "Some of the most famous archaeologists in the Northeast have practiced in Maine," but with little continuity until universities began more systematic investigations in the 1960s and 1970s. Before this the Robert S. Peabody Museum maintained dual interests in its home base in the Northeast as well as continent- and later hemisphere-wide explorations and problems. The archaeology of the Northeast benefited greatly from institutional continuity, breadth of scholarship, and the network of contributors. This essay has sampled some of the achievements through the museum's changing missions, academically and institutionally, emphasizing that our present knowledge is dependent on each of the missions and the continuity between them. With increasing numbers of archaeologists spending much of their careers retracing the work of others, the institutions and individuals who made it happen are to be congratulated and appreciated, then and now.

REFERENCES

Bacon, Anabel. 2009. "Warren King Moorehead: The Peabody Museum's First Curator, a Champion of Native American Rights." *Andover Bulletin* (Spring): 22–23.

Battle-Baptiste, Whitney. 2011. *Black Feminist Archaeology*. Walnut Hill CA: Left Coast Press.

Bourque, Bruce J. 1992. *Prehistory of the Central Maine Coast*. New York: Garland Publications.

———. 2012. *The Swordfish Hunters: The History and Ecology of an Ancient American Sea People*. Piermont NH: Bunker Hill Publishing.

Bull Brook Records (BBR). Original Bull Brook records, stamped with BBR catalog number, archived at the Peabody Essex Museum, Salem, Massachusetts.

Bullen, Adelaide K., and Ripley P. Bullen. 1945. "Black Lucy's Garden." *Bulletin of the Massachusetts Archaeological Society* 6, no. 2:17–28.

Bullen, Ripley P. 1950. "The Johnson's Spring Site." *Bulletin of the Massachusetts Archaeological Society* 11, no. 2:37–45.

Byers, Douglas S. 1939. "Warren K. Moorehead." *American Anthropologist* 41, no. 2:286–94.

———. 1954. "Bull Brook—A Fluted Point Site in Ipswich, Massachusetts." *American Antiquity* 19, no. 4:343–51.

———. 1955. "Additional Information on the Bull Brook Site, Massachusetts." *American Antiquity* 20, no 3:274–76.

———. 1979. *The Nevin Shellheap: Burials and Observations*. Papers of the Robert S. Peabody Foundation for Archaeology 9. Andover MA: Phillips Academy.

Byers, Douglas S., and Frederick Johnson. 1939. "Some Methods Used in Excavating Eastern Shell Heaps." *American Antiquity* 4, no. 3:189–212.

———. 1940. *Two Sites on Martha's Vineyard*. Papers of the Robert S. Peabody Foundation for Archaeology 1, no. 1. Andover MA: Phillips Academy.

Christenson, Andrew L. 2011. "Who Were the Professional North American Archaeologists of 1900? Clues from the Work of Warren K. Moorehead." *Bulletin of the History of Archaeology* 21, no. 1. Accessed February 20, 2013. http://www.archaeologybulletin.org/article/view/3/3.

Décima, Elena B., and Dena F. Dincauze. 1998. "The Boston Back Bay Fish Weirs." In *Hidden Dimensions: The Cultural Significance of Wetland Archaeology*, edited by Kathryn N. Bernick, 157–72. Vancouver: University of British Columbia Press.

Douglass, Andrew E. 1924. "Some Aspects of the Use of the Annual Rings of Trees in Climatic Study." In *The Smithsonian Report for 1922*, Publication 2731, 223–39. Washington DC: Government Printing Office. Originally published in *Scientific Monthly* 15, no. 1 (1922):5–21.

Eldridge, William. E., and Joseph Vaccaro. 1952. "The Bull Brook Site, Ipswich, Mass." *Bulletin of the Massachusetts Archaeology Society* 13, no. 4:39–43.

Hadlock, Wendell. 1939. "The Taft's Point Shell Mound at West Gouldsboro, Maine." *Bulletin of the Robert Abbe Museum* 5. Bar Harbor ME: Robert Abbe Museum.

Johnson, Frederick, ed. 1942. *The Boylston Street Fishweir: A Study of the Archaeology, Biology, and Geology of a Site on Boylston Street in the Back Bay District of Boston, Massachusetts*. Papers of the Robert S. Peabody Foundation for Archaeology 2. Andover MA: Phillips Academy.

———. 1946. *Man in Northeastern North America.* Papers of the Robert S. Peabody Foundation for Archaeology 3. Andover MA: Phillips Academy.

———. 1949. *The Boylston Street Fishweir II: A Study of the Geology, Paleobotany, and Biology of a Site on Stuart Street, in the Back Bay District of Boston, Massachusetts.* Papers of the Robert S. Peabody Foundation for Archaeology 4, no 1. Andover MA: Phillips Academy.

Knox, Arthur S. 1942. "Pollen Analysis of the Silt and the Tentative Dating of the Deposits. In *The Boylston Street Fishweir, A Study of the Archaeology, Biology, and Geology of a Site on Boylston Street in the Back Bay District of Boston Massachusetts,"* edited by Frederick Johnson, 105–29. Papers of the Robert S. Peabody Foundation for Archaeology 2. Andover MA: Phillips Academy.

Marlowe, Greg. 1999. "Radiocarbon Dating and American Archaeology, 1947–1948." *American Antiquity* 64, no. 1:9–32.

Moorehead, Warren K. 1891. "The Indian Messiah and the Ghost Dance." *American Antiquarian and Oriental Journal* 13, no. 3:161–67.

———. 1914. "The Red Paint People,—A Reply." *American Anthropologist* 16, no. 2:358–361.

———. 1922a. *The Hopewell Mound Group of Ohio.* Publications of the Field Museum of Natural History 211, Anthropology Series 6, no. 5. Chicago: Field Museum of Natural History.

———. 1922b. *A Report on the Archaeology of Maine: Being a Narrative of Explorations in That State, 1912–1920, Together with Work at Lake Champlain, 1917.* Department of Archaeology, Phillips Academy. Andover MA: Andover Press.

———. 1926. Letter to William Sumner Appleton dated April 25, 1926. Historic New England (formerly Society for the Preservation of New England Antiquities), institutional records IA001, Boston.

———. 1931a. Some Observations upon Anthropologists, Archaeologists and Hobbies. Presentation for the Explorers Club, A. & C. Boni, New York. Manuscript at the Ohio History Connection, Columbus, Warren King Moorehead Papers, MSS 106, box 2.

———. 1931b. *Archaeology of the Arkansas River Valley* with supplementary papers on *The Prehistoric Cultures of Oklahoma* by Joseph B. Thoburn and *The Exploration of Jacobs Cavern* by Charles Peabody. Department of Archaeology, Phillips Academy. New Haven: Yale University Press.

———. 1938. "Dean of American Archaeologists Retires from Active Labor." *Pennsylvania Archaeologist* 8, no. 3:51–54.

———. 2000. *The Cahokia Mounds.* Edited and with an introduction by John E. Kelly. Tuscaloosa: University of Alabama Press.

Norcini, Marilyn. 2008. Frederick Johnson's Canadian Ethnology in the Americanist Tradition. *Histories of Anthropology Annual* 4:106–34.

Ohio History Connection, Columbus, Warren King Moorehead Papers.

Robinson, Brian S. 1996. "A Regional Analysis of the Moorehead Burial Tradition: 8500–3700 B.P." *Archaeology of Eastern North America* 24:95–148.

———. 2001. "Burial Ritual: Groups and Boundaries on the Gulf of Maine: 8600–3800 B.P." PhD diss., Brown University.

———. 2006. "Burial Ritual, Technology, and Cultural Landscape in the Far Northeast: 8600–3700 B.P." In *The Archaic of the Far Northeast,* edited by David Sanger and M.A.P. Renouf, 341–81. Orono: University of Maine Press.

———. 2012. "The Bull Brook Paleoindian Site and Jeffreys Ledge: A Gathering Place Near Caribou Island?" In *Late Pleistocene Archaeology and Ecology in the Far Northeast,* edited by Claude Chapdelaine, 182–90. College Station: Texas A&M University Press.

Robinson, Brian S., Jennifer C. Ort, William E. Eldridge, Adrian L. Burke, and Bertran G. Pelletier. 2009. "Paleoindian Aggregation and Social Context at Bull Brook." *American Antiquity* 74, no. 3:423–47.

Rowe, John. 1940. *Excavations in the Waterside Shell Heap, Frenchman's Bay, Maine.* Excavator's Club Papers 1, no. 3. Cambridge MA: Harvard University.

Sanger, David. 1973. *Cow Point: An Archaic Cemetery in New Brunswick.* Papers of the Archaeological Survey of Canada 12. Ottawa: National Museum of Man.

Smith, Benjamin L. 1948. "An Analysis of the Maine Cemetery Complex." *Bulletin of the Massachusetts Archaeological Society* 9, nos. 2–3:20–71.

Smith, Walter B. 1926. *Indian Remains of the Penobscot Valley and Their Significance.* University of Maine Studies, Second Series 7. Orono: University of Maine.

Snow, Dean R. 1975. "The Passadumkeag Sequence." *Arctic Anthropology* 12, no. 2:46–59.

Spiess, Arthur E. 1985. "Wild Maine and the Rusticating Scientist: A History of Anthropological Archaeology in Maine." *Man in the Northeast* 30:101–29.

Wellman, Alice. 1984. "Lancaster Farm Bifaces and Ground Slate Points: An Exercise in Attribute Analysis." *Maine Archaeological Society Bulletin* 24, no. 2:3–33.

Willoughby, Charles C. 1898. *Prehistoric Burial Places in Maine.* Archaeological and Ethnological Papers of the Peabody Museum 1, no. 6. Cambridge MA: Harvard University.

———. 1935. *Antiquities of the New England Indians.* Peabody Museum of American Archaeology and Ethnology. Cambridge MA: Harvard University.

Chapter 5

Recent Research at Maine Sites

Nathan D. Hamilton and Donald A. Slater

An extensive reexamination of the Peabody Museum's assemblages from the Nevin and Richards Shellheaps at Blue Hill Bay, Maine, was recently conducted by Nathan Hamilton and his students at the University of Southern Maine.

Douglas Byers' and Frederick Johnson's 1936–38 excavations at Blue Hill Bay initiated a new methodology for excavation, recovery, and documentation of coastal "shell middens." They recorded detailed stratigraphy, cultural features, and spatial data for diagnostic stone tools, ceramics, and faunal remains (see Robinson, this volume). More than 17,000 Cartesian coordinates recorded stratigraphic detail and nearly 500 natural and cultural features. Nearly 500 square meters of midden profiles were documented using this new system. These well-documented excavations and the subsequent responsible curation of artifacts afford a unique opportunity to reexamine nearly 5,000 years of history in central Maine (see fig. 25).

Hamilton initiated several reexamination projects. These include the rescaling of all Archaic features in a computer-aided design (CAD) system to study the relationship of Moorehead Phase to Susquehanna Tradition occupations; the reexamination of 10,000 ceramic sherds for decoration and perishable impressions; petrographic and X-ray defraction studies of these sherds' clay and temper matrices; and a reassessment of the collection of 10,000 faunal remains from the sites.

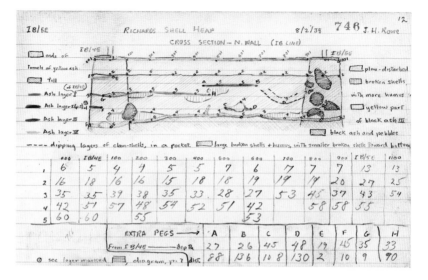

FIG. 25. Image of original field card of north cross section of unit 1B/5E at the Richards site, recorded August 8, 1938 (RSPM Card 746). Douglas S. Byers and Frederick Johnson records (01.03), archives of the Robert S. Peabody Museum of Archaeology.

In his reanalysis of the mapping data, Hamilton and his students manually rescaled all drawings, assigned feature numbers to each, then digitized and reassembled all materials into one composite map. The study establishes solid patterns of changes in site utilization and artifact and faunal refuse disposal from Moorehead Phase to Susquehanna Tradition and the multi-component Ceramic Period.

During the reexamination of the ceramic sherds, all materials were categorized by decorative and manufacturing attributes and classified according to the seven established ceramic periods from Maine (CP–CP7 or 3050–250 uncalibrated RCYBP), as defined by Petersen and Sanger (1991). The roughly 300 total vessel lots provide evidence of greater intensification of site use within the Middle Ceramic Period (CP2–CP4 or 2150–950 uncalibrated RCYBP), especially with dentate and cord-wrapped stick decorated ceramics.

Sherds from both the Nevin and Richards Shellheaps were thin-sectioned for petrographic microscopic analysis and powdered for X-ray defraction studies of mineralogical composition. Results demonstrate that the vessels' silt-clay matrix remained consistent. Comparing these matrices to a variety of Presumpscot formation glacio-marine clay sources from the central Gulf of Maine suggests that Nevin and Richards potters obtained raw silt and clay materials from immediately available Blue Hill Bay sources.

In 1937 at Nevin, Byers and Johnson recognized more clearly delineated stratigraphy and deeper archaeological deposits that revealed Moorehead Phase artifacts. During reanalysis of the Nevin and Richards faunal remains, Hamilton, his students, and archaeologists Dinah Crader and Arthur Spiess were able to identify approximately 90 percent of the specimens to genus and species, with more than fifty species of birds, mammals, fish, and shellfish represented. The deep Moorehead Phase deposits at Nevin contain one of highest diversities of faunal species known at sites in the Gulf of Maine. The assemblage is dominated by swordfish, cod, seal, and moose. But the presence of migratory animals and the thin sectioning and analysis of mammal teeth demonstrate that the Moorehead Phase residents lived at the site year-round. Faunal remains at Richards, on the other hand, are dominated by beaver and moose and display only a fall-winter-spring pattern of occupation.

Hamilton and colleagues have extracted new information about the ancient people of Blue Hill Bay that was not possible to gather during Byers' and Johnson's time. Microscopic and chemical analyses of ceramic and faunal remains determined at which seasons the sites were occupied and where raw materials were collected. New Geographic Information System (GIS) technologies allowed fragmentary mapping data to be reintegrated into a broader context of associated strata, features, and material culture. Analysis is ongoing and should continue to provide new insights into the Nevin and Richards sites.

REFERENCE

Petersen, James B., and David Sanger 1991. "An Aboriginal Ceramic Sequence for Maine and the Maritime Provinces." In *Prehistoric Archaeology in the Maritime Provinces: Past and Present Research*, edited by Michael Deal and Susan Blair, 113–78. Fredericton: Council of Maritime Premiers.

Chapter 6

A Retrospective Interpretation of the Origins of American Agriculture

Mary Eubanks

One of humanity's most important inventions is agriculture. This decisive step freed people from the quest for food and released energy for other pursuits. No civilization has existed without an agricultural base, either in the past or today. Truly, agriculture was the first great leap forward by human beings.
—Richard S. MacNeish, *The Origins of Agriculture and Settled Life*

Since its founding in 1901, the Robert S. Peabody Museum of Archaeology in Andover, Massachusetts, has been in the vanguard of interdisciplinary archaeological research to understand human-environmental interactions better. Following in the footsteps of the pioneering paleoecological work of his colleagues Douglas Byers and Frederick Johnson, Richard S. "Scotty" MacNeish assembled an interdisciplinary team to bring together multiple lines of scientific evidence to investigate the origins of agriculture and settled life in the Americas. This retrospective look at the landmark Tehuacán Archaeological-Botanical Project reviews its findings in light of twenty-first-century biocultural evidence for the origin and evolution of agriculture in Mesoamerica. Since maize, referred to as corn in the United States, was the grain upon which American civilizations were built, its domestication and evolution are central to understanding the origin of American agriculture. A number of events set the stage for the Tehuacán Valley project. The following pages present the highlights of significant research findings in the perspective of recent discoveries in archaeobotany, experimental genetics, and the sequencing of the maize genome.

The "Great Corn Hunt"

Setting the Stage in Tamaulipas

Reminiscing in the preface to his book *The Origins of Agriculture and Settled Life*, MacNeish [1991, xiii] tells this story:

> My first encounter with the problems of the origins of agriculture and settled life began one hot March afternoon in 1949 on a dusty "street" of Los Angeles, a tiny hamlet at the end of a rocky road in the Sierra de Tamaulipas, Mexico. . . . I pondered our season's work and thought that finding the first ceramic sequence for Mesoamerica made for a pretty good season. Tired but happy, I really perked up when I saw Alberto on the outskirts of town. [When I asked if he had brought the equipment and specimens and if the jeep was packed, he said,] "No, señor." [When I asked why not, he responded,] "Because we found what you said we might find." Alberto pulled out a box that contained a woven mat with three tiny corncobs tied with agave string. They had been excavated at a depth of 14 inches. I realized these tiny cobs were 3,000–4,000 years old—in 1949 this was the oldest corn ever found and a discovery that would change the course of my life.

This discovery was significant because maize (*Zea mays* L.) was the staff of life and essential staple crop that led to the origins of agriculture and settled life in the New World.

MacNeish sent the corncobs, which had been found in La Perra Cave in the northeastern Mexican state of Tamaulipas along the coast of the Gulf of Mexico, to Paul Mangelsdorf, a Harvard botanist working at the time on a corn project for the Rockefeller Foundation in Mexico. With a carbon-14 date of 4,445±280 BP (MacNeish 1991, xiv), the specimens were the oldest and most primitive maize remains Mangelsdorf had seen. Mangelsdorf invited MacNeish to Cambridge to discuss the tiny corncobs. At the meeting MacNeish, Mangelsdorf, and his associate Walton C. Galinat concluded that well-preserved prehistoric vegetal remains were essential

FIG. 26. (a) Archaeological specimen of *Tripsacum* from Tamaulipas, Mexico, 3200–2300 BCE. (b) Archaeological specimen of teosinte from Tamaulipas, Mexico, 2300–1600 BCE. The Archaeological Collection in the Harvard University Herbaria of Harvard University, Cambridge, Massachusetts.

for understanding the origin and evolution of corn, and the best way to solve this problem was to combine the skills of archaeologists with those of botanists. Thus began a truly interdisciplinary collaboration that would become a model for subsequent archaeological research. The investigation into the origin of corn soon included other crops, and MacNeish began to formulate a broad theoretical framework for crop domestication as a behavioral process leading to the development of agriculture with concomitant evolution of complex society—his lifelong work on "the origins of agriculture and settled life" (MacNeish 1991, 3–33).

In 1954 MacNeish returned to Tamaulipas to explore caves in Ocampo, seventy-five miles southwest of La Perra Cave. He excavated two caves (Romero and Valenzuela) that yielded well-preserved botanical materials. Mangelsdorf arrived at the lab in La Ciudad and set about sorting the corn from the other plant remains, which included beans, pumpkins, squash, and other domesticated plants. It is notable that Tamaulipas is the only place where both of the wild relatives of maize, teosinte and *Tripsacum*, have been found (figs. 26a and 26b). Among the remains was a remarkable specimen that is exactly like an F_2 *Tripsacum*-teosinte segregate I recovered in experimental crosses between the two genera (Eubanks 2001a, 498). There were also fossilized feces (coprolites). Mangelsdorf advised MacNeish to consult other specialists, including Hugh Cutler and Tom Whitaker (cucurbits), Lawrence Kaplan (beans), C. Earle Smith (New World domesticates), and Eric Callen (coprolites) (MacNeish 1991, 75–77).

By the end of the season MacNeish and Mangelsdorf concluded Tamaulipas was not where domesticated corn originated, and they launched "the great corn hunt" to try and find the cradle of maize. In 1957 MacNeish surveyed the Rio Balsas region of Guerrero; the next year he went to Honduras and Guatemala (Zacapá), then Chiapas (Santa Marta Cave) and Oaxaca (Mitla) in Mexico in 1959. He eliminated all these areas in favor of a location that had all the right conditions—a preceramic zone of occupation, great ecological diversity, preserved pollen and plant remains, and wild plants with potential to become domesticated (MacNeish 1991, 78).

The Tehuacán Archaeological-Botanical Project

In 1960 MacNeish conducted test excavations in a cave near Coxcatlán in the Valley of Tehuacán in southern Puebla, Mexico, where he found well-preserved plant remains in a preceramic context with good stratigraphy. With its dry climate, ever-flowing springs, and rich ecological diversity, the Tehuacán Valley seemed to him to be the most likely area to look for prehistoric corn and the origin of agriculture (MacNeish 1967a, 5). This was the beginning of the Tehuacán Archaeological-Botanical Project, sponsored by the Robert S. Peabody Museum of Archaeology and funded by the National Science Foundation and the Ford Foundation (Byers 1967, 3).

The Environment

The Tehuacán Valley is centrally located between the Valley of Oaxaca and the Valley of Mexico and has access to both the Gulf Coast and the Pacific Coast. It has a harsh dry season that became harsher as the climate warmed toward the end of the Pleistocene, when horses, antelopes, mammoths, giant jackrabbits, and giant turtles went extinct, reducing the animal food available from hunting. In other words, Tehuacán had all the conditions that MacNeish postulated for the transition from hunting and gathering to the stages leading to agriculture and settled life —foraging, incipient cultivation, and crop domestication (MacNeish 1991, 106–13).

The Tehuacán Valley has seven distinct ecological zones with resources that cannot be exploited from a single base camp (Flannery 1967, 132–39). These zones range in elevation, temperature regime, and annual precipitation, with the highest elevation characterized by lush vegetation and abundant animal life to areas that are deserts with Sonoran-like vegetation. Coxcatlán Cave (TC 50), Purrón Cave (TC 272), and Abejas Cave (TC 307) are located in the alluvial slope thorn-forest ecozone, where thorny trees, scrub, and grasses provide forage for herbivorous game. The travertine slopes—the desert zone—surround the El Riego oasis, a small set of cliffs with springs at the north end of the valley that have lush vegetation year-round and are a haven for animals in the dry season. San Marcos Cave (TC 254) and Teccoral Cave (TC 255) are located in the travertine slope ecozone, and El Riego Cave (TC 35) is in the oasis. The humid river bottoms along the Río Salado are warmer and offer permanent water, rich alluvial soils, and lush vegetation, while the surrounding valley steppe harbors many plant species with potential for domestication.

Archaeological Excavations in Tehuacán

Full-scale excavations began in the Valley of Tehuacán in 1961 and continued through 1963. The archaeological survey located 454 sites and 16 stratified sites with early village or pre-village preceramic remains that were tested or excavated. At least one site was tested in each of the seven ecozones. Of these sites, 60 preceramic components were identified as well as 40 preceramic surface sites. The project yielded dates from 20,000 BCE (Before Common Era) to 2,000 BCE and recovered more than 50,000 stone artifacts, more than 10,000 bones, 250 coprolites, and more than 100,000 plant remains (MacNeish 1967b, 290). Mangelsdorf and Galinat analyzed approximately 25,000 maize remains (Mangelsdorf et al. 1967,

178–200). Kaplan analyzed over 1,000 beans (Kaplan 1967, 201–11), and Cutler and Whitaker analyzed approximately 1,400 squash (*Cucurbita*) remains (Cutler and Whitaker 1967, 212–19). C. Earle Smith took on the task of analyzing thousands of specimens representing more than 60 species of food and fiber plants (Smith 1967, 220–255). A cotton boll (i.e., the seed capsule that contains the soft, fluffy cotton fibers) was analyzed by Stanley G. Stephens (1967, 256–60), and 250 coprolites were analyzed by Eric Callen (1967, 261–89). In the earliest levels large amounts of seeds of the wild grass *Setaria* were present, but they rapidly disappeared with the appearance and increased productivity of maize.

Prehistoric Maize Remains

MacNeish's selection of the Valley of Tehuacán in the "great corn hunt" proved to have been right on target in terms of recovery of well-preserved maize remains. The 24,860 prehistoric specimens were recovered from five caves: El Riego in the oasis north of the present-day city of Tehuacán; Tecorral and San Marcos, proximally located on the margin of the valley steppe and the travertine slope just south of the city, where food is available only in a brief wet season; and Coxcatlán and Purrón, in the alluvial slope ecozone (MacNeish 1991, 79). The well-preserved prehistoric remains from the Tehuacán Valley provide a continuous picture of maize evolution for 6,500 years; that is, from 7000 BP until European contact. Today, fifty years later, this collection is still the largest in number and the longest continuous sequence of plant remains recovered from any New World archaeological site.

The oldest cobs dated to the Coxcatlán Phase (7000–6500 BP) and had all the essential characteristics that distinguish domesticated maize from its closely related wild grasses teosinte and *Tripsacum*. Twenty-seven cobs were recovered from San Marcos Cave and 44 from Coxcatlán Cave. These cobs were 19–25 mm long and had 4–8 rows of kernels. There were 6 to 9 female flowers per row that produced 24–72 kernels on an ear. Two husk leaves enclosed the tiny ears. Like corn's wild relative *Tripsacum*, the ears were bisexual fragile spikes of pollen-producing flowers above the

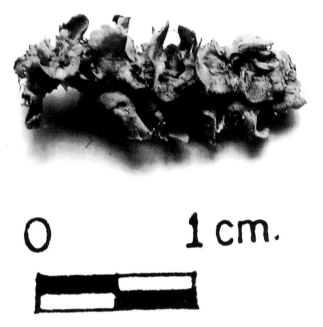

FIG. 27. Prehistoric maize cob from Coxcatlán Cave. This specimen illustrates the long, papery glumes that enclosed the kernels of early maize. Instituto Nacional de Antropología y Historia Laboratorio de Paleobotánica, Mexico DF. Photo by the author.

seed-producing female flowers. Long, soft, papery bracts referred to as glumes partially covered the round kernels (fig. 27), which were borne in pairs and were orange or brown in color. The ears appeared near the end or at the tips of branching stalks. At the time the pairing of the kernel rows, the soft tissue of the cob, and the papery glumes led Mangelsdorf, MacNeish, and Galinat to conclude that this was "wild maize" and that neither of corn's wild relatives, teosinte or *Tripsacum*, was the ancestor of maize (1967, 179–80).

For the sake of consistency in sequential cross-referencing with the early Tehuacán publications upon which much of this retrospectus is based, the uncalibrated radiocarbon dates from those publications are referenced herein. However, it is important to note that MacNeish's original dates for maize in the Coxcatlán and subsequent Abejas phases have been contested by Long and colleagues (1989), who obtained radiocarbon dates on twelve cobs MacNeish excavated from Coxcátlan and San Marcos caves. According to the new accelerator mass spectrometry (AMS) dates, the oldest maize from Tehuacán dates to 5640–3360 BP (3640–3360 cal BCE). The application of AMS to the Tehuacán samples was an innovation in the 1980s when this technique was first used by archaeologists, allowing for smaller sample sizes and the detection of lower levels of carbon-14 through a direct determination of the ratio of carbon-14 to carbon-12 atoms. Although MacNeish presented compelling reasons for rejecting the revised AMS dates (MacNeish 2001), many archaeologists accept the more recent dates in their discussions of maize domestication (Long and Fritz 2001). A subsequent AMS date for a maize cob fragment from the Tehuacán project is 5310 BP (Ramos-Madrigal et al. 2016), thus corroborating the AMS dates of Long and colleagues. Accordingly the oldest maize macroremains found in the archaeological record date to 6200 BP and are from Guila Naquitz cave in the neighboring state of Oaxaca, just south of the Valley of Tehuacán (Flannery 1986).

The subsequent Abejas phase (5500–4500 BP) yielded cobs that were quite similar to the oldest maize except that they were larger, with an average length of 49 mm. They had 8–10 rows of 15 kernels, so a single ear produced about 135 kernels. Mangelsdorf, MacNeish, and Galinat concluded that maize was in the early stages of cultivation by 5500 BP. This trend toward increased size and productivity continued for about 1,000 years (Mangelsdorf et al. 1967, 181).

Then in the Ajalpan phase (3500–2900 BP) a new type, designated "tripsacoid," appeared. The cob was hard, the glumes were stiff and short instead of soft and long, and the kernels were no longer covered by thin, papery glumes. A greater number of husk leaves covered the cob. This early tripsacoid corn was thought to be the result of hybridization between maize and a related wild grass, either teosinte or *Tripsacum*. Hybridization between early cultivated corn and early tripsacoid corn introduced new variation into the gene pool, leading to the next evolutionary step in maize domestication. Since the ancient indigenous maize races Chapalote and Nal Tel arose from crosses between primitive maize and tripsacoid maize, Mangelsdorf and colleagues referred to this precursor maize population as the Nal Tel–Chapalote complex (1967, 183–84).

By the Palo Blanco phase (2200–1200 BP, the Mesoamerican Classic period), another new form appeared, a slender popcorn in which the kernel starch expanded upon heating and burst into an edible morsel. This was the ancestral form of the ancient popcorn races Arrocillo Amarillo from Mexico and Pira Naranja from Colombia (Mangelsdorf et al. 1967, 187–95). Pira is represented on mold-made maize ears depicted on Zapotec urns from Oaxaca (Eubanks 1999). The mold-made maize replicas are positive casts from molds formed using actual maize ears. The depictions of corn in clay are botanical facsimiles of ancient maize. This was a period of cultural contact and trade between Mesoamerica and the north coast of South America (Chard 1950; West 1961). Maize was one of the traded commodities, consequently introducing new types (Bird 1984). Introgression of genes from these new types into Mexican maize gave rise to new races that were well established by the Postclassic (Eubanks 1999, 203).

Expansion of genetic diversity continued. By the Venta Salada phase (1300–460 BP), five more races appeared in the Valley of Tehuacán— Conico, Zapalote Chico, Tepecintle, Chalqueño, and an unidentified dent corn, a type of corn with a characteristic indentation in the kernel (Mangelsdorf et al. 1967, 197). Most of the highly productive corn grown in the United States Corn Belt today is a type of dent corn. The maize remains from the Tehuacán Valley reveal a continuous evolutionary sequence from the early domestication of maize to the contact period (fig. 28). The foundation for the rich heritage of maize diversity in the Americas was well established before the arrival of the Spaniards.

FIG. 28. Archaeological cobs from the Valley of Tehuacán illustrating the complete evolutionary sequence of maize domestication from 7000 BP up to contact with the Spanish. Photographic collection of the Robert S. Peabody Museum of Archaeology.

Tehuacán in Light of Twenty-First-Century Evidence

Evidence from recent research in experimental genetics, DNA studies, the sequencing of the maize genome, and archaeology sheds new light on the origin of maize and raises the question whether Tehuacán was the cradle of maize, as thought in the 1960s, or was it an important juncture at the crossroads of maize evolution?

The Teosinte Hypothesis

Maize is a plant that has been so domesticated it can no longer survive without human cultivation. There has been a long-running debate about the origin of maize beginning with George Beadle (1939, 1980), who believed maize arose from mutations to annual teosinte, and Paul Mangelsdorf (1974; Mangelsdorf and Reeves 1939), who believed that maize, like wheat, arose from hybridization between two or more wild grasses. Mangelsdorf originally proposed his tripartite hypothesis in which maize arose from a cross between an unknown wild maize and *Tripsacum,* another grass related to maize. According to Mangelsdorf, annual teosinte was a derivative from the cross between *Tripsacum* and wild maize and could not be the ancestor of maize. After the discovery of the perennial teosinte *Zea diploperennis* by Iltis and co-workers (1979) in the late 1970s, Mangelsdorf subsequently revised the tripartite hypothesis and proposed that annual teosinte arose from a cross between wild maize and perennial teosinte rather than *Tripsacum* (Mangelsdorf et al. 1981).

There is a large body of molecular evidence that indicates teosinte is the progenitor of maize (Doebley et al. 2006). The most widely held hypothesis favors annual teosinte from the Rio Balsas region, *Zea mays* ssp. *parviglumis,* as the progenitor (Matsuoko et al. 2002). For a review of the various hypotheses about the origin of maize, see Eubanks (2001b). A significant unresolved question is how the tiny teosinte spike of 5–7 shattering seeds in hard fruitcases transformed into the ear of maize with hundreds of kernels on a firm rachis. The teosinte hypothesis holds that accumulation of mutations in five genes over a long period gradually transformed teosinte's flowering spike into the multi-rowed maize ear with hundreds of kernels enclosed in husks (Bennetzen et al. 2001, 84–86). The accompanying table presents the five essential genes in which mutations had to occur for the transformation of the teosinte spike to the maize ear. Reasons why this explanation remains unsatisfactory are that spontaneous mutations in maize are rare (Stadler 1951), and the proposed mutations hinder the plant's ability to survive in the wild. The odds that a single harmful mutation will survive are approximately one in a million ($1:1 \times 10^6$). The odds that mutations in all five genes that transform teosinte into maize would occur are on the order one in a million trillion trillion ($1:1 \times 10^{30}$). Furthermore, no natural mutations in any of the five genes have been found in teosinte (Wilkes 2004, 45), and none of the putative mutations have been experimentally reconstructed (Kellogg and Birchler 1993, 415–39).

Five critical genes in the transformation of the
teosinte spike to an ear of maize

TEOSINTE	GENE	MAIZE
Single-rowed spike of 7–9 seeds	*tr1*	Many rowed ear with hundreds of kernels
Shattering spike	*ri1/ph1*	Segments fused to form rigid cob
Seed encased in hard fruitcase	*tga1*	Fruitcase reduced to an open cupule structure
Single seed in a fruitcase	*pd1*	A pair of kernels in each cupule
Plant with many branches	*tb1*	Plant has single stalk

In addition to these concerns, the teosinte hypothesis has not been corroborated by the archaeological record. Teosinte remains that predate the oldest maize remains have not been found. There is no fossil evidence showing a long gradual transformation of the simple spike of teosinte with five to seven hard seeds into the complex, highly productive maize ear (MacNeish and Eubanks 2000, 3–20). The effect of introgression of teosinte genes into maize is hardening of the cob and glumes, but the earliest maize at Tehuacán had soft cob tissue and paper-like glumes (Mangelsdorf et al. 1967, 179). Using genome-wide resequencing of single nucleotide polymorphisms (SNPs) to characterize maize, teosinte lines, and *Tripsacum dactyloides* var. *meridionale* from Colombia, Hufford and colleagues (2012) found that introgression from both of maize's wild relatives, teosinte and *Tripsacum*, contributed to an increase in genetic diversity following domestication. These findings fit the evolutionary picture drawn from morphological study of the Tehuacán archaeological cobs (Mangelsdorf et al. 1967). The comparative genomic data also reveal that as many as sixty genes may have contributed to maize domestication.

The Recombination Hypothesis

Although the archaeological record in the Valley of Tehuacán revealed that hybridization between maize and teosinte gave rise to new genetic diversity, this occurred thousands of years after the first appearance of maize. So what role did teosinte play in the origin of maize? Two characteristic

FIG. 29. F$_2$ teosinte-*Tripsacum* recombinant compared to Galinat's drawing of ancient maize from Tehuacán. Photo by the author.

features of the other wild relative of maize, *Tripsacum* sp., which are found in the oldest maize from Tehuacán, may hold the key to the origin of maize. First, *Tripsacum* is bisexual with male flowers above the female flowers on the same spike. Likewise, the oldest maize ears from Tehuacán have staminate tips; that is, male flowers above the female flowers (illustrated in figure 29). Second, *Tripsacum* has a gene for paired kernels, referred to as twinning or polyembryony (Farquharson 1954) and illustrated in figure 30. This is significant because unlike the single grain inside each teosinte seedcoat, there are a pair of maize kernels in each cupule. In the transition from teosinte to maize, the hard seedcoat of teosinte was reduced to a small open cup-like unit referred to as a cupule. Many cupules fused together make up the maize cob that holds the grain. Since the gene for twinning already occurs in *Tripsacum*, it is probable the characteristic of paired kernels in maize was inherited from *Tripsacum* rather than derived from a mutation in teosinte.

Although a number of efforts were made, no one successfully crossed annual teosinte with *Tripsacum* (Mangelsdorf 1974, 70). In 1984 I tried crossing the newly discovered perennial teosinte from the mountains of Jalisco, Mexico, with *Tripsacum*. As a postdoctoral fellow at Indiana University studying the chromosomes of perennial teosinte-maize crosses, I realized the chromosome architecture of the new diploid perennial teosinte was distinctly different from maize and from annual teosinte and was similar to that of *Tripsacum*. There were *Tripsacum* plants from Lois Farquharson's PhD research on *Tripsacum* still growing at the Hilltop Experiment Station in Bloomington, Indiana. I brought *Tripsacum* pollen from the field and made a few hundred hand pollinations onto de-tasseled teosinte plants that were growing in the greenhouse and had had all their pollen-producing flowers removed. I recovered four plants that produced unusual spikes exhibiting some missing links in the transformation from the teosinte spike to the maize ear. The segments of the spike were fused instead of shattering, an important step in the transition to the cob structure of domesticated maize; the segments were alternately arranged like teosinte and *Tripsacum*, but each segment had two kernels instead of a single kernel, another step toward the paired kernel rows

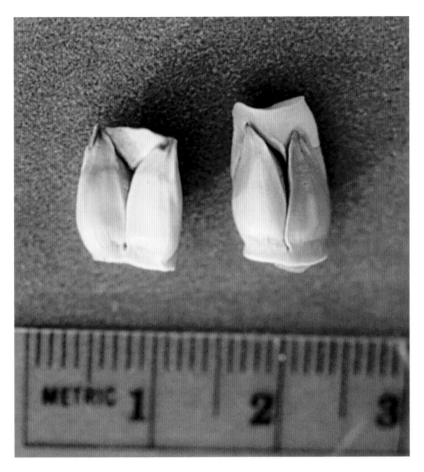

FIG. 30. *Tripsacum* segment exhibiting twinning, the precursor gene for paired kernels per cupule in maize. Photo by the author.

of domesticated maize; and the flowering spikes had staminate tips like early maize from Tehuacán. When I showed tiny ears from these plants to Walton C. Galinat, he immediately recognized them as teosinte-*Tripsacum* recombinants because of the distinct interspacing between the rachis segments, a characteristic of *Tripsacum*-maize introgression not found in maize-teosinte hybrids (Galinat 1970, 7). These missing link traits are seen in the tiny spike from one of my original plants illustrated in the center of figure 31 labeled F_1 below it. Galinat believed the teosinte-*Tripsacum* F_1

hybrids filled in critical missing links in the origin of corn (pers. comm., September 10, 1997).

Experimentally Reconstructed Prototype of Ancient Maize

Although this new discovery of crossability between perennial teosinte and *Tripsacum* revealed missing links in the transition to the ear of maize, suggesting that *Tripsacum* was involved in the origin of maize, it was not until I examined a segregating population from a second generation cross in which *Tripsacum* was the female parent and teosinte was the pollen donor that I recovered specimens with all the features of the oldest maize from the Valley of Tehuacán. It may help to understand the concept if you think of the second generation plants as the grandchildren from a mating between *Tripsacum* and teosinte. Some second generation ears have long soft glumes partially enclosing rounded orange kernels. They have eight rows of kernels with around nine kernels per row. The ears have a staminate tip, and the cob is enclosed in two leaf-like husks. When I showed specimens of these F_2 segregates on a visit to Galinat in his office at the Waltham Experiment Station in 1997, he immediately pulled out his diagrammatic reconstruction of "wild maize" published in the Tehuacán report (Mangelsdorf et al. 1967, 200), pointed to the drawing, and exclaimed, "That's it! You have experimentally reconstructed a prototype of the oldest maize from Tehuacán." This experimentation demonstrates a feasible evolutionary pathway for the origin of maize (fig. 31) and illustrates how human selection and cultivation of naturally occurring recombinants between the two wild relatives of maize could have led to the sudden appearance and rapid domestication of maize as seen in the archaeological record. Advocates of the teosinte hypothesis discount this explanation for the origin of maize by claiming the crosses are not credible (Bennetzen et al. 2001), in spite of the fact that DNA fingerprinting verified the plants are true recombinants between the perennial teosinte and *Tripsacum* parents (Eubanks 1997, 2001a, 2001b, 2001c).

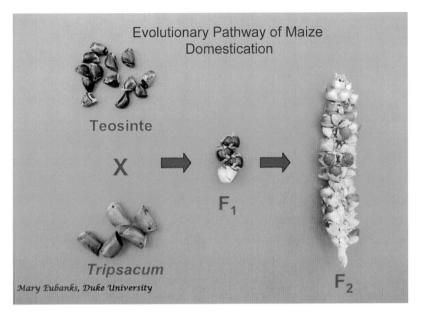

Evolutionary Pathway of Maize
Domestication

Teosinte

X ➡ F₁ ➡

Tripsacum

Mary Eubanks, Duke University

F₂

FIG. 31. Proposed evolutionary pathway for the origin of maize. Photo by the author.

Supporting Archaeological Evidence

The Tehuacán cobs were radiocarbon dated to around 7000 BP. This date is consistent with Piperno and Flannery's AMS dates on cobs from Guilà Naquítz rockshelter in Oaxaca that date to around 6200 BP (Piperno and Flannery 2001, 2101–3). Since Oaxaca is a southward extension of the Tehuacán Valley, it is quite feasible that maize was in Tehuacán by 7000 BP. This is also consistent with recent microfossil evidence, reported by Piperno and colleagues from the Río Balsas Valley in the neighboring state of Guerrero. The rationale to look for evidence of the origin of maize in the Río Balsas area was that *parviglumis* teosinte, thought by some to be the wild progenitor of maize (Matsuoko et al. 2002), grows extensively in the area of the river's drainage. Archaeologists reasoned that this was the most likely place to find evidence of human use of teosinte and the transition from teosinte to domesticated maize. The authors found phytolith evidence that maize was present by around 10,000–7500 BP. They found no evidence of teosinte at the preceramic site, which had a long sequence of human occupation beginning in the early Archaic (Piperno et al. 2009, 5019). If teosinte had been exploited by humans in prehistory and was the progenitor of maize, it should have been identified among the starch grains and microfossils at the Río Balsas early site. That is not what they found. Teosinte starch grains and phytoliths are quite distinct from those of maize. Piperno and colleagues found only evidence for maize. This picture fits the archaeological evidence from Tehuacán and Oaxaca. It may be interpreted to support the MacNeish and Eubanks (2000, 15–17) hypothesis that maize originated from human selection and cultivation of naturally occurring recombinants between *Tripsacum* and teosinte. Although MacNeish and Eubanks proposed a highland origin, the evidence from the Río Balsas indicates a lowland origin is just as likely. The fact that the greatest concentration of *Tripsacum* diversity is in the Río Balsas basin, where it occurs in the same ecological zones with teosinte (Wilkes 1965) signals possibility that natural recombinants could have grown there. The jury is still out on where exactly cultivated maize originated or if it had more than one origin.

Evidence from Molecular Genetics

Recent DNA sequencing of a cob fragment (Tehuacán 162) from the Tehuacán project revealed that the 5,310-year-old specimen is related to the ancestor of modern maize and is distinct from the wild ancestor *parviglumis* teosinte (Ramos-Madrigal et al. 2016). This finding from paleogenomics is consistent with other evidence for early maize domestication. To address the question of the origin of maize at the molecular level, I conducted restriction fragment length polymorphism (RFLP) genotyping of six teosinte species, seven *Tripsacum* species, three ancient maize races found at Tehuacán (Nal Tel, Chapalote, and Pira), Pollo (another ancient maize race from South America), and two modern maize inbreds using 140 molecular markers dispersed throughout the maize genome (Eubanks 2001a). This is the only molecular study to date that included a broad sampling of *Tripsacum* species and provides comparative genomic data for *Tripsacum* as well as teosinte. If maize derived from recombination between two or more progenitors, the

DNA fingerprint should reveal alleles shared exclusively between teosinte and maize, alleles shared exclusively between *Tripsacum* and maize, and alleles shared among all three taxa. DNA analysis of all these taxa revealed 36.4 percent of the alleles in maize are shared exclusively with teosinte, 20.2 percent are shared exclusively with *Tripsacum*, and 43.4 percent are found in maize, teosinte, and *Tripsacum* (Eubanks 2001a, 504–7). These findings support the recombination hypothesis and are consistent with findings from the sequencing of the maize genome. The 32,000-gene blueprint revealed that maize is an allotetraploid, meaning it derived from two progenitors (Schnable et al. 2009, 1112). The maize genome project also revealed that the ancient indigenous land race Palomero Toluqueño has at least twelve genes related to heavy-metal detoxification and stress tolerance, traits not present in teosinte and modern maize (Vielle-Calzada et al. 2009, 1078). In a molecular-marker breeding program to transfer nitrogen-use efficiency from *Tripsacum* into maize, Eubanks demonstrated that some of the same stress-tolerant genes not found in teosinte derive from *Tripsacum* (Eubanks and Richter 2008). A recent genome-wide study examining 55 million single nucleotide polymorphisms (SNPs) to characterize 103 *Zea* lines, including 17 accessions of *Zea mays* ssp. *parviglumis*, two of *Zea mays* ssp. *mexicana*, and one of *Tripsacum dactyloides* var. *meridionale* from Colombia, also found there is significant overlap in key gene content in maize and *Tripsacum* (Chia et al. 2012). The molecular data revealed no large-scale structural variations between *Zea* and *Tripsacum*. The authors concluded that the greater chromosome number of *Tripsacum* is a result of chromosome fissions. This concept lends feasibility to the Eubanks hypothesis that the reduction in chromosome number in teosinte-*Tripsacum* recombinants occurs by fusions of *Tripsacum* chromosomes when aligning with *Zea* chromosomes. This phenomenon, which is well documented in animals (McClintock 1984), also occurs in plants (Jenkins and White 1990; Lord and Richards 1977; White et al. 1988). Recent advances in maize genomics leave the door open to the possibility that the recombination hypothesis may be a reasonable explanation for the sudden appearance of maize in the archaeological record and its subsequent rapid evolution.

In summary, a half century after the Tehuacán Valley project, the 24,860 maize specimens recovered from five dry caves and rockshelters still provide an unprecedented, continuous record of 6,000 years of maize evolution, the emergence of agriculture, and the development of settled village life. Thirty years after the Tehuacán project, experimental crosses between *Tripsacum* and teosinte reconstructed the missing link in the origin of maize and replicated a precise prototype of the oldest maize from Tehuacán. We now know that the ancient specimens Mangelsdorf, MacNeish, and Galinat called "wild maize" were probably maize in the early stages of human selection and domestication (MacNeish and Eubanks 2000, 16). DNA studies and the sequencing of the maize genome have confirmed that maize has two progenitors instead of one. Although we do not know where primordial maize (i.e., teosinte-*Tripsacum* recombinants) was exploited by hunters and gatherers, nor where domesticated maize (i.e., second generation segregates) first appeared, archaeological investigations have corroborated the antiquity of maize in Tehuacán, Oaxaca, and the Río Balsas. If not Tehuacán, the archaeological evidence still points to the probable birthplace of maize as this general region of the southern highlands of Mesoamerica, anywhere south of Tamaulipas and north of Chiapas, or the lowlands of the Rio Balsas. The recombination experiments demonstrate how the transformation of teosinte into maize could have happened rapidly, within a few generations of intercrossing, when humans began selecting and cultivating primordial maize recombinants. The findings from breeding experiments, new data from genomics, and the evolutionary sequence of maize from Tehuacán support a complex evolutionary picture of maize domestication. MacNeish pointed out that "the notion that corn descended from its closest wild relative, teosinte (Doebley 1990, Doebley et al. 1997), is still being defended, but it is far too simple and linear" (Ferrie 2001, 725).

A half century later the Robert S. Peabody Museum of Archaeology's Tehuacán Valley project continues to shine new light on our understanding of the role of humans in the transformation, evolution, and dispersal of maize as well as the origins of agriculture and settled life. The work still has practical significance for applications that can help solve problems today. Experimental prototypes of ancient maize allow us to recapture ancient

FIG. 32. Richard S. "Scotty" MacNeish (left) and Walton C. Galinat (right) forty years after the Tehuacán Valley Archaeological-Botanical Project. Photo by the author.

genes that can be employed for breeding hardier maize (Eubanks 2006, 315). This resurrected genetic diversity gives breeders new resources to adapt maize for sustainable agriculture and enhances security of one of the world's most important grain crops at a time when Earth is undergoing anthropogenic global climate change.

Acknowledgments

With gratitude, I recognize the work and unique insights of Richard S. "Scotty" MacNeish and Walton C. Galinat that have contributed greatly to my professional development and ideas expressed herein (fig. 32). I thank James A. Neely for his help in preparing this essay and comments on the manuscript. A special thank you to Malinda Blustain for the invitation to participate in the "Rising from the Ashes" symposium held at the Society for American Archaeology meeting (April 2, 2011) and to Marshall Cloyd for his loyal and generous support of the Robert S. Peabody Museum of

Archaeology. My thanks to Ryan Wheeler and an anonymous reviewer for valuable comments that substantially improved the manuscript. I am grateful to the National Science Foundation for its support of my research under grant nos. 9660146, 9801386, DEB-94–15541 and IBN-9985977.

REFERENCES

Beadle, George W. 1939. "Teosinte and the Origin of Maize." *Journal of Heredity* 30:245–47.

———. 1980. "The Ancestry of Corn." *Scientific American* 242:112–19.

Bennetzen, J., E. Buckler, V. Chandler, J. Doebley, J. Dorweiler, B. Gaut, M. Freeling, S. Hake, E. Kellogg, R.S. Poethig, V. Walbot, and S. Wessler. 2001. "Genetic Evidence and the Origin of Maize." *Latin American Antiquity* 12:84–86.

Bird, Robert McKelvy. 1984. "South American Maize in Central America." In *Pre-Columbian Plant Migration*, edited by Doris Stone, 39–66. Papers of the Peabody Museum of Archaeology and Ethnology, Harvard University 76. Cambridge MA: Harvard University Press.

Byers, Douglas S., ed. 1967. "Editor's preface." In *The Prehistory of the Tehuacán Valley*, vol. 1: *Environment and Subsistence*, edited by Douglas S. Byers, v–vi. Austin: University of Texas Press.

Callen, Eric O. 1967. "Analysis of the Tehuacán Coprolites." In *The Prehistory of the Tehuacán Valley*, vol. 1: *Environment and Subsistence*, edited by Douglas S. Byers, 261–89. Austin: University of Texas Press.

Chard, Chester. 1950. "Pre-Columbian Trade between North and South America." *Papers of the Kroeber Anthropological Society* 1:1–27.

Chia, Jer-Ming, Chi Song, Peter J. Bradbury, Denise Costich, Natalia de Leon, John Doebley, Robert J. Elshire, Brandon Gaut, Laura Geller, Jeffrey C. Glaubitz, Michael Gore, Kate E. Guill, Jim Holland, Matthew B. Hufford, Jinsheng Lai, Meng Li, Xin Liu, Yanli Lu, Richard McCombie, Rebecca Nelson, Jesse Poland, Boddupalli M. Prasanna, Tanja Pyhäjärvi, Tingzhao Rong, Rajandeep S. Sekhon, Qi Sun, Maud I. Tenaillon, Feng Tian, Jun Wang, Xun Xu, Zhiwu Zhang, Shawn M Kaeppler, Jeffrey Ross-Ibarra, Michael D. McMullen, Edward S. Buckler, Gengyun Zhang, Yunbi Xu, and Doreen Ware. 2012. "Maize HapMap2 Identifies Extant Variation from a Genome in Flux." *Nature Genetics* 44:803–07.

Cutler, Hugh C., and Thomas W. Whitaker. 1967. "Cucurbits from the Tehuacán Caves." In *The Prehistory of the Tehuacán Valley*, vol. 1: *Environment and Subsistence*, edited by Douglas S. Byers, 212–19. Austin: University of Texas Press.

Doebley, John. 1990. "Molecular Evidence and the Evolution of Maize." *Economic Botany* 44, no. 3 (supplement):6–27.

Doebley, John F., Brandon S. Gaut, and Bruce D. Smith. 2006. "The Molecular Genetics of Crop Domestication." *Cell* 127:1309–21.

Doebley, John, Adrian Stec, and Lauren Hubbard. 1997. "The Evolution of Apical Dominance in Maize." *Nature* 386, no. 3:485–88.

Eubanks, Mary W. 1997. "Molecular Analysis of Crosses between *Tripsacum dactyloides* and *Zea diploperennis* (Poaceae)." *Theoretical and Applied Genetics* 94:707–12.

———. 1999. *Corn in Clay: Maize Paleoethnobotany in Pre-Columbian Art*. Gainesville: University Press of Florida.

———. 2001a. "The Mysterious Origin of Maize." *Economic Botany* 55:492–514.

———. 2001b. "The Origin of Maize: Evidence for *Tripsacum* Ancestry." *Plant Breeding Reviews* 20:15–66.

———. 2001c. "An Interdisciplinary Perspective on the Origin of Maize." *Latin American Antiquity* 12:91–98.

———. 2006. "A Genetic Bridge to Utilize *Tripsacum* Germplasm in Maize Improvement." *Maydica* 51:315–27.

Eubanks, Mary, and Daniel Richter Jr. 2008. "Enhancing Nitrogen Use Efficiency in Corn through Introgression of Low N Tolerance from Eastern Gamagrass." Poster presented at the joint annual meeting of the Geological Society of America, American Society of Agronomy, Crop Science Society, and Soil Science Society, October 5–9, 2008, Houston TX.

Galinat, Walton C. 1970. *The Cupule and Its Role in the Origin and Evolution of Maize*. Bulletin of the Massachusetts Agricultural Experiment Station 585. Amherst: University of Massachusetts.

Farquharson, Lois I. 1954. "Apomixis, Polyembryony and Related Problems in *Tripsacum*." PhD diss., Indiana University.

Ferrie, Helke. 2001. "An Interview with Richard S. MacNeish." *Current Anthropology* 42:715–34.

Flannery, Kent V. 1967. "Vertebrate Fauna and Hunting Patterns." In *The Prehistory of the Tehuacán Valley*, vol. 1: *Environment and Subsistence*, edited by Douglas S. Byers, 132–77. Austin: University of Texas Press.

———. 1986. *Guilá Naquitz: Archaic Foraging and Early Agriculture in Oaxaca*. New York: Academic Press.

Hufford, Matthew B., Xun Xu, Joost van Heerwaarden, Tanja Pyhäjärvi, Jer-Ming Chia, Reed A. Cartwright, Robert J. Elshire, Jeffrey C. Glaubitz, Kate E. Guill, Shawn M. Kaeppler, Jinsheng Lai, Peter L. Morrell, Laura M. Shannon, Chi Song, Nathan M. Springer, Ruth A. Swanson-Wagner, Peter Tiffin, Jun Wang, Gengyun

Zhang, John Doebley, Michael D. McMullen, Doreen Ware, Edward S. Buckler, Shuang Yang, and Jeffrey Ross-Ibarra. 2012. "Comparative Population Genomics of Maize Domestication and Improvement." *Nature Genetics* 44:808–11.

Iltis, H. H., J. F. Doebley, R. Guzmán, and B. Pazy. 1979. "*Zea diploperennis* (Gramineae): A New Teosinte from Mexico." *Science* 203:186–88.

Jenkins, G., and J. White. 1990. "Elimination of Synaptonemal Complex Irregularities in a *Lolium* Hybrid." *Heredity* 64:45–53.

Kaplan, Lawrence. 1967. "Archaeological *Phaseolus* from Tehuacán." In *The Prehistory of the Tehuacán Valley*, vol. 1: *Environment and Subsistence*, edited by Douglas S. Byers, 201–11. Austin: University of Texas Press.

Kellogg, Elizabeth A., and James A. Birchler. 1993. "Linking Phylogeny and Genetics: *Zea mays* as a Tool for Phylogenetic Studies." *Systematic Biology* 42:415–39.

Long, Austin, Bruce F. Benz, D. J. Donahue, A.J.T. Jull, and L. J. Toolin. 1989. "First Direct AMS Dates on Early Maize from Tehuacán, Mexico." *Radiocarbon* 31:1035–40.

Long, Austin, and Gayle J. Fritz. 2001. "Validity of AMS Dates on Maize from the Tehuacán Valley: A Comment on MacNeish and Eubanks." *Latin American Antiquity* 12:87–90.

Lord, R. M., and A. J. Richards. 1977. "A Hybrid Swarm between the Diploid *Dactylorhiza fuchsii* (Druce) Soó and the Tetraploid *D. purpurella* (T. & T. A. Steph.) Soó in Durham." *Watsonia* 11:205–11.

MacNeish, Richard S. 1967a. "An Interdisciplinary Approach to an Archaeological Problem." In *The Prehistory of the Tehuacán Valley*, vol. 1: *Environment and Subsistence*, edited by Douglas S. Byers, 14–24. Austin: University of Texas Press.

———. 1967b. "A Summary of the Subsistence." In *The Prehistory of the Tehuacán Valley*, vol. 1: *Environment and Subsistence*, edited by Douglas S. Byers, 290–309. Austin: University of Texas Press.

———. 1991. *The Origins of Agriculture and Settled Life*. Norman: University of Oklahoma Press.

———. 2001. "A Response to Long's Radiocarbon Determinations That Attempt to Put Acceptable Chronology on the Fritz." *Latin American Antiquity* 12:99–104.

MacNeish, Richard S., and Mary W. Eubanks. 2000. "Comparative Analysis of the Río Balsas and Tehuacán Models for the Origin of Maize." *Latin American Antiquity* 11:3–20.

Mangelsdorf, Paul C. 1974. *Corn: Its Origin, Evolution and Improvement*. Cambridge MA: Harvard University.

Mangelsdorf, Paul C., Richard S. MacNeish, and Walton C. Galinat. 1967. "Prehistoric Wild and Cultivated Maize." In *The Prehistory of the Tehuacán Valley*, vol. 1:

Environment and Subsistence, edited by Douglas S. Byers, 178–200. Austin: University of Texas Press.

Mangelsdorf, Paul C., and Robert G. Reeves. 1939. *The Origin of Indian Corn and Its Relatives.* Bulletin of the Texas Agricultural Experiment Station 574:1–315.

Mangelsdorf, Paul C., Lewis M. Roberts, and John S. Rogers. 1981. *The Probable Origin of Annual Teosintes.* Publications of the Bussey Institution 10. Cambridge MA: Harvard University.

Matsuoko, Y., Y. Vigouroux, M. M. Goodman, G. J. Sanchez, E. Buckler, and J. Doebley. 2002. "A Single Domestication for Maize Shown by Multilocus Microsatellite Genotyping." *Proceedings of the National Academy of Sciences* 99:6080–84.

McClintock, Barbara. 1984. "The Significance of Responses of the Genome to Challenges." *Science* 226:792–801.

Piperno, Dolores R., and Kent V. Flannery. 2001. "The Earliest Archaeological Maize (*Zea mays* L.) from Highland Mexico: New Accelerator Mass Spectrometry Dates and Their Implications." *Proceedings of the National Academy of Sciences* 98:2101–03.

Piperno, Dolores R., Anthony J. Ranere, Irene Holst, Jose Iriarte, and Ruth Dickau. 2009. "Starch Grain and Phytolith Evidence for Early Ninth Millennium B.P. Maize from the Central Balsas River Valley, Mexico." *Proceedings of the National Academy of Sciences* 106:5019–24.

Ramos-Madrigal, Jazmín, Bruce D. Smith, J. Victor Moreno-Mayar, Shyam Gopalakrishnan, Jeffrey Ross-Ibara, M. Thomas P. Gilbert, and Nathan Wales. 2016. "Genome Sequence of a 5,310-Year-Old Maize Cob Provides Insights into the Early Stages of Maize Domestication." *Current Biology* 26:1–7.

Schnable, Patrick S., Doreen Ware, Robert S. Fulton, and colleagues. 2009. "The B73 Maize Genome: Complexity, Diversity, and Dynamics." *Science* 326:1112–15.

Smith, C. Earle. 1967. "Plant Remains." In *The Prehistory of the Tehuacán Valley,* vol. 1: *Environment and Subsistence,* edited by Douglas S. Byers, 220–55. Austin: University of Texas Press.

Stadler, L. J. 1951. "Spontaneous Mutations in Maize." In *Cold Spring Harbor Symposium in Quantitative Biology* 16:49–63.

Stephens, Stanley G. 1967. "A Cotton Boll Segment from Coxcatlán Cave." In *The Prehistory of the Tehuacán Valley,* vol. 1: *Environment and Subsistence,* edited by Douglas S. Byers, 256–260. Austin: University of Texas Press.

Vielle-Calzada, Jean-Philippe, Octavio Martínez de la Vega, Gustavo Hernández-Guzmán, Enrique Ibarra-Lacletter, Cesar Alvarez-Mejía, Julio C. Vega-Arreguín, Beatriz Jiménez-Moraila, Aracelia Fernández-Cortés, Guillermo Corona-Armenta, Luis Herrera-Estrella, and Alfredo Herrera-Estrella. 2009. "The Palomero Genome Suggests Metal Effects on Domestication." *Science* 326:1078.

West, Robert C. 1961. "Aboriginal Sea Navigation between Middle and South America." *American Anthropologist* 63:133–35.

White, J., G. Jenkins, and J. S. Parker. 1988. "Elimination of Multivalents during Meiotic Prophase in *Scilla autumnalis*. I. Diploid and Triploid." *Genome* 30:930–39.

Wilkes, H. Garrison. 1965. "*Tripsacum* Population Studies." *Maize Genetics Newsletter* 39:71–71.

———. 2004. "Corn, Strange and Marvelous: But Is a Definitive Origin Known?" In *Corn: Origin, History, Technology and Production*, edited by C. Wayne Smith, Javier Bertrán, and E.C.A. Runge, 3–63. Hoboken NJ: John Wiley & Sons.

Chapter 7

Trials and Redemption at the Peabody Museum

Malinda Stafford Blustain

Like many museums, the Peabody has had ups and down that were a consequence of both internal and external factors. When times were tough the museum was forced to clarify its mission and role at Phillips Academy. Twice in recent years the museum had to confront very challenging financial issues while simultaneously trying to develop its educational program. These difficult times helped lay the foundation for the success that the institution enjoys today. By creating an environment within which frank discussion and innovative ideas can be voiced, the museum is now integrated into the academic program at Phillips Academy.

Around 1950 archaeology, along with other social sciences, benefited from a profusion of new funding. In 1949 the Rockefeller Foundation expanded its involvement in social and cultural issues throughout the developing world (Rockefeller Foundation n.d.). The National Science Foundation was established in 1950 and in 1954 created the Social Science Division, which became a major source of funding for archaeology (National Science Foundation n.d.; Patterson 1999, 163). In 1951 the Viking Fund changed its name to the Wenner-Gren Foundation for Anthropological Research and became a mainstay of funding in the discipline (Wenner-Gren Foundation n.d.). Peabody curators and directors Frederick Johnson, Douglas Byers, and Richard S. "Scotty"

MacNeish were quick to take advantage of these new resources, initiating decades of reliance on funding from private foundations and the federal government.

The very fruitful collaboration between Johnson and MacNeish began in the 1960s and continued until Johnson's death in 1994 (MacNeish 1996). Their work in the Tehuacán Valley of Mexico is perhaps the best known project. Never one to do things on a modest scale, MacNeish employed an interdisciplinary host of scientific professionals and local excavators in pursuit of the origin of corn (see Eubanks, this volume). In 1960 John Kemper, the Phillips Academy headmaster, named MacNeish a research associate of the Robert S. Peabody Foundation for Archaeology so that the Tehuacán Archaeological-Botanical Project funds could be administered by the foundation. Between 1960 and 1968 MacNeish was awarded a total of more than $400,000 from the National Science Foundation and the Rockefeller Foundation. At the time it was considered big money.

After the Tehuacán project MacNeish began investigating early corn in Ayacucho, Peru. Again MacNeish brought in twenty international scientists and students. Fieldwork lasted from 1969 through 1971 and was the genesis of many of Scotty's most colorful and entertaining stories (Ferrie 2001).

In 1970 MacNeish was appointed Peabody Foundation director. In the midst of planning and directing huge field projects, Scotty also found the time to design a comprehensive year-long curriculum in introductory anthropology and archaeology for Phillips Academy. He renovated one of the museum's galleries to amplify the themes in his courses. Phillips Academy students not only benefited from Scotty's considerable expertise in the classroom but also learned the La Perra technique while excavating at the Andover dump (fig. 33).

It is important to note that MacNeish and Johnson were fulfilling the mandate of the school. In 1914 the "Panel of Eminent Experts"—whose membership was Franz Boas, W. H. Holmes, Hiram Bingham, and F. W. Putnam—had issued a report stating that the Department of Archaeology (as it was called at the time) should focus on research, with particular emphasis on answering the "big questions" in American archaeology (see transcript of their report in Blustain 2008). Kidder, Byers, Johnson, and

FIG. 33. The Andover town dump served as a training ground for several generations of archaeologists, beginning with Alfred V. Kidder, who practiced his stratigraphic method on the sloping deposits, recognizing that they looked like the deep midden at Pecos. Later MacNeish held several field schools for Phillips Academy students there. This photo shows the dig conducted in 1974. Photographic collection of the Robert S. Peabody Museum of Archaeology.

MacNeish took this mandate seriously (see Richardson and Adovasio, Cordell, and Eubanks, this volume).

Phillips Academy appreciated the prestige it received as the foundation's parent institution. In 1969 a Phillips Academy trustee, George H. W. Bush, spoke admiringly of MacNeish's important research in Mexico, his revitalization of exhibitions at the Peabody, and the benefits being derived by Andover faculty and students (excerpt from trustee meeting notes of April 25–26, 1969, Trustees of Phillips Academy).

Money Matters

Understanding how the Peabody is funded is critically important to this narrative. The founder, Robert S. Peabody, directed that his considerable financial gift be kept independent of, and managed separately from, the rest of the school's endowment. Today the Peabody Museum, along with the Addison Gallery and the academy's other outreach programs, are expected to be largely self-supporting. For example, at present less than a third of the Peabody's budget comes as a budget allocation from Phillips Academy, and the rest derives from endowment income and from funds raised for operating expenses each year. This ratio has fluctuated through time.

Trouble Brews

As long as external funds were available to pay for important, ambitious projects, all was well. But then, as now, periods of financial uncertainty occurred. During the 1970s the national economy experienced a downturn and high rates of inflation (Wenner-Gren Foundation n.d.; also see Casteel 1980, documenting decreased NSF funding around this period, and Patterson 1999 on the political economy of American archaeology). MacNeish began to have difficulty securing the money needed to keep his programs running. To continue operations in the field and at home, MacNeish drew heavily on the foundation's endowment; withdrawals of at least $226,000 were made between 1969 and 1975. He had by this time founded the "Friends of the Foundation," a donor group. Unfortunately the generosity of the Friends diminished with the economic downturn and could not provide the supplementary revenue he needed. His annual report for 1975 cites difficulties stemming from lack of support for research in the Palo Blanco region of the Tehuacán Valley through the "rapidly diminishing funds of the Friends of the Foundation."

The $40,000 awarded to MacNeish in 1975 for research at Santa Marta Cave in Chiapas was returned to NSF after the site was disturbed by Mexican archaeologists, and he would not work there, and the National Endowment for the Arts did not grant funds for renovation of the exhibits, so this was paid for by the foundation. MacNeish remarked, "As you are well aware, the financial situation of the world in general, and the Peabody Foundation in particular, has been in rather bad shape for the last couple of years" (MacNeish 1975).

A double-dip recession in the early 1980s, along with a stock market decline, made matters worse, leaving the foundation's coffers at their lowest level in decades. The trustees of Phillips Academy, charged with fiduciary responsibility for the founder's gift, became concerned about the large and expensive scale of international fieldwork and the erosion of the foundation endowment. In 1983 the research program ended, and MacNeish left Phillips Academy.

For the remainder of the decade the Peabody Foundation had no public or research program. Day-to-day management of the Peabody Foundation and its facility was very capably undertaken by Eugene Winter, who made the building and collections accessible to public school groups, researchers, and any Phillips Academy students and faculty wishing to use them. But compared to its heyday, the museum was dormant.

By the late 1980s the school's faculty and the Board of Trustees took a renewed interest in reviving the museum. The imminent passage of the Native American Graves Protection and Repatriation Act (NAGPRA) added considerable weight to their case. In September 1990 James W. Bradley assumed the directorship of the foundation, the name of which he changed to its current one, the Robert S. Peabody Museum of Archaeology.

Bradley faced a broad mandate from the trustees. He was to jump-start the museum's outreach to the school and the public at large. He was to ensure compliance with NAGPRA. He was expected to raise funds to bring the building up to code. Perhaps most important in the eyes of the trustees, he was to rebuild the museum's endowment. The model in that regard was the Addison Gallery of American Art, the Peabody's sister institution at Phillips Academy. During the 1980s the Addison had built a sizable endowment that freed it from the need to raise funds for day-to-day operation, leaving only the obligation to find funding for its first-class programs in exhibitions and outreach. The expectation was that Bradley would do the same for the Peabody.

And so during the 1990s Bradley began building the Peabody's current program. He was successful in stimulating interest in the museum among faculty and students. In some ways this feat was harder than it sounds. The previous directors' focus on research had yielded acquisitions that were scientifically very important but that to the untrained eye were difficult to comprehend. And in truth, while the Peabody's collection has many wonderful objects, it also contains hundreds of thousands of bits and pieces of stone and bone and pottery. For trustees, administrators, faculty, students, and donors accustomed to the standard of art at the Addison Gallery of American Art, tiny corn cobs, broken pots, debitage, and antler tines with use-wear aroused little interest.

Nevertheless, Bradley managed to insinuate the Peabody's resources into the new curricula being designed for several academic departments. He also removed outdated exhibitions and began a program of rotating exhibitions in the museum's galleries.

Bradley moved the museum forward in other directions as well. He made friends with trustees and alumni and instigated a public membership program. He hired museum professionals to bring collections management up to the standards of the American Association of Museums (now the American Alliance of Museums). He put together a development team to support his fundraising efforts. Perhaps his greatest contribution was with NAGPRA (see Bradley, this volume). He developed national models of NAGPRA compliance, served on the NAGPRA Review Committee, and created cooperative educational programs such as the Pecos Pathways program that made the museum partners with descendant communities (see Randall and Toya, this volume).

This level of activity, however, required significant infusions of cash.

Bradley was resourceful in attracting large federal grants for NAGPRA. Other grants were found for collections management and operational support. But a large staff and an ambitious program took their toll. External funding and budgeted contributions from the academy were not enough to make ends meet without significant endowment draw. Finally in 2002 the Peabody's future was once more in doubt, and the Board of Trustees called for a "pause" in order to assess the situation once again.

That year, at the 2002 annual meeting of the Society for American Archaeology in Denver, Dena Dincauze, a past president of the society, set up a meeting to discuss the so-called pause. Members of the Peabody Visiting Committee and museum staff reported on what was about to happen in Andover (see Sykes, this volume). The important outcome was that the Phillips Academy administration received more than one hundred letters written by archaeologists, tribal members, museum professionals, and the lay public in support of the Peabody Museum.

Troubles Resolved

The hiatus served to facilitate the deliberations of two consecutive committees. The first was a Peabody Planning and Assessment Committee, an internal body composed of trustees, administrators, alumni, faculty, members of the Peabody Visiting Committee, and Peabody staff. They assessed the quality of the museum's collection relative to those of other archaeological museums in the United States. They also appraised its potential usefulness to the academic program at Phillips Academy, considered alternative futures for the collection, and assessed the museum's financial viability.

After nine months of deliberation the committee recommended support of a small professional staff until 2004 to continue the ongoing inventory of the collection and fulfillment of NAGPRA obligations.

A second committee, the Peabody Planning Committee, was convened in 2002 to continue the assessment and planning process. Membership was expanded to include Emerson Baker II, a Phillips Academy alumnus and historical archaeologist, and David Hurst Thomas, a curator of archaeology at the American Museum of Natural History. This new body was

FIG. 34. The Peabody Advisory Committee seated around the library table in the museum during their fall 2011 meeting. Photo by Donald A. Slater for the Robert S. Peabody Museum of Archaeology.

charged with determining whether the Phillips Academy community had interest in integrating the Peabody Museum into its academic program. The committee also sought to identify financial strategies for the collection and for use of the building, and finally, to develop a course of action to make the Peabody a viable operation once again. Among the thirteen recommendations they produced in 2004 were the following:

> to continue the museum's current lean operation and to refocus its mission on service as an academic resource for Phillips Academy;
> to embed the Peabody's operations within the school by refocusing the Peabody's resources on Phillips Academy students and faculty;
> to change the structure so that the Peabody director reports to the academy's dean of studies;

FIG. 35. Phillips Academy Bio 600 student Jennifer Evans with her independent project based on analysis of ancient bird feathers in the Peabody Museum collection. Photo by the author.

> to appoint an internal education committee staffed by faculty to guide the Peabody's integration into the academic program;
> to retain the collection and manage it with the assistance of Phillips Academy work-duty students and unpaid interns from local universities and colleges.

Oversight of the collections program came under the purview of a Collections Committee, members of which would be drawn from external and internal sources. Native American, scholarly, and public access to the collection would continue, but no ambitious public programming was to be encouraged. A progress report was requested in four years.

By 2008 much had been accomplished (Blustain 2008). A very active and engaged Peabody Advisory Committee (fig. 34) replaced the old Visiting Committee. In addition to earlier Visiting Committee members, new Andover faculty and alumni and several more archaeologists and museum professionals became active in the oversight and planning of the museum's affairs. Freed from public programming and its attendant fundraising obligations, the Peabody was able to focus on NAGPRA compliance and on broadening its relationships with students and faculty. Peabody staff designed a multidisciplinary course in Human Evolution and more than fifty single-class curriculum units. They have supervised student independent projects (fig. 35); developed a Native speakers and a Native artists series; and launched a second expeditionary learning program in Mexico, Belize, and Peru (see Slater and Hamilton, this volume) and a third to France (see Gallou, this volume).

The Peabody collections are now perceived by faculty and students to be a rich repository of information and treasures pertaining to more than 12,000 years of human experience in the Americas. The Peabody has become integrally tied into the academy.

A comprehensive strategic plan for FY 2009–13 was approved by the Board of Trustees. By 2011 the majority of goals put forward in that strategic plan had already been accomplished, fully two years ahead of schedule.

So the Peabody's story is presently a happy one. Thanks to the foresight of Phillips Academy trustees, increasing interest and support from faculty and students, and expert guidance from a very engaged Advisory Committee, the Peabody found a steady course through its troubles. Now, due to the generosity of alumni donors, the museum has just completed a near total renovation of its interior spaces, and the endowment continues steady growth. All this was nearly inconceivable only four years ago. The Peabody Museum is now on solid ground and for the first time in decades can look forward to continuing its present stable trajectory well into the future.

REFERENCES

Blustain, Malinda Stafford. 2008. "Strategic Plan, FY2009–2013, Report of Progress, FY2004–2008." Robert S. Peabody Museum of Archaeology, Phillips Academy, Andover, Massachusetts.

Casteel, Richard W. 1980. "National Science Foundation Funding of Domestic Archaeology in the United States: Where the Money Ain't." *American Antiquity* 45, no. 1:170–80.

Ferrie, Helke. 2001. "An Interview with Richard S. MacNeish." *Current Anthropology* 42, no. 5:715–35.

MacNeish, Richard S. 1975. "Annual Report, Robert S. Peabody Foundation for Archaeology, 1975." Accessed October 19, 2016. https://archive.org/details/robertspeabodymu1975rich.

———. 1996. "Frederick Johnson 1904–1994." *American Antiquity* 612:269–73.

National Science Foundation. n.d. "A Timeline of NSF History: 1940s–2000s." Accessed March 4, 2013. https://www.nsf.gov/about/history/overview.50.jsr.

Patterson, Thomas C. 1999. "The Political Economy of Archaeology in the United States." *Annual Review of Anthropology* 28:155–74.

Robert S. Peabody Museum of Archaeology. Richard S. MacNeish records (1950s–early 1980s) 01.04. Andover: Phillips Academy.

Rockefeller Foundation. n.d. "Moments in Time: 1940–1949." Accessed March 4, 2013. http://www.rockefellerfoundation.org/about-us/our-history/1940–1949.

Trustees of Phillips Academy. 1969. "Unpublished notes from Trustee meeting of April 25–26, 1969." Phillips Academy Archives, Andover, Massachusetts.

Wenner-Gren Foundation. n.d. "The Story and People of Wenner-Gren." Accessed March 4, 2013. http://www.wennergren.org/history/story-and-people-wenner-gren.

Chapter 8

Negotiating NAGPRA

REDISCOVERING THE HUMAN SIDE OF SCIENCE

James W. Bradley

My appointment as director of the Robert S. Peabody Foundation, as it was then known, began on September 1, 1990. Even before I started I knew this would be a difficult job. Basically my charge was to bring the museum back to life after years of decline (see previous chapter) and to rebuild a positive relationship with Phillips Academy as well as the museum and archaeological communities. In short, I was to return the Peabody to the kind of national, even international, prominence it had enjoyed under previous directors. No small task. Two months later the Native American Graves Protection and Repatriation Act (NAGPRA) was signed into law, and I found that my priorities had changed.

The NAGPRA Process

For those not familiar with NAGPRA, perhaps the best explanation is that it changed museums in this country in a fundamental way, especially in terms of their relationship with Native American people. NAGPRA required all museums that received federal funds to inventory their collections for human remains, funerary objects, sacred objects, and objects of cultural patrimony related to Indian people. These inventories were to be sent to the culturally affiliated, federally recognized Indian tribes and a process of consultation was to be initiated. The goal of consultation was to determine the most appropriate way to repatriate these ancestral remains and objects. Rightly or wrongly, most museums believed that they had title to all the materials in their collections. NAGPRA changed this, essentially giving title, and therefore legal control, to these four sets of materials back to the descendants in the communities involved.

Museums faced few choices. One could fight NAGPRA, ignore the new law and hope it would go away, or utilize it as the extraordinary opportunity it was. For me, there was never any question which way to go.

First and foremost, I needed the academy's attention, and NAGPRA was the perfect lever. At that time the position of museum director reported directly to the Board of Trustees via the headmaster, and there was much that needed their attention. Frankly, things were a mess. I had no real idea of the size of the collections (former director Richard "Scotty" MacNeish had told me there were more than a million objects). The museum had no staff other than a receptionist and virtually no operating funds. NAGPRA provided an excellent justification for staff and funding. I was also fortunate to be able to hire Malinda Blustain as collections manager and Leah Rosenmeier as repatriation coordinator.

Malinda and Leah made a huge difference and soon brought the museum back to a professional level of operation. However, their work also highlighted the enormity of complying with NAGPRA. We had little intellectual control over our own collections, and as we learned more, our apprehensions were confirmed. The museum held a huge amount of material subject to NAGPRA requirements—far more than we had expected. The vast majority of items were from the continental United States, and a significant percentage had come from mortuary contexts. It was also clear that we had many assemblages of immense archaeological importance. These included the materials from A. V. Kidder's excavations at Pecos, Warren K. Moorehead's work at Etowah, and the Late Archaic assemblages from New England excavated by Douglas Byers and Frederick Johnson as well as Moorehead. It soon became apparent that to comply with NAGPRA we would have to work with tribes and professional colleagues across the country and to make decisions on cultural affiliation ranging from the absolutely straightforward—the Pueblo of Jemez—to the completely ambiguous. NAGPRA compliance was going to be an enormous undertaking. Now, more than twenty-five years later, the museum has completed more than four hundred consultations.

All this led the R. S. Peabody to take an active, even aggressive, approach to repatriation. We felt it was our responsibility to make the first move, to reach out to the tribes whose materials we had and begin the conversation. It did not always go well, but having no choice, we persevered in our efforts to find grounds for mutual understanding. Over time I found that the consultation process usually went through four stages:

STAGE 1. The first stage was adversarial, sometimes polite, sometimes not. The tribe's position was usually an unconditional demand to have everything returned. We were generally stuck with trying to explain compliance under federal law. These initial meetings were often frustrating and difficult.

STAGE 2. With any luck, however, discussion eventually moved to a second stage. Here each side began to realize how differently we viewed the process and, more important, how little we knew about each another. While these meetings often retained an edge of distrust and skepticism, they also included more open questioning. For tribes, this meant a clearer understanding about why sites had been excavated and what had been learned from the materials collected—something that had seldom been shared with them before. For us, it was a revelation to learn, from their point of view, how much harm excavation and scientific inquiry could cause within a community. This meant there were wounds to heal, not just negotiations to be concluded. I often left these meetings feeling that, tough as compliance was for us, it was far more difficult for the tribes.

STAGE 3. If things had progressed this far, the third stage was one I began to anticipate with pleasure. At this time we really started to learn about one another and even become friends. A key indicator of this stage was when the silence ended and the good-natured teasing began. Nevertheless, these were important meetings, where real understanding began to occur. For tribes, this meant realizing more clearly what was subject to the law and what was not as well as how much material was actually involved— usually far more than they realized. This was often when tribes began to understand how much time and money the museum had spent caring for its collections. In other words, they realized that we too valued these objects, even if for different reasons. For my part, I began to understand how much knowledge about these objects survived in present-day Native communities, and how important they still were. The objects were not just things from the past. They were often considered to be part of the living community and needed to be treated as such. Interestingly, these meetings were also characterized by an avid interest in archaeology and what it could tell Indian people about their ancestors and past ways of life. These meetings were exhausting but deeply satisfying. We frequently went out to eat together afterward.

STAGE 4. The fourth stage focused on finding the right repatriation solution. By this time we had become partners, working together to make the best possible choices. One of the great things about NAGPRA is that it does not mandate a specific, one-size-fits-all solution. As long as the tribe and the museum agree, they can essentially do what they want. This stage became the opportunity for friends and colleagues to discover that creative solutions can produce remarkable results.

There is no better example of this than the repatriation agreement that emerged from our consultation with the Pueblo of Jemez (fig. 36). This had been a long and often difficult process, one in which Jemez took the lead in coordinating the claims of several tribes, while we assumed the responsibility for reassembling the record of Kidder's work and the widely scattered collections. The process took more than six years to accomplish. It also required time for the right solution to emerge. In the end, this is what the Pueblo decided:

1. Kidder's excavations should not have taken place. The ancestral remains should never have been disturbed.
2. However, since they had been, there must be a reason why this had been allowed to happen. The Pueblo's task was to find out that reason.
3. Archaeological excavation broke the spiritual bond between the ancestors and their associated funerary objects. Since the Pueblo had no ceremonies for reestablishing that bond, simply reburying

FIG. 36. Pecos Governor and Jemez Second Lieutenant Governor Ruben Sando (left), Jim Bradley, and Martin Toya of Jemez Pueblo begin the repatriation process at the Peabody Museum on May 20, 1999. Photo by Bethany Versoy, photographic collection of the Robert S. Peabody Museum of Archaeology.

the objects would not solve the problem. New decisions would be required.

4. In terms of the human remains, these ancestors would be reburied along with a small number of objects that were considered to be "living tribal members." The reburial would take place within the Pecos National Historical Park, as near the original location as was feasible.

5. Members of the present-day community would have the opportunity to offer their own gifts to these ancestors, creating a new spiritual bond in place of the one that had been broken.

6. The rest of the associated funerary objects were considered "gifts from the ancestors" to the present-day community. These gifts had been given to help the people, now and in the future, remember

who they are and where they came from, especially at times when pressures from the outside world threaten tribal identity.

7. Since the museum had been a "good surrogate parent" to the objects, and had the professional ability to curate them, the Pueblo asked the R. S. Peabody to enter into a long-term curation agreement for the continued care of their property. The result was that except for the human remains and some fifty objects, nearly all the Pecos collection stayed right where it was—in Andover and at the Pecos National Historical Park.

8. This agreement was part of a broader understanding, a commitment to ongoing, active relations between Jemez and the museum. One visible aspect of this partnership has been Pecos Pathways. This annual exchange program brings together students from Philips Academy, Jemez Pueblo, and the town of Pecos, New Mexico, to learn about each other, their communities, and archaeology (see Randall and Toya, this volume).

Repatriation

On May 20, 1999, the formal repatriation ceremony was held at the Robert S. Peabody Museum. Barbara Landis Chase, head of Phillips Academy, read a formal proclamation turning custody of the materials in the museum's collection over to the Pueblo of Jemez (fig. 37). A similar agreement was also signed with the Peabody Museum of Archaeology and Ethnology at Harvard University, where the human remains had been stored. Later that day all the remains and other objects to be repatriated were loaded into the enormous 18-wheel tractor-trailer that would take them back to Pecos, New Mexico.

The following day Leah Rosenmeier and I flew to Albuquerque and drove to Pecos for the reburial ceremony at the Pecos National Historical Park. Much of the material subject to NAGPRA was there (on long-term loan from Andover), and during the consultation process, we had all agreed that the reburial should be as close to that original site as possible. With the help of Superintendent Duane Alire, a trench had been excavated in a secure location and the area prepared for the reburial.

FIG. 37. Head of School Barbara Landis Chase officially transfers the ownership of Pecos materials in the Peabody collection to the people of Jemez; Jim Bradley holding proclamation and Raymond Gachupin looking on. Photo by Bethany Versoy, photographic collection of the Robert S. Peabody Museum of Archaeology.

The reburial ceremony took place on May 22, 1999. Leah and I were there to facilitate this last step in the repatriation process. I was also honored with an invitation to participate as a representative of the museum. It was an intensely powerful and emotional event. Over the course of that day, I managed to scribble down some notes. In reflecting on them now, several years later, I am even more aware of how extraordinary that day was.

4:00 A.M. This is not a time of day with which I am familiar. Still, I'm dressed and ready to go, even reasonably coherent considering there is no coffee.

4:30 A.M. Leah and I arrive at the park. It is silent and dark, a wash of stars across the sky the only light. The waxing moon set hours ago. I can't even see the familiar shape of the cliffs to the west. Park headquarters is quiet; only the night-shift rangers are present. I open the office door and am overwhelmed by the smell of ripe melons, cartons of them stored overnight for this afternoon's feast. Leah heads to the collections storage building to be sure the objects for reburial are ready. I get some coffee started. Joshua Madalena, one of the Jemez religious leaders, arrives, all focus and purpose, and disappears after Leah. The first faint bands of dawn are visible through the banked clouds in the east.

5:30 A.M. Birdsong and other sounds increase with the light. Rangers from the National Park Service Event Management Team arrive, set up, and depart. I am most useful staying out of the way and making more coffee. The smell of coffee now equals that of melon. Bill Whately, the tribal preservation officer, arrives. He and Joshua leave for the burial trench with several boxes. A beam of sunlight catches the top of the cliff and brings color back into the world. Each time I look up, it has slid a little farther down the buff-orange-red rock face.

6:15 A.M. The pace of activity grows. Outside, several carloads of Jemez women arrive and prepare for cooking. Lots of conversation and jokes in their language, Towa; comments about the morning chill and requests for water in English. Leah is still in the collections building finalizing the inventory. The paperwork must be perfect. More people are appearing: members of the Pecos Eagle Society joking around and taking pictures, a pickup truck from the Jemez Black Eagle Singers, its windows painted with slogans like "Pecos Bound" and "Return to Graceland." Suddenly Martin Toya, head of the Pecos Eagle Watchers Society, is there. He greets me warmly, then leaves to call his members to order. Coffee break is over.

7:30 A.M. Leah is finally done and joins me to watch events unfold. For now, our part is over. I set up chairs for the elderly people and bring them coffee. Everyone is focused on the progress of the truck carrying the remains and the 300 people who have walked the 80 miles from Jemez to Pecos, preparing the way for the return of the ancestors (fig. 38). The rangers say they have just entered the park.

FIG. 38. Many members of the Jemez community spent days walking the eighty miles from Jemez to Pecos, where they joined the tractor trailer that transported the ancestral remains and artifacts back to the Pecos National Historical Park for reburial, May 1999. Photo by Ira Block, courtesy of National Geographic Society.

8:00 A.M. The truck arrives and is greeted by perhaps 200 Jemez folks, infants to elders, all in their finest regalia. If ribbon shirts and blankets, silver and turquoise, are indicators of power, then this is the spiritual center of the universe today.

The truck is a huge 18-wheeler lent by a Cherokee-owned firm in Oklahoma. I last saw it parked in front of the Peabody Museum at Harvard. Chief Ranger Gary Hartley, who with Joshua Madalena and Michael Loretto accompanied the remains on the long drive back to Pecos, is the escort. Jemez Governor Raymond Gachupin, Pecos Governor Ruben Sando, and the rest of the Jemez leadership follow. The Event Management Team estimates that 2,000 people are waiting behind them.

As the truck turns and backs down the dirt road toward the trench, Joshua leads a group of young men into the collections building. Each emerges with an object for reburial and follows the truck. There is no joking now.

9:00 A.M. The temperature rises with the sun, as does the smell of juniper, piñon and sage. The sky is a hard bright blue. Most of the unloading and reburial seems to be done. This is remarkable. It takes time to move 2,000 sets of human remains. In addition, the remains needed to be taken from the boxes in which they had been transported and placed in the dirt. Once all the remains are in the trench, they are covered with a layer of earth. A plume of reddish dust indicates the initial covering has begun. Delegations from the other tribes who participated in this repatriation begin assembling to pay their last respects.

10:00 A.M. It's time for the people of the Pueblo of Jemez to visit the burial site. War Chief Pete Toya asks the museum representatives to come forward, and he introduces us to the crowd in Towa (fig. 39). Since we have cared for those ancestral remains, we are considered surrogate parents. We start to leave as the line forms, but Pete asks us to stay. The Eagle Watchers Society members are coming back, dusty and tired after their labors. Martin Toya comes forward, takes both my hands, and thanks me for helping to bring the ancestors home. He hugs me and introduces me to other members of the society, starting with the eldest. Each greets me with a courtesy and intensity that excludes all other thought.

By this time, Jemez people have begun to return from the burial site and join the queue. I suddenly realize I am at the head of a receiving line for hundreds of people. It is intensely emotional. Many people are weeping openly, others are somber. Yet each person takes my hands, hugs me, and thanks me. Many of the older people, their brown wrinkled faces wet with tears, bless me. Only the younger teenagers seem a little uncertain how to behave. I thank people in turn for their patience and good wishes; I tell the kids never to forget this day because soon the life of the community will be in their hands.

FIG. 39. Jemez War Chief Pete Toya in front of burial trench at Pecos National Historical Park, May 1999. Photo by Ira Block, courtesy of National Geographic Society.

As people continue to return, the line becomes amorphous. People gather in knots and start to tell stories. Two sisters stop, one too emotional to speak; the other, a nun, tells of an event several years ago when a Catholic priest visited the Pecos mission and performed a brief service to release the spirits trapped there. At the conclusion, she said, there was a gust of wind out of the church and it was clear to all present that something had been freed. Still, she continues, that was nothing compared to today.

Finally it is our turn. As the last of the Jemez people return, we are invited to pay our respects. As surrogate parents, we are family now; we would not have been asked otherwise. Stuart Gachupin leads us down the now well-trodden path toward the burial trench. It is 10 feet wide, 6 feet deep, and 600 feet long. Only the reddish earth is visible; everything else has been covered. I stand for a few moments, stoop and throw a handful of powdery red soil into the pit, then walk back toward park headquarters alone. All along the way are huge piles of empty boxes, each meticulously labeled with provenience information and storage codes.

11:00 A.M. It is time for the program to begin. A stage has been set up in the parking lot, and people are gathered on all sides, especially where there is shade. Leah and I have been asked to come up to the stage and are seated in the front row. There are prayers, welcomes, and expressions of appreciation. Most are in Towa. It is strange to be a participant in a program when you don't understand the language. In the background, the roar of diesel engines signals that the burial trench is being filled. Duane Alire, the superintendent at Pecos, says it took four days for two backhoes to dig that trench. It will take two days to backfill it.

It is midday now, and I'm really cooked up here on stage. The sunscreen was sweated off long ago, but it really doesn't matter. The walkers who accompanied the remains from Jemez to Pecos have been asked to come forward. Many hobble from blisters and cramped muscles. I know several of them. They are thanked and the Black Eagle Singers honor them with a new song. It is a mass of people, swaying, weeping and hugging. But these are cleansing emotions, joy and relief, and when people finally return to their seats, there is a sense of completeness, of closure.

As the presentations and acknowledgments go on, clouds build and the sky darkens over the western cliffs. A good thing too. I am quite well done. The shadows from the clouds, and the breezes they bring, are truly a gift from the heavens. But there is more. Soon plumes of rain sweep down from the purple-black sky, turning portions of the intensely colored landscape into a gray scale of silhouettes. Here, rain is a blessing that brings life to a beautiful but otherwise barren world. One squall passes north of us; another, rumbling deeply, goes south. The Native people all notice and nod.

Finally, War Captain David Yepa begins the concluding prayer. As he does, the wind suddenly picks up. Fierce gusts bend the junipers, and red dust is drawn up into great columns, towering versions of the blanket-wrapped figures standing around me. Perhaps this is all coincidence, perhaps not, but the sense of the moment is overwhelming, and eyes remain closed for more reasons than the swirling dust. David's prayer ends, the dry squall passes. It is time to celebrate and eat.

2:30 P.M. The line is long, but there is plenty of food, as there always is at a Jemez feast: chili verde, posole, Jemez enchiladas, tamales, red chili with meat, potato salad, fry bread, horno-baked bread, bread pudding, feast day cookies, and, of course, ripe melon. It does not begin to rain until everyone has finished.

Much changed during the eleven years I served as director of the museum, for me personally, for the museum, and within the broader archaeological and museum community. As David Hurst Thomas (2000, 276) observed in his book *Skull Wars*, now "perhaps we can rediscover a more human side to our science and come to value once again the importance of face-to-face relationships with those whose ancestors we wish to study." I could not agree more strongly. To return to the beginning, and my charge as director: I was asked to bring the Peabody back to life and to national prominence. Little did I realize that NAGPRA would be the means by which that would occur. But thinking back on it now, it could not have happened in a better way.

REFERENCES

For additional readings on Pecos Pueblo, Kidder's excavations, NAGPRA, and the Jemez consultation, please see the following:

Kidder, Alfred V. 2000 [1924]. *An Introduction to the Study of Southwestern Archaeology*, reprint edition. New Haven: Yale University Press.

Levine, Frances. 1999. *Our Prayers Are in This Place: Pecos Pueblo Identity over the Centuries*. Albuquerque: University of New Mexico Press.

Morgan, Michèle E. 2010. *Pecos Pueblo Revisited: The Biological and Social Context.* Papers of the Peabody Museum of Archaeology and Ethnology, Harvard University 85. Cambridge MA: Peabody Museum Press.

National Park Service. 2004. "National Park Service Partnership Case Studies: Repatriation and Reburial of Ancestors." Accessed December 31, 2012. http://www .nps.gov/partnerships/repatriation_pecos.htm.

Robbins, Catherine C. 2001. *All Indians Do Not Live in Teepees (or Casinos).* Lincoln: University of Nebraska Press.

Tarpy, Cliff. 2000. "Pueblo Ancestors Return Home." *National Geographic Magazine* 198, no. 5:118–25.

Thomas, David Hurst. 2000. *Skull Wars: Kennewick Man, Archaeology, and the Battle for Native American Identity.* New York: Basic Books.

Chapter 9

Pecos Pathways

A MODEL FOR LASTING PARTNERSHIPS

Lindsay Randall and Christopher Toya

Pecos Pathways is an expeditionary learning program that grew out of Native American Graves Protection and Repatriation Act (NAGPRA) consultations between the Robert S. Peabody Museum of Archaeology, Pecos National Historical Park, and the Pueblo of Jemez. A mutual interest in the education of young people and a desire to continue the relationship between the three organizations led to its creation. Each June students from Phillips Academy, Jemez Pueblo, and Pecos, New Mexico, travel, live, and learn together. The informal interactions spark deep friendships, cross-cultural sharing, and meaningful lessons about the importance of place and how the past informs both the present and the future.

Introduction

The Pecos Pathways program helps bring together students from three very different communities: Phillips Academy in Andover, Massachusetts, a private boarding school made up of "students from every quarter"; the Pueblo of Jemez in New Mexico, with descendants of the people of Pecos Pueblo; and Pecos, New Mexico, which is a primarily Hispanic American community. For three weeks each June, ten high school students from these three communities travel together to learn in an engaging and hands-on manner about ancestral and contemporary Native communities as well as about archaeology (fig. 40). This expeditionary learning program illustrates

FIG. 40. Pecos Pathways participants and Jemez tribal members at Soda Dam on the Jemez River, 2004. Photo by Donald A. Slater for the Robert S. Peabody Museum of Archaeology.

one way in which tribes, museums, and archaeologists can create and foster positive relationships with one another. By working collaboratively toward a goal such as the education of young people, tribes, museums, and archaeologists move beyond the sometimes tense relationships that can form between these disparate groups.

Pecos Pathways helps develop an appreciation of the relationship between the Robert S. Peabody Museum of Archaeology (RSPM), the Pueblo of Jemez, and Pecos National Historical Park (PNHP). The program was developed around the shared history and unique aspects of each institution. As students learn how these communities are linked, they move beyond simple histories into thought-provoking discussions about such topics as NAGPRA and cultural relationships.

Expeditionary learning, sometimes called experiential learning, is a way to engage students with meaningful learning outside a traditional classroom setting. Students learn through hands-on activities and collaborative interactions with other individuals and then critically reflect on what they are learning in order to make meaning of it. Expeditionary learning also creates an atmosphere in which students are able to develop relationships with each other and with adults, which in turn encourages positive risk taking and allows them to continue to build confidence (Wurdinger 2005).

Background of Pecos Pathways

In 1991 the RSPM, PNHP, Peabody Museum of Archaeology and Ethnology at Harvard University (PMAE), and Jemez Pueblo began consultation regarding the human remains and the objects excavated by Alfred Kidder from the ruins of Pecos Pueblo. These conversations were concluded in May 1999, when the remains of the people of Pecos were reinterred, and control over the artifacts from Pecos was returned to their descendants, the people of Jemez Pueblo. The Pecos repatriation is, to date, the largest single repatriation to take place since the implementation of NAGPRA (Reed 2004; Tarpy 2000).

While many institutions and tribes are still in consultation about artifacts, sometimes rather contentiously, the cooperation between the organizations involved with the Pecos repatriation demonstrates the potential of such collaborations. The Pecos repatriation shows that NAGPRA does not have to be a burden; instead, it can serve to open doors between disparate communities.

After tirelessly working to ensure that the NAGPRA repatriation was done properly, three of the four main organizations decided that they wanted to continue the partnership. They agreed that the best way to do so was through the youth of their respective communities. This gave rise to the Pecos Pathways program. Pecos Pathways was seen as an opportunity to educate future leaders and expose them to new people and ideas. In order to guide the development of Pecos Pathways, clear goals for the program were outlined and agreed upon by the three participating organizations. These goals are:

To connect youth from Jemez Pueblo, Phillips Academy, and Pecos, New Mexico.

To give youth a firsthand opportunity to learn about diversity.

To use traditional Native voices to emphasize that the story of Native people is one of continuity, reaching from the past to the present and future.

To use the story of Pecos Pueblo as a means to educate high school students about topics such as continuity and change within communities, the relationship of people and their environment, and how archaeology helps us understand past and present human cultures in order to make intelligent decisions for the future.

To empower Pueblo youth regarding their sense of past and future and to provide them with an opportunity to become advocates for their culture.

Facets of the Program

Although Pecos Pathways has evolved dramatically since its inception, its core focus on students has not. It was originally conceived as a weeklong program, during which students spent their time almost exclusively at PNHP. However, in an effort to augment student learning, the trip was expanded in 2001 and 2003 to two and then to three weeks to allow for the incorporation of homestays with Jemez families, excursions to Jemez ancestral sites, and a week in New England.

The first week of the program is hosted by the Jemez community. Traditionally, Jemez is closed to the public, mindful of the privacy of those who live there. It does not encourage tourist visits other than to its Visitor Center. By embracing the Pecos Pathways program the people of the Pueblo welcome students and trip leaders into their homes for the duration of their visit. Each day tribal elders and community members work with the students to teach them not only about Jemez culture and traditions but also about the history of the Pueblo (fig. 41). Group excursions to ancestral sites, discussions about history, and storytelling are integral to this part of the trip.

One important and far-reaching aspect of this expansion of the program

FIG. 41. Pecos Pathways students learning to play shinny stick, a traditional Pueblo game similar to field hockey, 2009. Photo by Marla Taylor for the Robert S. Peabody Museum of Archaeology.

is the conversations that are generated throughout the three weeks. One student remarked that it is impressive that "kids from such different backgrounds can have such great conversations" together (E.S., pers. comm., 2010). These conversations can have a profound effect on the group as information is exchanged and long-held beliefs are challenged by new friendships and experiences. These discussions and their positive effects are central to what makes Pecos Pathways such a successful educational learning program. However, it must be noted that because Jemez is a closed community, certain information still cannot be shared with those from outside the Pueblo. Instead of allowing this to create rifts or to undermine the "get-to-know-you" aspect of the program, it is used as a learning tool to teach the students and adults from Andover and Pecos that it is appropriate for certain information to be restricted. This knowledge is always met with understanding and respectfulness by those not from Jemez.

During the second week the group travels to PNHP. There they are introduced to the specifics that link the Jemez, Pecos, and Andover communities. While at Pecos students learn how some Pecos traditions have continued at Jemez. For example, the second lieutenant governor of Jemez also holds the office of governor of Pecos. Students then receive a tour of the Peabody Museum collection that is housed at the park. This collection consists largely of the non-funerary artifacts from Kidder's Pecos excavation, on long-term loan from the Robert S. Peabody Museum so that they are available to Jemez community members, researchers, and park staff. Until his death in 2014, participants had an opportunity to meet Rudy Busé, Kidder's grandson. From Rudy they heard firsthand accounts about his grandfather as well as family anecdotes from his mother, who spent her childhood at Pecos while her father excavated the Pueblo. Activities at the park range from a tour of the Pueblo to a nature walk and working with park rangers by assisting them with preservation work on the ruins of the 1717 Spanish mission (fig. 42).

The week in New England brings a noticeable change in the focus of the program. Since the program is no longer in the Southwest, students learn about Native American tribes in New England, with specific emphasis on collaborative archaeology between the tribes and archaeologists. During past programs students have spent two days working at archaeological sites with Kevin McBride on the Mashantucket Pequot Reservation in southern Connecticut (fig. 43). Students have also taken a tour of the Mashantucket Pequot Museum guided by a tribal member. Interaction with Mashantucket Pequot tribal members, both at the dig and in informal settings, has exposed students to the reality that Native American cultures exist and thrive in the eastern United States. They also more fully understand what identifies a person as Native American.

At the end of Pecos Pathways all students are asked to write an essay describing their experience and what they have learned. (To protect the identity of students, only their initials and year in which they participated in the program are given.) One of the most positive outcomes of the program has been how it creates and fosters both meaningful friendships and an authentic learning experience in a manner that "really lasts a lifetime"

FIG. 42. Students from Phillips Academy, Jemez Pueblo, and Pecos help to reinforce walls of the Spanish mission convent at Pecos National Historical Park. Photographic collection of the Robert S. Peabody Museum of Archaeology.

(J.M.D.R., pers. comm., 2010), as one former student remarked eleven years after participating in the program. When asked to reflect on their favorite aspect of the program, students often do not cite a specific event but instead refer to the incredible friendships they made. As one student wrote, "All of the trips and activities we did would have meant nothing without the amazing group of people we had on this trip" (E.S., pers. comm., 2010). Students also talk about how the trip fundamentally changed how they view other people. One student wrote, "I came to understand that if we all take a minute and listen, stereotypes will be broken, ignorance will become knowledge, and people will see each other for who they truly are, people" (A.A., pers. comm., 2002). These responses are typical of program participants and speak to the level of learning in which the students are engaged, formally and informally, throughout the trip. Pecos Pathways invites students to move beyond their preconceived impressions of each other—elitist boarding school student, typical Indian as portrayed by

FIG. 43. Pueblo of Jemez student Craig Lucero excavates on the Mashantucket Pequot Reservation in Connecticut, 2009. Photo by Marla Taylor for the Robert S. Peabody Museum of Archaeology.

Hollywood, poor Latino immigrant—to forge friendships that would not have been initiated in any other context.

Pecos Pathways as a Model

The relationships that exist among tribes and museums and archaeologists are often strained due to the conflicting attitudes toward who controls collections and objects and the manner in which these items should be treated. The implementation of NAGPRA has often highlighted some of these contentious relationships. However, the relationship that is enjoyed between the RSPM, Pueblo of Jemez, and PNHP defies such typically contentious interactions. As a whole, all participants of Pecos Pathways leave the program with valuable knowledge that will help them to grow as individuals.

Archaeology is, by its nature, fairly removed from the culture and people being studied. Students often learn about the past in a passive manner, through books and online sources. Pecos Pathways, on the other hand, provides a unique form of active learning. Through interactions with the Jemez community, students from Phillips Academy and Pecos are able to view history and archaeology from an angle that makes the human side more tangible. A realization that the "ancient" culture that archaeologists and historians study is still in existence is often new to the Phillips Academy and Pecos students, and a major goal of the program is to foster respect for the story of Native peoples. An Andover student who experienced the trip in 1999 stated, "One of the biggest revelations I had this week was thinking deeply about the human aspect of archaeology" (M.O., pers. comm., 1999). This same student revealed that his own reflection on the issue was caused by a story from a peer at Jemez about mummified human remains that were removed.

Pecos Pathways not only engenders understanding among the non-Pueblo students; it promotes the growth of the Jemez students within their own culture. The Jemez community has a deep and rich heritage, but often young people on the reservation have not learned a great deal about it. As one Jemez student said, "This experience made me think about our Indian tradition more than ever. I learned more in Pecos Pathways than in my own classroom" (Z. T., pers. comm., 2011). Other Jemez students echoed these sentiments: "Because of Pecos Pathways I learned more about the past and the history of how people lived and what they did to survive. No one would have ever taught me about the history of Jemez, Pecos, and Boston" (J. P., pers. comm., 2011), and "The first week was the best because we learned a lot about my culture" (K. W., pers. comm., 2010).

Janice Tosa (pers. comm., 2010), student program and outreach coordinator at Jemez Pueblo, states, "The most important thing Jemez students learn from the program is building a strong cultural identity." Tosa argues that this experience allows students to build a "strong self identity" and become "more comfortable with who they are as a Jemez person," thereby teaching them to be proud of their heritage. Students from Jemez who take part in Pecos Pathways also have a better understanding of contemporary issues within the Pueblo, which encourages them to grow into young adults who will be proactive in their community. The youth of Jemez are the future leaders of their community. As they learn more about their own culture and history, they gain important information and ideas that will help them to lead the Pueblo effectively as they mature. The students begin to embrace the idea that "the history of our people is our language, in it the history is carried on" (Janice Tosa, pers. comm., 2010). They begin to realize that to survive as Jemez people, they must not lose their history or their language.

Although the Pueblo of Jemez, the Robert S. Peabody Museum, and the Pecos National Historical Park each focus on different aspects when educating youth, Pecos Pathways is successful because it challenges all the groups to focus on common goals and ideology and to work with one another in a respectful manner. This cooperation creates more communication and better information flow, leading to a higher level of trust that allows the adults of the groups to share more about themselves and their communities than they otherwise might.

Conclusion

Expeditionary learning in any form is a powerful educational tool because it enables students to gain knowledge through firsthand experience.

Interacting with topics in this manner gives students the tools they need to comprehend better the secondary material, such as readings, that they are given in the classroom. This manner of dual instruction ensures that students are more readily able to recall what they learned and apply it to a variety of situations (Wurdinger 2005). After the conclusion of Pecos Pathways, one student remarked, "The difference between learning through Pecos Pathways and learning in a classroom is that you won't forget it because, along with learning, came great experiences" (K.G., pers. comm., 2012). Another student also noted, "For years I've sat in my history class bored. I never cared, never understood I guess. But during this trip I experienced history, I lived it. This program instilled within me a newfound appreciation for history. I learned more these few weeks than I expected I would, and I loved every moment of it. It was an experience like no other" (N.G., pers. comm., 2012). The sentiments of these students, echoed by other participants of the program throughout the years, demonstrate how expeditionary learning is an effective method to reach students, especially those who might struggle with traditional learning models, and have them positively engage with educational topics in a meaningful and lasting manner.

Additionally, all relationships and interactions among tribes, museums, and archaeologists are unique, and the expeditionary learning model of Pecos Pathways might not be appropriate for every situation. How Pecos Pathways came to be formed and developed, however, can offer an example of ways to guarantee positive interactions and meaningful relationships that have the potential to last through several generations. Respectful interactions and positive dialogue between tribes and diverse non-Native organizations can educate future leaders from each group, which is a powerful tool indeed.

REFERENCES

Reed, Judy. 2004. "Repatriation and Reburial of Ancestors." Accessed November 19, 2010. http://www.nps.gov/partnerships/repatriation_pecos.htm.

Tarpy, Cliff. 2000. "Pueblo Ancestors Return Home." *National Geographic Magazine* 198, no. 5:118–25.

Wurdinger, Scott D. 2005. *Using Experiential Learning in the Classroom: Practical Ideas for All Educators.* Lanham MD: Scarecrow Education.

Chapter 10

Teaching Science at the Peabody Museum

Jeremiah Hagler

The Peabody Museum is the only active archaeology museum housed on the campus of a secondary school. As such, it presents many unique educational opportunities for students at Phillips Academy. The faculty and the museum staff have used various approaches to expose students to the great range of archaeological and historical objects housed in the museum's collection. This interaction also encourages students to explore ideas about the evolution of humankind and the development of human culture.

The interdisciplinary nature of archaeology offers perspective on traditional academic subjects (see Conkey, this volume). Further, having access to the expertise of the museum staff offers unprecedented opportunities for students to engage in deeper exploration and learning in all academic fields.

Through the museum's extensive collection, students are given the opportunity to make visual and sometimes tactile contact with prehistoric and historic artifacts, giving additional depth to their experience in the classroom. Viewing an actual Acheulean handaxe that was knapped and used by *Homo erectus* adds meaning for students who are learning about human evolution. When students attempt to knap tools in flint-knapping exercises, the challenges faced by early humans using such technology take on new significance. Having the artifacts close at hand is invaluable.

Three main approaches to integrating the museum into the academic

FIG. 44. Students participate in the Cranial Morphology activity at the Peabody Museum. Photo by Ryan Wheeler for the Robert S. Peabody Museum of Archaeology.

curriculum are: the curriculum unit, new courses (like Human Origins), and collaborative research projects.

Curriculum Units

The most widely used educational tool is the curriculum unit. A catalog produced by Curator of Education Lindsay Randall for academic year 2016–17 lists forty-six of these period-long, self-contained educational presentations that have been actively used in many courses (fig. 44). All of them are developed and presented by museum educators, either in the classroom or, ideally, within the museum itself. Many of these units actively use the museum collection, and all draw on the expertise of the museum staff. The description for one popular unit—It's aMAIZEing!—is reproduced here:

> Students learn how and why corn was domesticated, and the implications (both good and bad) that corn agriculture has on human cultures in the Americas. In the activity "It's Corny," students examine corn specimens

from the Peabody's collection and rate them based on desirable qualities such as cob size and kernel size.

Nearly all ninth-graders take History 100 (introductory world history course), in which students can use museum artifacts and hands-on activities to learn more about different cultures. For example, "Blubber: It's What's for Dinner!" and "Maps and Dreams" give students insight into the prehistoric past and the settlement of America. In History 200 the units "Cultures in Contact" and "The little Spots allow'd them: Landscapes and Slavery in New England" promote understanding of economic and cultural interactions. Through integration of curriculum units into these courses, nearly all students at the academy are exposed to both the field of archaeology and the museum.

Curriculum units are also used in other departments. "Forensic Anthropology" and "Going Viral" are used in the Division of Natural Sciences; units on trigonometry, statistics, and radiocarbon dating are used in math and the sciences; and "Objects and Meaning in Portable Art" is used in the art department. The completed catalog of learning opportunities for academic year 2016–17 is available as a pdf file on the website of the Robert S. Peabody Museum of Archaeology.

Collaborative Projects

Collaborative research projects between the Peabody Museum and students increase cooperation between the museum and academic departments. Independent research projects offer individual students an opportunity to engage in deep research on topics of their own choosing under the tutelage of a faculty member.

In 2002 my collaborations with the museum began through these independent projects. In the course Molecular Biology Laboratory Research, students undertake original, independent molecular biology research projects. Two research projects focused on ancient DNA: Trudi Cloyd, Class of 2003, attempted to isolate, amplify, and sequence DNA from several pre-contact dog bones to investigate the genetic ancestry of Native American dog populations. A second set of projects, initiated by Jen Evans, Class of

2004, and further developed by Christiana Hollis, Class of 2005, used tiny amounts of bird feather shaft from an ancient feather headdress excavated from the Etowah mounds in 1926 in an attempt to isolate, amplify, and sequence bird DNA (see fig. 35 in Blustain, this volume). Their goal was to identify the species of bird represented in the headdress and thereby gain insight about the origin of these feathers. Both projects gave students a real taste of science in action. Other research projects that have engaged the museum collections and utilized the expertise of museum educators include "The Role of Woman in Prehistory" and "The Next Step: The Choctaw a Century After the Trail of Tears."

Human Origins Course

Collaboration between the Peabody Museum staff and Phillips Academy faculty in the development of new interdisciplinary courses from scratch has further perpetuated integration of the museum and academic departments. The Interdisciplinary Science course Human Origins was developed in 2007 from the ground up as a cooperative effort between the Peabody and the Department of Biology and is taught with two or more teachers present in the classroom every day (one from the Peabody and one from Biology). The real beauty of this approach is that the instructors come at the subject matter from unique backgrounds and perspectives. Students can experience the very real interaction of well-educated and knowledgeable scholars disagreeing (amicably, of course) about the material they are teaching, giving students valuable insight into how science and other forms of intellectual inquiry work (fig. 45).

A portion of our syllabus from the 2011 winter term of Human Origins demonstrates that within a span of five days the seniors taking this course considered various perspectives on the role of sexual selection in human evolution, discussed the origins of art and language, performed a laboratory experiment focusing on catchment, and had a conversation about the origins of food. This wide-ranging and in many ways freewheeling approach to teaching has made this course one of the most popular at the school.

Teaching and learning have been part of the Peabody Museum since its founding in 1901. Robert S. Peabody envisioned an institution where

FIG. 45. Students in the class Human Origins, fall 2016, use calipers and mathematical formulas to explore the concept of race. Photo by Ryan Wheeler for the Robert S. Peabody Museum of Archaeology.

students would learn about the relatively young field of archaeology, something that he thought was missing from the Phillips Academy curriculum. We know very little about the classes offered by Warren K. Moorehead and Charles Peabody in the first decades of the museum's history. After 1915 the focus was almost entirely on research. Douglas S. Byers occasionally offered a year-long anthropology and archaeology course during his tenure, and we know he taught it at least twice during the 1950s. When Richard "Scotty" MacNeish became associated with the museum in the 1960s, he reintroduced the course, which he and his curators taught throughout the 1970s and into the early 1980s. The current approach to teaching has experimented with lots of ways to deploy the museum's resources in the classroom, including term-long courses, science-based student projects, and curriculum units that fit within one or two class periods. Recent trends include more term-long courses being offered at the museum, taught in conjunction with academy faculty, and classroom projects that span a week or more during a term.

Chapter 11

Experiential Learning and the New Peabody Museum

Donald A. Slater and Nathan D. Hamilton

Although the Peabody Museum's focus has shifted toward education in recent years, this does not preclude the institution from also supporting research. In fact, the museum continues its distinguished program of archaeological inquiry—but primarily in tandem with experiential education programs. Indeed, its staff recognizes that fieldwork and the use of modern techniques to reanalyze museum collections present rich opportunities to engage students in hands-on learning. In addition to recent work with existing Peabody collections, since 2005 the museum has conducted new research through the Rebecca Nurse Homestead Archaeological Project and the Central Yucatán Archaeological Cave Project, while also developing three pedagogically driven expeditions: Maya Cosmos, the Bilingual Archaeological Learning Adventure in Mesoamerica (BALAM), and Human Understanding through Archaeology and Cultural Awareness (HUACA) in Peru. This essay explores the intersection between research and experiential education within the context of the revitalization of the Peabody Museum.

Rebecca Nurse Homestead

In 2006 the Rebecca Nurse Homestead Archaeological Project was launched in Danvers, Massachusetts. This project was the result of a partnership between the Peabody Museum, the University of Southern Maine (USM), and the Danvers Alarm List Company (DALCO), and fulfilled these organizations' common goal of initiating a local field school that would harmoniously involve students, the general public, and local scholars.

Originally inhabited by Native Americans, the site of the Homestead is now best known for one of its seventeenth-century residents, Rebecca Nurse, who was accused of sorcery during the 1692 Salem Witch Trials (Baker 2007, 95–96, 183–84; Boyer and Nissenbaum 2011). The consequent infamy led to a long record of public interpretation and preservation at the site. As a result, detailed plans, maps, photographs, and documentation of the Homestead's features were compiled under the Works Progress Administration (1936) and the Historic American Buildings Survey (HABS MA-239) (Library of Congress 1938). These data record the site's changing land-use patterns over time and afford a unique opportunity to examine the long-term use of a site in eastern Massachusetts. In addition, the Homestead's popularity provides an excellent venue for an archaeological project designed to engage the public.

The house standing on the property today is traditionally dated to 1678 (Library of Congress 1938; Perley 1928, 113–14) but also may include construction materials from earlier structures at the Homestead. Project excavations south of the house have determined that the present structure occupies roughly the same location as the original "great house" constructed on the property by Townsend Bishop circa 1636. The appearance of the house today represents an early twentieth-century restoration by preservation architect Joseph Everett Chandler (Damon 1928; Lindgren 1995, 94; Trask 2002, 30).

DALCO owns and operates the Homestead as a historic site and a living history museum. In 2006 collaboration between DALCO, the Peabody, and USM led to reconnaissance and archaeological test excavations. The next year this program was formally integrated into Phillips Academy Upper and Lower Summer Institute courses, including the nationally recognized course Dig This: Unearthing the American Past (Phillips Academy 2009). Archaeological investigations involved middle- and high-school-age participants working in an integrated fashion alongside USM students, Peabody staff, and the public at large (fig. 46). In addition to excavations, students

FIG. 46. Phillips Academy students begin excavations at the Nurse Homestead front yard. Photo by Nathan D. Hamilton.

also participated in other hands-on activities such as laboratory work, analysis, and the presentation of final interpretive reports.

In the 1980s DALCO restored the front yard and removed stone walls and flower and herb gardens constructed in the 1920s by the Society for the Preservation of New England Antiquities (now called Historic New England). Despite soil disturbances created by these landscaping efforts, important seventeenth-century deposits remain intact, as does material evidence of a Middle to Late Woodland Native American occupation. Surface finds elsewhere at the site indicate that Native Americans utilized the land as early as 5000 BP (Watson 2014).

The Rebecca Nurse Homestead Archaeological Project reflects a strong commitment to engaging the public. This has been demonstrated by its sponsorship of educational and family programs such as "Trails and Sails," an event held annually by the Essex National Heritage Commission. Since 2011 the program has variously included lectures, interpretive discussions, participatory excavation of test pits, and a visit by the Towne Family

FIG. 47. BALAM students and chaperones climb Structure 10 at the ruins of Becan, Mexico. Photo by Donald A. Slater.

Association (a group comprising modern descendants of Rebecca Nurse). A small exhibit opened in the Nurse House in 2012 featuring information about the project's excavations as well as artifacts recovered from the site.

Experiential Learning and Research in Latin America

Founded in 2005, the Bilingual Archaeological Learning Adventure in Meso-america, or BALAM—the word for jaguar in several Mayan languages—is an interdisciplinary archaeological and language immersion expeditionary learning program sponsored by the Peabody Museum, the Phillips Academy Spanish Department, and the academy's Tang Institute Learning in the World program. Led by history and social science instructor Donald Slater, formerly a Peabody Museum educator, and Spanish instructor Mark Cutler, BALAM gives approximately ten Phillips Academy students the opportunity to travel throughout the Maya region to study the ancient and modern culture of the Yucatán Peninsula (fig. 47).

BALAM is a dual-purpose program. It introduces students to archaeological research and field skills, including reconnaissance, mapping, excavation, introductory Global Positioning System (GPS) and Geographic Information-tion System (GIS) training, and iconographic analysis. At the same time participants are immersed in the linguistic and cultural milieu of Meso-america. BALAM students have assisted Jaime Awe, director of the Belize Valley Archaeological Reconnaissance Project, and now former director of the Belize Institute of Archaeology, by participating in excavations at the Maya sites of Cahal Pech and Baking Pot. In addition BALAM has included visits to ceremonial caves, archaeological sites such as Tikal, Calakmul, and Palenque, and modern Maya villages such as Yaxunah, Zinacantan, and San Juan Chamula. Students are encouraged to engage local people in conversation, both to practice Spanish and to learn basic phrases in Mayan languages, all while exchanging cultural information and experiences.

Despite the success of this program, drug-related violence in Mexico and the resultant U.S. Department of State travel warning led to Phillips Academy's cancelation of BALAM 2011 and 2012. After a successful recon-naissance mission in June 2012, as an alternative, the trip's pedagogical goals have been relocated to Peru—one of the few regions in the Americas that can provide students with a comparably rich immersion experience in archaeological research, the Spanish language, and vibrant Native American culture. This iteration of the trip was named the Andean HUACA Project, with the Quechua term *huaca*, meaning "sacred place," also serving as an acronym for "Human Understanding through Archaeology and Cultural Awareness."

In 2013, 2015, and 2017 HUACA students variously hiked the Inca Trail to Machu Picchu, visited other important sites such as Chavín de Huán-tar, Chan Chan, and Túcume, and explored the impact of colonialism in Cusco (fig. 48). Most significantly, perhaps, HUACA has forged a rela-tionship with the indigenous Q'eros Nation in Peru through the Willka Yachay NGO. In 2015 eleven students and three instructors from Phillips Academy joined Willka Yachay director Hannah Rae Porst and fourteen students and educators from Q'eros for a three-day cultural exchange in a remote mountain village north of Cusco. To continue the partnership, in 2017 HUACA participants made the eight-hour drive, horseback ride,

FIG. 48. ʜᴜᴀᴄᴀ students descend from the crest of Warmi Wañusqa (Dead Woman's Pass). At nearly 14,000 feet in elevation, it is the highest point along the twenty-six-mile Inca Trail to Machu Picchu. Photo by Donald A. Slater.

and hike from Cusco to the Q'eros village of Qochamoqo for a five-day visit. Through shared meals, soccer games, dancing, and lengthy *despacho* ceremonies, these exchanges fostered a deep sense of cultural understanding and appreciation between the groups, which illustrated the commonalities as well as the many differences in participants' life experiences.

Phillips Academy has recently lifted its restriction on travel to southern Mexico. As such, Slater led a student group to Yucatán during the 2017 spring break. This new trip, Maya Cosmos, will serve as a light version of ʙᴀʟᴀᴍ and is attached to a new elective on ancient and modern Maya spirituality and cosmology offered by Slater at the Peabody Museum. After the completion of the course, students traveled immediately to Yucatán, where they had the opportunity to witness modern Maya religious rituals and explore sacred caves and ruins studied during the class.

Ultimately the goal of these expeditionary programs is not to produce a crop of new archaeologists each year but to allow students to experience cultural diversity, to learn the basics of scientific field inquiry, and to be exposed to situations not possible in the classroom. In fact, these programs have served as many students' first trip outside the United States. Perhaps the most significant result of the program is raising awareness among young participants of the importance of global cultural and historic resources, with the hope of this leading to a lifelong sense of stewardship regardless of each student's future plans. Alumni of these programs consistently cite their experience as life changing and as a catalyzing event that alters their worldview and occasionally even their career path.

As of 2017 the future is bright for these programs. With increased support through the Peabody Museum and Tang Institute at Phillips Academy, there are plans for BALAM, HUACA, and Maya Cosmos to run for years to come.

The Central Yucatán Archaeological Cave Project

As part of BALAM and Maya Cosmos, students travel to sites investigated by the Central Yucatán Archaeological Cave Project (CYAC), which is directed by Slater. Although foreign high school students are not permitted to assist with archaeological fieldwork in Mexico, they may engage in behind-the-scenes tours of CYAC sites such as Aktun Kuruxtun and Aktun Jip, to learn more about the project and to acquire an experiential education on the role caves played in ancient Maya religion and cosmology.

The broad research goal of CYAC, as conducted under the auspices of the Proyecto de Interacción Política del Centro de Yucatán (PIPCY), is to study ancient cave ritual and its relationship to landscape, power, and control among the ancient Maya (Slater 2014a, b). Specifically, CYAC has built a GIS of caves in the Yaxcaba region, studying the power wielded by the local ruling class to control access to caves located both within the core of sites and in their hinterland, while also investigating the different ways space within caves was used (Slater 2014a, b). Investigations have revealed that the area's caves contain artifacts that date from approximately 900 BCE through the time of Spanish arrival. Features within the caves— petroglyphs (fig. 49) and architectural modifications such as pathways, floors, walls, and stairways, and even a solar observatory—suggest intensive ceremonial use of these sacred spaces (Slater 2014a, b).

In addition to field visits for students, CYAC's research has been brought

FIG. 49. The Petroglyph Chamber at Aktun Kuruxtun, Mexico. Photo by Donald A. Slater.

into the lecture halls and classrooms of Phillips Academy during English, Spanish, and history and social science courses. Discussion of caves' roles in Maya origin stories, ancient ideologies, and modern religion have presented students with practical examples from the field, which complement studies on a variety of topics, ranging from anthropology to literary analysis and creative writing. CYAC's research has also been featured as part of the Massachusetts Archaeological Society Northeast Chapter monthly lecture series held at the Peabody Museum. Furthermore, Slater has worked with recent alumni to guide further archaeological studies at the college level.

Conclusion

Although we have presented only highlights of the recent Peabody Museum experiential learning and research program, we feel its vibrancy and diversity of scope are clear. The programs described continue the museum's deep-rooted tradition of research and scholarship, while pushing its current educational goals to the next level. They are but one way of encouraging academic use of the Peabody's resources and the development of new projects that actively connect the museum and the Phillips Academy community with external groups. By embracing this balance between research and pedagogy, the museum serves Phillips Academy students and faculty, the scholarly and Native communities, and the general public in a manner that is sustainable and honors the achievements of past Peabody scholars and the wisdom and legacy of its founder.

Acknowledgments

Donald Slater would like to dedicate this paper to Mark Cutler and the students of BALAM, HUACA, and Maya Cosmos 2006–17. Many thanks to the Abbot Academy Association, the Tang Institute, and the Phillips Academy Financial Aid office for their major role in funding our expeditionary programs and making them available to all students regardless of financial need. CYAC was funded by NSF grant No. BCS-1111508, National Geographic grant No. W81–09, Brandeis University, the Cave Research Foundation, the Explorers Club, and the Cleveland Grotto of the National Speleological Society and was made possible through PIPCY Directors Travis Stanton and Aline Magnoni as well as Javier Urcid, Charles Golden, and the hard work of individuals too numerous to mention here. You know who you are—thanks!

Nathan Hamilton would like to thank Deborah Cutten, Gina O'Leary, Tanya Justin, Dinah Crader, Arthur Spiess, and Steve Polloch for analysis related to the Nevin and Richards sites. He would also like to thank Kevin Clark, Arthur Cluesmitzer, Lindsey Weeks, and Heather Froskour for supervising work at the Nurse Homestead and for conducting analysis on excavated materials.

Both authors thank Malinda Blustain and Ryan Wheeler for their support, partnership, and friendship as well as for helpful comments on this essay. We thank the Danvers Alarm List Company and Nurse Homestead staff for their collegiality and friendship through our collaborations. Finally, we would like to thank all of the past researchers who have worked with the Robert S. Peabody Museum. Your legacy lives on.

REFERENCES

Baker, Emerson W. 2007. *The Devil of Great Island: Witchcraft and Conflict in Early New England*. New York: Palgrave Macmillan.

Boyer, Paul, and Stephen Nissenbaum. 2011. "The Salem Witchcraft Papers, Volume 2: Verbatim Transcripts of the Legal Documents of the Salem Witchcraft Outbreak of 1692," edited by Paul Boyer and Stephen Nissenbaum, University of Virginia. Accessed November 28, 2011. http://etext.virginia.edu/etcbin/toccer-new2?id=BoySal2.sgm&images=images/modeng&data=/texts/english/modeng/oldsalem&tag=public&part=38&division=div1.

Damon, Frank C. 1928. "Antiques in Nurse House All Genuine; Some Very Valuable." *Salem Evening News* (Salem MA), November 15.

Library of Congress. 1938. "Rebecca Nurse Place, Historic American Buildings Survey, Engineering Record, Landscapes Survey." Accessed November 28, 2011. http://www.loc.gov/pictures/item/ma0609/.

Lindgren, James Michael. 1995. *Preserving Historic New England: Preservation, Progressivism, and the Remaking of Memory*. Oxford: Oxford University Press.

Perley, Sidney. 1928. *A History of Salem, Massachusetts*, vol. 3. Salem MA.

Phillips Academy. 2009. "Hands-On Archaeology Course at Phillips Academy Receives National Attention." Accessed September 14, 2011. http://www.andover.edu/About/Newsroom/Pages/Hands-OnArchaeologyCourseatPhillipsAcademy-ReceivesNationalAttention.aspx.

Slater, Donald A. 2014a. "Into the Heart of the Turtle: Caves, Ritual, and Power in Ancient Central Yucatán, Mexico." PhD diss., Brandeis University.

———. 2014b. "Linking Cave, Mountain, and Sky: A Subterranean Observation Point for the Sunrise on the Day of Solar Zenith Transit in Yucatán, Mexico." *Latin American Antiquity* 25, no. 2:198–214.

Trask, Richard B. 2002. *Danvers*. Charleston MA: Arcadia Publishing.

Watson, Jessica E. 2014. "Lithic Debitage and Settlement Patterns at the Rebecca Nurse Homestead." *Northeast Anthropology*, nos. 81 and 82:23–47.

Works Progress Administration. 1936. "Rebecca Nurse Place, Danvers, Essex Co., Mass., Survey No. 239, Official Project No. 465-214-3-414." Accessed July 3, 2012. http://www.loc.gov/pictures/collection/hh/item/ma0609.sheet.00001a/resource/.

Chapter 12

Reflections and Stories

Using Archaeology as a Basis for Learning
HOW ARCHAEOLOGY CAN TEACH ALMOST ANYTHING!

Margaret Conkey

The Society for American Archaeology (SAA) Principles of Archaeological Ethics note that outreach and education are key principles of archaeological practice. Archaeologists should reach out to, and participate in cooperative efforts with, others interested in the archaeological record, with the aim of improving the preservation, protection, and interpretation of the record. In particular, archaeologists should undertake to: (1) enlist public support for the stewardship of the archaeological record; (2) explain and promote the use of archaeological methods and techniques in understanding human behavior and culture; and (3) communicate archaeological interpretations of the past. Many publics exist for archaeology, including students and teachers; Native Americans and other ethnic, religious, and cultural groups who find in the archaeological record important aspects of their cultural heritage; lawmakers and government officials; reporters, journalists, and others involved in the media; and the general public. Archaeologists who are unable to undertake public education and outreach directly should encourage and support the efforts of others in these activities. (Society for American Archaeology Executive Board 1996).

Outreach usually refers to the activities that archaeologists do to bring archaeology into wider circles, ranging from the elementary school to the local women's club and the communities where we work. It can also have a broader connotation. The program that has developed at Phillips Academy in conjunction with the Robert S. Peabody Museum brings archaeology into a wider public and/or educational sphere and integrates it into the actual pedagogy and curriculum. This has gone even further than archaeology in history, biology, sociology, or art classes, all of which are testimonies to the idea of this chapter—that archaeology can be used to teach about almost anything. The even more ambitious step that the Peabody-plus-Phillips Academy has taken includes the many years that they have run the exchange program with Pueblo peoples and, more recently, the Piette Program: a summer trip of several weeks to France, where Phillips Academy students are plunged into language and cuisine but also museums, excavation sites, and history from the Neanderthals to contemporary politics. The story of how this program got started is itself a story of how one so-called discipline (such as archaeology) is embedded in and informs other disciplines, in this case the study of the French language. In this twenty-first century of heightened interest and concern with cultural patrimony, heritage, and the provocative question of who "owns" the past, when the museum received an inquiry regarding artifacts held at the Peabody Museum, it became a French language lesson, a cultural heritage lesson, and eventually a summer program touching on multiple worlds of learning. The inquiry came from the French national antiquities museum, the Musée d'Archéologie Natio-nale (MAN). The artifacts in question are the famous "painted pebbles" from the French site Le Mas d'Azil, attributed to the Mesolithic period of around 11,000 years ago. The response to the MAN entailed the French class writing back—in their best French!—to the museum and beginning the arrangements for the return of the pebbles. The painted pebbles had been the product of excavations at Le Mas d'Azil by the energetic French researcher Édouard Piette, for whom an entire room at the MAN is named. It holds most of his amazingly rich collection of portable art objects from the Upper Paleolithic of the Pyrenean region in France, and for this reason the travel study program, still ongoing for Phillips Academy students, is named for him—the Piette Program.

The Peabody Museum's approach to archaeology in the classroom is similar to a service-learning course that we taught at the University of California at Berkeley (see Nassaney and Levine 2009 on service-learning and archaeology). Like the programs at the Peabody Museum, the Berkeley course stressed multidisciplinary learning. Undergraduates spent three hours a week in local after-school programs in under-served middle schools, using archaeology and digital storytelling/computer skills as their subject matter. In teaching this course we had to discuss what it is about archaeology that makes it such a compelling arena for learning and for the development of basic skills in so many different fields. We developed the following list:

Archaeology focuses on material-based, tangible objects.
Archaeology is a highly visual discipline.
Archaeology encourages creativity and the imagination.
Archaeology promotes observational skills.

Archaeological objects viewed in their context = people. The objects (data) don't speak for themselves; they are ambiguous and open to multiple interpretations. In this way archaeology encourages critical thinking. It helps make people aware of constructivist history and of the fact that history is written by and in multiple voices—multivocality. Archaeology helps people become aware of the existence of different interpretations for the same object and/or event. It encourages them to share interpretations. The Internet and digital publications play an increasingly effective and important role in helping people make interpretations.

The Berkeley experience shows how archaeology can be more than a source for outreach. Through the service-learning course at Berkeley students learn the responsibilities of being "stakeholders" of cultural heritage. And along the way the Berkeley service-learning course develops what in California are termed the Middle School Education Standards for literacy, critical thinking, and constructivist history. The different fields of inquiry that are part of the archaeological process are wide-ranging: from mathematics, geology, biology, and chemistry to materials science, arts analysis, architecture, and many more. One can get a veritable multidisciplinary education just from "doing archaeology." In fact, one Berkeley professor volunteered as the Science Club sponsor for a local middle school, and each club meeting engaged with a different science (botany, geology, zoology, chemistry, math . . .) but using an archaeological example and approach.

Given the expanding wealth of forensic methods and analytical tests now being used by archaeologists—from DNA analyses to soil geochemistry, various dating methods, residue analyses, and such, many specialty fields can be taught through archaeological examples!

The often conflicting interpretations of archaeology help people realize that with or without written sources, ethnicity and cultural (in modern familiar terms) attributions are ambiguous. This leads students to many avenues toward multiculturalism: exploration of alternative ways of life, tolerance for difference, exercise in "stepping in" and "stepping out," and awareness raising of cultural values that are assumed to be "natural" or "true." As more and more educational institutions confront the need to serve increasingly diverse populations and to develop ways to "teach" about diversity in lifeways, opinions, practices, expectations, and "ways of being in the world," there is no doubt that these can all be understood through examples from archaeology, especially as it is rooted in an anthropological context. It has been said that "anthropology makes the world safe for human differences." More specifically, archaeology can inform on such things as how social and economic inequalities arise in varied historical and social contexts. It can infer the organization and divisions of labor as well as how varied governmental structures emerged, developed, and declined. It can show how environmental events had differential impacts on past human communities and how different cultures have coped with environmental events, change, and disasters. It can outline the different trajectories of cultural contacts and migrations, and it can zoom in to the daily lives and microhistories of small-scale groups and individuals, to lay bare, so to speak, the core of daily practices in many different contexts, including relations among different groups that may be those based on varied identities, such as age, ethnicity, sex/gender, or religious or other dimensions of social personae.

While the ethical principles of contemporary archaeology point to a centrality of "outreach," this is far too simple of a term and far too limited a way to characterize the ways in which archaeology can work in the contemporary world, even if its topic is about past human lives from thousands of years ago. Rather, archaeology is not only "about" but is itself a public engagement and can or should be found at all levels, for all ages, and for all communities. There is no doubt that the practice of archaeology has expanded its reach in fruitful and important ways (see Sabloff 2008 on "Action Archaeology in the Modern World"), and we no longer think "we" hold specialized knowledge to share with others in a somewhat one-way "outreach." Rather, when archaeology is incorporated into the biology class or located inside and within communities, it begins to reach a new potential while allowing us all to learn something new, exciting, and even revelatory—about the past but also about ourselves, the present and how we might best approach the future. What goes on with the Peabody Museum and the classrooms and programs of Phillips Academy is an excellent example of how far archaeology has come with its deep engagement with the educational process and the potentials of its field for infusing pedagogy, curriculum, and learning for the global demands of the twenty-first century.

Perspectives from Indian Country

Hillary Abé

The Peabody Museum and Phillips Academy offer contemporary Native students an opportunity to fashion new avenues of cross-cultural dialogue between museums, Indigenous peoples, and the community-at-large. At the same time their programs help to educate the broader school community on current Native issues.

When a student from a Native American community acquires an education, that student is taking a direct part in the process of nation building. Many Native students leave home to seek an education that will ultimately be used to serve their community, the Native nation. Indian Country comprises an immensely diverse range of communities, each with different languages, cultures, and traditions. The vast majority of these communities are, in fact, sovereign nations. It is in the direct interest of these nations to have an educated citizenry to maintain all the functions of society. Thus one of the most important things we can do as nations is to offer youth many opportunities to enrich their intellectual and spiritual growth. Educated Native students are likely to become leaders of tribal governments, health professionals serving in our clinics, business leaders, engineers, biologists, historians, and teachers. Native students and communities are hungry for collaboration and exchange that includes a healthy dialogue between cultures.

During the two years I worked for Phillips Academy the academy and the Peabody Museum participated directly in this process of nation building. Though only three Native students attended the academy then—one from the Prairie Band of Potawatomi Nation and two students from the Navajo Nation— I do not doubt that they will one day be intellectual and professional leaders in their communities. The support and resource opportunities these students encountered during their one-year stay at Andover will continue to inform them throughout their lives. The Peabody Museum played a significant role in the growth and support for these students; the museum facilities were a wide-open space where they were made to feel welcome. The three students—LeManley, Forrest, and Tristin—spent much time in the museum, even performing their obligatory work duty for the school within the museum's collections. They left the academy to participate in competitive college programs and become better prepared to serve their communities. Their view of archaeological institutions has been altered, and they made a lasting impact on what the Peabody Museum sees as part of its mission; both parties are better for the experience.

Modern archaeological institutions would seem an unlikely place to find this sort of willing exchange—at least in the minds of many Native people. I first visited an archaeology museum with my father when I was eight years old. This museum had a large collection of items from my community. As we peered into the cases labeled "Hidatsa," the name of my tribe, my father pointed out items he thought had originally belonged to his great-grandmother or other relatives he had known. Were they bought? Were they taken? Which relative of mine crafted and wore those moccasins or grew in that cradleboard? Many Native people have these questions but are too uncomfortable to ask them aloud. Until very recently, the field of archaeology lacked Native voices. During my time at Phillips Academy, I was the only self-identifying Native American faculty member. The students we recruited are certainly among only a handful of students from Native backgrounds who have ever graduated from Andover. One of the reasons they were able to succeed was because of the support and mentorship they received from the museum staff (fig. 50). Along with the ideas and programming the museum already had in place, it was clear that they were interested in cultivating cross-cultural dialogues with Indigenous communities.

This willingness to communicate across barriers meant that we could leverage the museum's long experience and deep history in Indian Country to help support Native students on campus and to educate the Phillips Academy community at large about contemporary Native peoples. Since students and faculty had rarely had an opportunity to interact with Native people, it added a layer of stress for our students to be asked embarrassing questions about their Native-ness. It was a comfort to know that the museum had already been undertaking the task of engaging the academic community in a variety of ways about contemporary Native peoples.

When I first learned about the programs the Peabody Museum had already initiated, I was impressed. First, the museum's successful effort to consult with tribes in order to fully comply with NAGPRA was a sign that they were already ahead of the curve in communicating and interfacing with Native tribes. Next, the cultural exchange program called Pecos Pathways, through which Phillips Academy students visit and learn from the people of Jemez Pueblo (see Randall and Toya, this volume), piqued my interest. When I learned that Jemez students also had the opportunity to come to New England to experience a stint out East, I was thoroughly excited. The Pecos Pathways program and the demonstrated commitment to pursuing consultations with the tribes serve as strong examples to me of how the Peabody Museum has made a point to facilitate learning among and between individuals from Indigenous and non-Native backgrounds. The greatest asset this museum has demonstrated is the mix of valuable information it offers students. The museum offers students classes and

FIG. 50. Tristin Moon, Phillips Academy Class of 2010, Jane Thomas, Phillips Academy Class of 2010, and another Andover student at the Phillips Academy Log Cabin with Native American storyteller Manitonquat of the Assonet Band of the Wampanoag. Photo by Donald A. Slater.

information dealing with archaeology and anthropology, and it seeks to bridge the gap between deeply rooted historical knowledge and understanding it in the context of contemporary Native peoples. Valuing the presence, experience, and knowledge that contemporary Native people can bring to the table is important.

It was a new experience for archaeologists to interface regularly with contemporary Native peoples, an outgrowth of compliance with NAGPRA. Cross-cultural communication is often challenging. The cultural innuendos and subtleties of navigating Native communities can be confusing to outsiders. Similarly, students who come from close-knit reservation communities often feel alienated when attempting to mesh with mainstream values in higher education settings. Though this is an uncomfortable process for many, the learning potential is great. When Malinda Blustain, while director of the Peabody Museum, attended the National Indian Education Association annual convention to learn about Native education, she stepped out of her comfort zone. The willingness on the part of the Peabody Museum staff to learn and create dialogue that doesn't fit within the established scope of archaeology is a welcome sign of the larger growth taking place in the field. As Indigenous archaeology becomes more commonplace and more Native people have an interest in the application of anthropology and archaeology to expand the knowledge of their communities, this type of growth and experimentation can only yield more ideas and possibilities for future collaboration. What better way to engage Native communities than by offering youth opportunities for learning and support? When the history of Native people has been such a key component in the development of the field of archaeology, who better to help cultivate that future than the Native people who are already invested in the histories pertaining to them? This type of innovation and readiness to explore possible collaborations with Native communities enriches the dialogue and promises new partnerships and knowledge.

I am hopeful that the cross-cultural work of this museum can help set the tone for future collaborations between educational institutions, Native students, and archaeological institutions. This process is long overdue. The Peabody Museum stands as an example of an institution willing to test the waters of cross-cultural dialogue. The museum staff has become one of the strongest advocates for recruiting Native students to take full advantage of the educational opportunities offered at Phillips Academy. What makes this museum particularly ripe for the task of intercultural communication is the willingness to learn alongside, and with, Native communities and their members.

The Piette Program in France

Claire Gallou

This essay charts the origins of a successful collaboration between Phillips Academy faculty and the Peabody Museum, one that connected the museum's history with modern-day pedagogy around language, history, art, and archaeology. In 2009 the museum was contacted by a representative of the Musée d'Archéologie Nationale (MAN) of Saint-Germain-en-Laye near Paris. M. Guillaume Goujon was searching collections in New England institutions in order to locate materials from the MAN that were on outstanding loan. The visit was followed by a long letter that included charts, copies of century-old formal letters, and excerpts from current French laws. Collections Manager Marla Taylor arranged for a meeting with museum director Malinda Stafford Blustain and me. The objective was to translate the letter and associated documents as well as correspondence from the museum's archive.

Blustain and I agreed that advanced students would take charge of the entire project. Language teachers endeavor to address language and culture together. Indeed, language was at the heart of the MAN's letter: it requested the repatriation of painted pebbles from the Mesolithic era that have long figured in research and debate over early symbol systems and in why the much-celebrated cave art of the preceding period was no longer being produced. These painted pebbles seemed to herald a new and different visual culture (fig. 51). It was a perfect opportunity: a linguistic project providing students with real-life experience in French while also

FIG. 51. Painted pebbles collected by Édouard Piette from Mas d'Azil Cave prior to their return to France. Photographic collection of the Robert S. Peabody Museum of Archaeology.

helping the museum sort out a complex situation. The translation project became an integral part of the syllabus of two courses, French 520 and French 600. Students in French 600 compared their alternate translations of the MAN letter and then collaborated to produce a final version—the project involved the theory of translation, the controversial role of the translator, and translation techniques.

The translation of the MAN letter and archival correspondence supported the museum's decision that the artifacts should be returned to France. They had been sent to the museum as a "deposit" in the 1920s, which meant a long-term loan. In addition, sending them to America was apparently a mistake in the first place. The original owner of the collection of painted pebbles, French jurist and antiquarian Édouard Piette, had formally requested that the pebbles never leave the Musée d'Archéologie Nationale. In spring 2010 a new group of French 520 students benefited from a unit on translation. They translated a few more letters from the 1920s so that

FIG. 52. Phillips Academy students on the third Piette Program in France posing with a cutout of Édouard Piette at Mas d'Azil Cave, June 2016. Photo by Ryan Wheeler for the Robert S. Peabody Museum of Archaeology.

the archives would be complete, and they learned how to craft a formal, technical letter to the MAN in response to its repatriation request. Again the students decided on the best ways to convey the Peabody's position. They learned about compromise, misunderstandings, and idioms.

Blustain and I made a trip to France in July 2011. There we repatriated the painted pebbles and other artifacts, and also mapped out a student trip that would include archaeological sites, museums, and participation in an archaeological excavation near the Mas d'Azil site where Piette had found the pebbles. We envisioned a historical component to the trip as well that would include the World War II memorial site in Caen and Renaissance castles of the Loire Valley. The trip became a new plan for an interdisciplinary summer program.

Since the repatriation of the painted pebbles in 2011 we have taken students to France three times (fig. 52). Each trip begins with a visit to the MAN outside Paris. There we have toured the exhibitions, viewed the reserve collections, chatted with conservators, and visited the Piette Room, where glass and wood cases display Piette's collections exactly as he wished. In each corner of the room are cabinets with painted pebbles from Mas d'Azil; more are stored in the reserves. Beyond the other sights of Paris—Notre-Dame, the Louvre, and Versailles—we follow an itinerary much like the scouting trip with time in Normandy and the Loire Valley as well as visits to the decorated caves of the Dordogne and the Pyrenees. In the Pyrenees students have participated in excavations at the open-air Magdalenian site of Peyre Blanque. The trip is now a fixture of Phillips Academy's Learning in the World Program and an important addition to the museum's expeditionary learning trips to New Mexico, Peru, and Mexico (see Slater and Hamilton, and Randall and Toya, this volume).

Just Down the Road

A FORMER STUDENT'S PERSPECTIVE ON THE PEABODY MUSEUM
AND ITS APPROACH TO SECONDARY EDUCATION

Kristi Gilleon

As a college archaeology major, I can say that the Peabody Museum is unique in the breadth and quality of its educational activities and can serve as a model for other archaeology museums seeking to establish a close educational relationship with students.

Work Duty Experience

Every Andover student is obligated to spend one hour each week doing work duty on campus. Since I loved history and archaeology, I chose the Peabody Museum for my work duty. I began by helping to catalog the enormous collection of books and archives of Scotty MacNeish. By doing so I provided a valuable service to the ever-busy museum as well as learning how a museum operates and how archaeologists catalog and track artifacts and archival material.

Other work duty students and I learned about the history and lives of

FIG. 53. Kristi Gilleon exploring the ruins at Bandelier National Monument. Photo by Donald A. Slater.

various peoples. Rather than reading about how prehistoric groups in the Americas made and used lithic tools, we were handed a heavy chert core and an antler billet and were shown how to flintknap. Similarly, hurling darts across the lawn with an atlatl was remarkably effective in teaching us what it must have been like to hunt ancient bison in the prehistoric Americas.

Work duty students could attend monthly lectures held by the Northeast Chapter of the Massachusetts Archaeological Society. Museum staff also led off-campus field trips that ranged from local excursions to three-week-long learning programs in foreign countries.

Expeditionary Learning

The museum's devotion to education outside the classroom is perhaps best exemplified by two expeditionary learning programs, Pecos Pathways and

BALAM (see Randall and Toya, and Slater and Hamilton, this volume). In summer 2005 I traveled with four other Andover classmates to the Pueblo of Jemez in New Mexico to join students from the Pueblo and Pecos, New Mexico, for the annual Pecos Pathways program (fig. 53). We each stayed with a Jemez family who lived on the reservation. I was treated to a rare tour of the Pueblo and also made bread in my host mother's handmade *horno* or oven. Next we went to Pecos National Historical Park and participated in an excavation that turned up scores of ancient pottery sherds and animal remains, which provided us with clues about the daily lives of individuals living at the mission during the colonial period. Our time on Pecos Pathways also included trips to important archaeological sites. We developed a deep understanding of the history of Native people in the American Southwest.

Pecos Pathways also brings Jemez and Pecos students to New England to explore its history. Participating in Pecos Pathways ensures that I will never think of history or archaeology the same way again.

In 2006 I took part in the Bilingual Archaeological Learning Adventure in Mesoamerica (BALAM), led by Donald Slater of the museum and Mark Cutler of the Spanish department. After visiting Maya sites such as Coba and Tulum along the coast, we moved to the interior of the Yucatán and were based in the Calakmul Biosphere Reserve, traveling to many important Maya sites.

At each site Mr. Slater discussed Maya architectural styles, how archaeologists can determine when a site was occupied, and the role religion and cosmology played in a site's layout and spatial design. We traveled to San Ignacio, Belize, to help an archaeological team excavate at the site of Cahal Pech. We learned about the phases of archaeological research by actually doing the work: we learned basic mapping techniques, set up standard excavation units, then participated in digging, sifting, and screening and in recording our finds. It gave me a deep appreciation for the remarkable difference archaeology makes in bringing the ruins of history into the present.

By participating in Pecos Pathways and BALAM, I found that my original interest in archaeology and history became a serious intention to become an archaeologist one day.

College and Beyond

In college I took as many anthropology classes as I could. Through my experiences at the Peabody I developed a strong sense of connection to the material I study. While my classmates jot down notes, I remember uncovering a canine tooth in the red soil of the Pecos mission. And during classroom explanations of Central American archaeology, I think back to the ceremonial cave I visited while on BALAM and the centuries-old pottery placed there as an offering, still largely intact.

My participation in Pecos Pathways and BALAM also instilled in me an understanding of the importance of hands-on learning and real world experience. I am eager to continue my education as a developing archaeologist by following the Peabody's model: travel, do, learn.

What makes the Peabody Museum exceptional is that it finds new ways to use its collections, personnel, and professional connections to educate and make lasting impressions on its students. The Peabody Museum's commitment to making interaction with archaeology available to students has made all the difference for me.

From Research to Education

THE PEABODY-PHILLIPS ACADEMY CONNECTION

Rebecca Miller Sykes

Phillips Academy and the Peabody Museum have coexisted on the Andover, Massachusetts, campus for more than a century and have recently experienced the most productive and promising relationship of their shared history.

Robert Singleton Peabody envisioned that his 1901 gift would build a facility and establish a department of archaeology (Moorehead 1906,

27). The academic department was never realized, and while the Peabody Museum was very important to the field of American archaeology over its first eighty years, it had a relatively modest impact on the experience of students at Phillips Academy. Fritz Allis, an iconic Phillips instructor and author of a history of the school, wrote in 1979:

> Despite attempts to make the Archaeology Department and its museum attractive to the [Andover students], the institution has always been something of an anomaly. From the first it was clear that Dr. Moorehead and his staff would devote most of their time to archaeological research, and this they did with distinction. The difficulty was that most of their sites were far from Andover.... Elective courses in archaeology were offered from the start till 1917, but the number of boys actively engaged in the subject remained small. Some four or five each year usually became vitally interested and often accompanied the staff on summer expeditions.... Probably in deference of Robert Singleton Peabody's original wishes, the Trustees have preferred to engage highly trained professionals and encourage them to proceed with their research rather than people whose main interest would have been in teaching archaeology. (Allis 1979, 355)

The Peabody Museum seemed to have little to offer the academy. By the advent of the Native American Graves Protection and Repatriation Act (NAGPRA) in 1990, the museum had been dormant for seven years, operating by appointment only and available almost exclusively to scholars. NAGPRA made it necessary for Phillips Academy to hire staff to design and implement a repatriation plan. Ironically, while the legislation created a compliance burden, it also breathed life into the museum (see Bradley, this volume).

Peabody Director James Bradley used NAGPRA initiatives as an opportunity to educate Phillips Academy students and faculty about the cultural and ethnographic treasures in the museum and the people with whom the objects were affiliated. Bradley hired Leah Rosenmeier, and together they created a repatriation effort that became nationally recognized and garnered several sizable federal grants. One of the enduring innovations coming out of the tribal consultations was Pecos Pathways, a travel learning and exchange program (see Randall and Toya, this volume). Marcelle Doheny, instructor in history and social science, was enthralled by the educational possibilities the Peabody represented. She collaborated with Rosenmeier to develop curriculum units for the required ninth grade history course. Matching archaeological objects to the lessons amplified the students' study of written history and made it tangible. Doheny also recognized and capitalized on the fact that the Peabody not only had a collection illustrating American history but was in itself a history lesson. Three examples stand out:

1. In 1908 Theodore Roosevelt appointed Moorehead—the Peabody's curator and second director—to the Board of Indian Commissioners, a group that investigated illegal seizure of reservation land by lumber and land companies (Fritz 1985).
2. In 1935 the inaugural meeting of the Society for American Archaeology took place at Phillips Academy, and the Massachusetts Archaeological Society had its start there in 1939 (Griffin 1985; Robbins 1949).
3. During his tenure as Peabody director, Richard S. MacNeish investigated the origins of domesticated corn and was widely heralded for his contribution to the field (Ferrie 2001).

Despite the compelling history and interest from many Phillips teachers, by 2000 the museum's fiscal health was in deep decline. The Peabody had been unable to attract adequate funds to sustain a program beyond its repatriation activities, and the future of the museum was imperiled. In fall 2001 Head of School Barbara Chase appointed a committee to assess the Peabody's future viability. The committee included a charter trustee; the school's chief financial officer; Malinda Blustain, then interim museum director; Marcelle Doheny; myself, as chair; and the person who was to become the Peabody's greatest guardian angel, Marshall P. Cloyd, Class of 1958. It was during this period of review that the academy heard from many members of the SAA. The Peabody Planning and Assessment Committee report in spring 2002 asserted the value of the collection and noted the imperative to continue NAGPRA consultations. Our committee asked that the school supplement the museum's endowment for an additional two years, during which a practical, long-term financial and operational plan could be finalized.

As acting head of school in 2002, I charged a second group—the Peabody Planning Committee—consisting of trustees, alumni, faculty, and administrators—to answer several questions, including: Does the Academy wish to integrate the Peabody Museum further into its curriculum and activities? And, if so, how and to what extent?

The committee's answer was a resounding "yes." Additionally, the committee opined:

> The motivation for greater Academy use of the Peabody's resources must come from classroom teachers, academic departments and the residential program rather than from the museum itself. We also recognize that the brisk pace of faculty life and decades of limited interaction between the Peabody and the Academy pose obstacles. Still, there are instructors in science, history, art, English and the residential course "Life Issues" who are increasingly interested in strengthening connections with the Peabody. Collaboration with these faculty has already resulted in the reworking of previous collections-based curriculum units and the development of new ones. (Peabody Planning Committee 2004).

Before 2004 we tried many things—including public programming and costly exhibitions—but ultimately what worked was weaving the Peabody into the educational program, especially into diploma requirements. We knew it was unlikely that stand-alone archaeology courses would draw sufficient numbers of students to justify large budget allocations. Teachers from several disciplines worked closely with the Peabody staff to identify resources for diploma requirements, electives, and independent projects. (See Hagler and Gallou, this volume.)

Phillips Academy faculty has long aspired to offer students interdisciplinary and multidisciplinary experiences, and the Peabody is uniquely qualified to contribute to this initiative: By its very nature, archaeology is multidisciplinary and forces those who study it to think across disciplines. The museum staff has enjoyed an increasingly close and cordial working relationship with teaching colleagues from a variety of departments. More than fifty curriculum units have been developed. In 2004 Malinda Blustain and then Dean of Studies John Rogers created the Peabody Education Oversight Committee, composed of the director of the school's library and six teaching faculty members who serve as effective ambassadors to their departments.

Not many colleges, much less schools, have archaeological museums on or near their campuses. What aspects of our experience might other institutions apply to their programs? I suggest three:

1. Time. Use the time you have. Attach lessons in archaeology to courses that already exist, preferably required courses. Figure out how lessons can be enhanced by the archaeological perspective.
2. Relevance. Present lessons through words, objects, and people to which or whom students can relate. Teach about your local area and its indigenous people and storied past.
3. Buy-in. Create buy-in across constituencies. Build a coalition of supporters who represent every stakeholder group, including teachers, administrators, alumni, and funders with existing affiliation to and appreciation for archaeology.

Developing such programs is culturally and educationally invigorating. Archaeology can integrate with existing curricula to bring excitement to the classroom, to bridge different disciplines, and to encourage critical thinking. Because of archaeology's multidisciplinary focus, it provides an ideal platform for learning in a variety of divergent subjects. Archaeological sites and objects speak to the kind of outreach envisioned by the Society for American Archaeology—one where the value of places and things fosters a sense of preservation, a connection with the past, and understanding of other cultures.

Open Doors

A RETROSPECTIVE ON THE ROBERT S. PEABODY MUSEUM

Abigail Seldin

As a student at Phillips Academy, I found my experiences at the Peabody Museum both crystallized my passion for anthropology and launched my academic career. Equipped with a foundation in archaeology and hands-on curatorial experience, I co-curated an exhibition at the University of Pennsylvania Museum of Archaeology and Anthropology as an undergraduate, its first show to be co-curated by individuals of Native American descent.

Examining the history of the Robert S. Peabody Museum offers many lessons for museums, archaeologists, and students regarding institutional stewardship and creative learning strategies. While a student at Phillips Academy during the beginning of the Peabody's renaissance, I was offered the opportunity to curate a revised version of its exhibition Pecos Pueblo: Crossroads of Cultures. This project was conceived to meet a challenging programming goal and was ultimately completed through student participation. Throughout my experience curating Pecos Pueblo, I witnessed the Peabody Museum's primary values in action: relevance, flexibility, and inclusion.

The Values of the Peabody

In 2002, facing the possibility of closing its doors, the Peabody staff focused much attention on proving the museum's relevance to its key constituencies—the faculty, staff, students, and trustees of Phillips Academy. Among the many ideas for demonstrating relevance and developing key programming was the revision and reinstallation of the Pecos exhibition. Centering on the development and demise of the occupation at Pecos Pueblo, the exhibition displayed numerous artifacts excavated at Pecos. Originally it occupied the second floor of the museum. Director Malinda Blustain thought a reinstalled exhibition could be a strong component of museum programming, providing a connection point for Pecos Pathways alumni as well as a recruiting tool for future student participants (see Randall and Toya, this volume). Perhaps most important, the exhibition could also provide a key opportunity to connect with the curricula at Phillips Academy, thereby enhancing existing academy programming and bringing faculty and students into the museum. Thus the Pecos exhibition opportunity arose because it filled a need. The development of the exhibition was guided neither by obscure interest nor by individual passion but by an institutional goal for service to key constituencies, including the museum's partners at Pecos Pueblo.

Reinstalling Pecos Pueblo: Crossroads of Cultures offered an excellent opportunity to appeal to key groups and fulfill the museum's obligation to its Pecos partners to be good stewards of the collection at Andover. However, numerous challenges stood in opposition to the plan. In accordance with the Native American Graves Protection and Repatriation Act (NAGPRA), a number of items had been repatriated or removed from display (see Bradley, this volume). Further, the exhibition was rendered completely inaccessible by changing fire codes in Massachusetts; the second floor lacked a second staircase, and the museum did not have funds to build another egress. Even with the removal of a number of objects, the exhibition remained much too large for the first floor gallery. To revise and reinstall the exhibition on the first floor would require staff time that the institution could not spare.

My involvement with the reinstallation began during an informal staff meeting in January 2005. When I asked if I could help, Malinda offered the project to me as an independent study opportunity. Malinda's focus on flexibility and commitment to relevance created an opportunity to address a key institutional need by involving students in museum activities. My responsibilities included fully rewriting the exhibition script, selecting some new objects for exhibition, and helping with the installation. Ultimately my work expanded to include modest fundraising and assembling a work crew of fellow students to assist with repainting cases and exhibition installation (figs. 54, 55). The work took considerable extracurricular time, and I earned an independent course credit for my continuing work during

FIG. 54. Abigail Seldin and a crew of fellow students clean and paint display cases for the exhibit. Photo by Donald A. Slater.

the term. The Parents of Students of Phillips Academy provided a small grant to help offset the exhibition costs.

From a student's perspective, the opportunity to curate the new version of the Pecos Pueblo exhibition was invaluable, both for the experiences it provided and for the credibility it gave me as a budding anthropologist. The project introduced me to the real challenges of creating a site-based experience for an audience. The raw materials for the exhibition included a script that needed to be rewritten and shortened, a different pool of objects from those identified in the existing script, and a beautiful diorama in need of a new case. Most seriously, there was no funding. Grappling with these issues yielded a unique opportunity to learn about the actual process for creating an exhibition. Hands-on experience of this kind is extremely rare for university students and almost unheard of for those in high school. When

FIG. 55. Close-up view of the Pecos Pueblo diorama originally constructed in 1940 by artist Stuart Travis. Photo by Ryan Wheeler for the Robert S. Peabody Museum of Archaeology.

I matriculated to the University of Pennsylvania in fall 2005, my experience at the Peabody helped me access a graduate level curatorial seminar, and ultimately to curate my own gallery exhibition at the Penn's Museum of Archaeology and Anthropology as an independent research project. This exhibition, Fulfilling a Prophecy: The Past and Present of the Lenape in Pennsylvania, was the foundation for my successful Rhodes Scholarship application in 2009 and acceptance to Oxford's doctoral program. After a successful three-year run at the Penn Museum, Fulfilling a Prophecy was installed at the Lenape Nation Cultural Center in the Bachmann Publick House, Easton, Pennsylvania, in October 2011.

Perhaps the most important values I saw in action at the Peabody Museum were those of inclusion and collaboration. The focus on meeting community needs at the Peabody extended beyond serving local constituencies to collaborating with the source communities for its collections, as the Peabody continues to do through Pecos Pathways and complying with

NAGPRA. I encountered the legacy of both programs as I selected new objects to fill the holes left by objects repatriated or permanently removed from display. When I asked Director Blustain to tell me about NAGPRA, she began by stating, "NAGPRA is a wonderful thing," thereby illustrating the Peabody's commitment to inclusion and collaboration as guiding values, rather than its submission to legally mandated commitments. The dedication of the staff to these values influenced my nascent understanding of the issues at play. Their guidance helped shape my understanding of the rights of indigenous and source communities, the special relationship they have to museums, and the obligation museums have to them.

Values for the Future

Though the opportunities the Peabody Museum granted me while I was a student opened doors, it is the values I observed firsthand that remain with me. These values—flexibility, relevance, and inclusion—have the potential to guide the way institutions interact with their constituencies. The Peabody Museum helps the stories of generations past come back to life. And those stories have brought the museum back from the ashes. As institutions continue to recover from challenges of the past few years, it is these principles of flexibility, relevance, and inclusion that can lead to a brighter future.

REFERENCES

Allis, Frederick S., Jr. 1979. *Youth from Every Quarter: A Bicentennial History of Philips Academy, Andover.* Hanover NH: University Press of New England.

Ferrie, Helke. 2001. "An Interview with Richard S. MacNeish." *Current Anthropology* 42, no. 5:715–35.

Fritz, Henry E. 1985. "The Last Hurrah of Christian Humanitarian Indian Reform: The Board of Indian Commissioners, 1909–1918." *Western Historical Quarterly* 16, no. 2:147–62.

Griffin, James B. 1985. "The Formation of the Society for American Archaeology." *American Antiquity* 50, no. 2:261–71.

Moorehead, Warren K. 1906. "Sketch of Mr. Robert Singleton Peabody." In *A Narrative of Explorations in New Mexico, Arizona, Indiana, Etc., Together with a Brief*

History of the Department, edited by Warren K. Moorehead, 26–29. Department of Archaeology Bulletin 3. Andover MA: Phillips Academy.

Nassaney, Michael S., and Mary Ann Levine, eds. 2009. *Archaeology and Community Service Learning.* Gainesville: University Press of Florida.

Peabody Planning Committee. 2004. "Report to the Board of Trustees," Phillips Academy, Andover.

Robbins, Maurice. 1949. "A Brief Review of the Progress of the Massachusetts Archaeological Society." *Bulletin of the Massachusetts Archaeological Society* 10, no. 3:50–53.

Sabloff, J. A. 2008. *Archaeology Matters: Action Archaeology in the Modern World.* Walnut Creek CA: Left Coast Press.

Society for American Archaeology Executive Board. 1996. Principles of Archaeological Ethics. Accessed January 4, 2017. http://www.saa.org/AbouttheSociety/PrinciplesofArchaeologicalEthics/tabid/203/Default.aspx.

Contributors

Hillary Abé, BA. Hillary is a citizen of the Mandan, Hidatsa, and Arikara Nation of Fort Berthold, North Dakota. A 2008 graduate of Dartmouth College with a focus in Native American studies, he served as an admission counselor, English teaching fellow, swimming coach, and house counselor during his time at Phillips Academy. Hillary now works for College Horizons, a national nonprofit that provides college access and success programs for Native American, Alaska Native, and Native Hawaiian youth.

James M. Adovasio, PhD, DSc. Jim is currently a research associate of the Senator John Heinz History Center in Pittsburgh and a research affiliate of Southern Methodist University in Dallas. He has served as director of the Mercyhurst Archaeological Institute, dean of the Zurn School of Science, and provost at Mercyhurst University and was professor of anthropology at the University of Pittsburgh. His research on perishable material culture—especially basketry, textiles, and cordage—is well known, as is his work in geoarchaeology and human adaptation during the Lake Pleistocene and Early Holocene. His excavations at Meadowcroft Rockshelter have been widely recognized as the earliest well-dated evidence of human habitation in North America.

Malinda Stafford Blustain, MA. Malinda has worked in curation and collections management at Harvard University's Peabody Museum of Archaeology and Ethnology, the Florida Museum of Natural History, and the Jackson Homestead museum in Newton, Massachusetts. She was the assistant state archaeologist in Kentucky and has worked as an analyst on expeditions in Egypt and Honduras. She is best known for her leadership at the Robert S. Peabody Museum, first as curator (1992–2002) and then as director (2002–12). After retiring Malinda and her husband, Harvey, moved to Gorkha, Nepal, to teach English as a foreign language. They now reside in Eugene, Oregon.

James W. Bradley, PhD. Jim is the founder and president of ArchLink, an independent, individually owned business, linking archaeology with education and preservation. He received his PhD from the Maxwell School at Syracuse University in 1979. He served on the staff of the Massachusetts Historical Commission from 1979 to 1990 and on the NAGPRA Review Committee from 1997 to 2003 and was director of the Robert S. Peabody Museum from 1990 to 2001.

Margaret Conkey, PhD. Meg is class of 1960 professor emerita at the University of California, Berkeley, where her research has focused on issues of gender and feminist perspectives in archaeology, studies of Paleolithic art, and fieldwork at a late Paleolithic site in the French Pyrénées. She served as president of Society for American Archaeology from 2009 to 2011.

Linda S. Cordell, PhD. Linda (1943–2013) was a senior scholar at the School for Advanced Research on the Human Experience in Santa Fe, New Mexico, and external faculty at the Santa Fe Institute. Before then she was director of the Museum of Natural History at the University of Colorado, Boulder. She previously taught archaeology and anthropology at the University of New Mexico and was Irvine Curator of Anthropology at the California Academy of Sciences. A member of the National Academy of Sciences and the American Academy of Arts and Sciences, she received the A. V. Kidder medal for eminence in American archaeology from the American Anthropological Association, and a Lifetime Achievement Award from the Society for American Archaeology. Linda's publications on the archaeology of the Southwest are well-known to scholars and the general public.

Mary Eubanks, PhD. An alumna of Abbot Academy (1965), which merged with Phillips Academy in 1973, Mary was a 2000 recipient of Phillips Academy's highest alumni honor, the Claude Moore Fuess Award for distinguished contribution to public service, in recognition of her lifelong work in science and education. Mary has served as an adjunct professor in the biology department at Duke University. Her research focuses on the origin and evolution of maize, finding important implications in the early domestication of corn for modern-day corn breeding and for issues of global food security. Her book *Corn in Clay: Maize Paleoethobotany in Pre-Columbian Art*, won the Society for Economic Botany's Mary Klinger Award in 2001.

Claire Gallou, DEA, PhD. Claire has a doctorate in comparative literature from UCLA, with research interests in contemporary poetry, translation, and literary theory. She has taught a variety of subjects at the middle school to college and adult professional levels. She teaches French at Phillips Academy, where she also serves as a house counselor.

Kristi Gilleon, BA. Kristi is a graduate of Phillips Academy (2007) and the University of Montana (2011) and studied philosophy at Georgia State University. She began her involvement at the Peabody Museum as a work duty student and subsequently participated in the full range of its educational activities, including the expeditionary learning program that took students to Mexico and Belize in an effort to deepen their Spanish skills and introduce them to ancient and contemporary life in Latin America.

Jeremiah Hagler, PhD. Jerry is a biology instructor at Phillips Academy, where he currently teaches advanced biology, collaborates on several interdisciplinary science electives, and acts as faculty supervisor for many student independent research projects each school year. He has degrees from the Cornell Graduate School of Medical Sciences and conducted post-doctoral work at Harvard University. His classes frequently utilize the hands-on resources at the Robert S. Peabody Museum.

Nathan D. Hamilton, PhD. Nate received his PhD from the University of Pittsburgh and has been teaching archaeology and anthropology since 1987 at the University of Southern Maine, where he is associate professor of archaeology. His research interests include historic and American Indian archaeology of New England, maritime adaptations, and analysis of basketry and textiles.

Lindsay A. Randall, MA. Lindsay is the curator of education at the Robert S. Peabody Museum of Archaeology. She has taught at the Hartford Old State House Museum and was an intern in the collections department at Plimoth Plantation before joining the staff of the Peabody in 2008. Her interests include the history and prehistory of New England, especially European–American Indian interactions. She also spends time guiding kayak expeditions along the New England coastline.

James B. Richardson III, PhD. Jim is professor emeritus of anthropology at the University of Pittsburgh and curator emeritus of anthropology at the Carnegie Museum of Natural History. His archaeological interests include the rise of complex societies, the impact of climate change on cultural development, geoarchaeology, maritime and riverine adaptations, historic archaeology, ethnohistory, and museology. He has a long-term research program in Peru and also works extensively in western Pennsylvania and Martha's Vineyard, Massachusetts.

Brian S. Robinson, PhD. Brian (1953–2016) was associate professor in the Anthropology Department and the Climate Change Institute the University of Maine. He was known for his work on northern and coastal hunter-gatherers, the cultural history of northeastern North America, mortuary ritual, and anthropological theory. His dissertation research at Brown University provided a reanalysis of the Moorehead burial tradition, with a focus on groups and boundaries in the Gulf of Maine between 9,000 and 4,000 years ago.

Abigail Seldin, D.Phil. Abigail is a Phillips Academy graduate (2005) and summa cum laude graduate of the University of Pennsylvania, where she received an MA in anthropology. As a Rhodes Scholar she studied social anthropology at the University of Oxford. She has served as a fellow in cultural heritage tourism in the office of strategic planning and research at the Hong Kong Tourism Board, co-founded College Abacus, and currently works in the nonprofit sector in Washington DC.

Donald A. Slater, PhD. Donald received his PhD in anthropology and archaeology from Brandeis University in 2014, where he focused his research on ancient Mesoamerica. He was named a National Geographic Explorer in recognition of his fieldwork at Maya cave sites in Yucatán, Mexico. He has worked as a museum educator at the Robert S. Peabody Museum and is now an instructor in history and social science at Phillips Academy.

Rebecca Miller Sykes, AB, MSW. Becky Sykes joined the faculty of Phillips Academy in 1976 and most recently served as associate head of school. She has held posts in education or social work at a variety of institutions. She was formerly a trustee at Simmons College in Boston and the Museum of African-American History in Boston. Becky now leads the Oprah Winfrey Charitable Foundation.

Christopher Toya. Chris is a Jemez Pueblo tribal member and archaeologist who serves as the traditional cultural properties manager for the pueblo. Chris also is actively engaged in traditional knowledge and cultural preservation programs in his community and serves on the Native American Advisory Group of the Crow Canyon Archaeological Center. He has been involved with all aspects of Pecos Pathways, one of the Robert S. Peabody Museum's longest running and most successful expeditionary learning programs.

Ryan J. Wheeler, PhD. Ryan has a background in field and laboratory archaeology as well as extensive experience in the leadership of archaeological organizations. As Florida's state archaeologist he led efforts to design and develop the Miami Circle Park, commemorating the significant Tequesta site preserved through community efforts. His research interests include everything from ancient dugout canoes to shell mounds and the archaeology of the recent past. He became the eighth director of the Robert S. Peabody Museum in 2012.

Eugene C. Winter Jr. Gene (1927–2014) was a retired teacher and principal best known for his long association with the Massachusetts and New Hampshire archaeological societies. He received the SAA's 2005 Crabtree Award for distinguished service as an avocational archaeologist spanning more than fifty years. He also was the first recipient in 2011 of the Eugene Winter Award for distinguished volunteer service at the Robert S. Peabody Museum, where he served as honorary curator until his passing in 2014.

Index

Page numbers in italic indicate illustrations.
RSPM *refers to Robert S. Peabody Museum of Archaeology.*

animals: bird DNA studies, *155*, 187–88;
bison and Folsom point discovery,
56–58, *57*; bone carvings, 48–49; dog
population study, 187; domestication
of, 28, 29; of Maine sites, 117–19; of
Mesoamerican sites, 72n7; paleoeco-
logical approach on, 19–20, 65, 125;
from Pecos archaeological sites, 215
Anishinaabeg, 13
Antiquarian, 9
Antiquities Act (1906), 85
Appleton, William Sumner, 105–6
archaeobotany. *See* agricultural origins
of Mesoamerica; maize
Archaeological Institute of America, 7,
84, 87
Archaeologist, 9
archaeology, application and outreach
using, 201–5
Ashley, Margaret, 108
Awe, Jaime, 195
Ayacucho Archaeological-Botanical
Project (Peru), xviii, xxi, 29, 65, *65*,
72n7, 148
Ayacucho phase, 66
Aztec Ruins (New Mexico), 26, 89

Baker, Emerson, II, 153
Baker, Vernon G., 26
BALAM. *See* Bilingual Archaeological
Learning Adventure in Mesoamer-
ica (BALAM)
Bancroft, Cecil F. P., 44
Bandelier National Monument, *214*
basketry, 25
Battle-Baptiste, Whitney, 26
Beadle, George, 130
Belize archaeological sites, 66, 195, 215

Belize Archaic Archaeological Recon-
naissance, 66
Belize Valley Archaeological Recon-
naissance Project, 195
Bilingual Archaeological Learning
Adventure in Mesoamerica
(BALAM), *194*, 194–97, 214–16
Bingham, Hiram, III, 12, 17, 49, 148
bird DNA studies, *155*, 187–88
bison and Folsom point discovery,
56–58, *57*
*Blanket Statements: A Brief History of
American Indian Trade Blankets*
(exhibition), 32, 33
Blue Hill Bay (Maine). *See* Nevin site
(Maine); Richards site (Maine)
blues music, 71n6
Blustain, Malinda Stafford, xvi, *xvii*, 33,
34–35, 160, 218
Boas, Franz, 11, 17, 86, 148
bone carvings, 48–49
Bourque, Bruce, 108
Boylston Street Fish Weir (Massachu-
setts), 21–22, 54–56, *55*, 112. *See also*
Massachusetts archaeological sites
Bradley, James W., *xvii*, *31*; career
of, xxi, xxii, 30–34; professional
affiliations of, 70n1; repatriation
work by, 151–53, 159–71, *163*; research
work of, 67, *67*, 67–68; summary of
RSPM directorship of, 151–53, 217–18
British Academy of Sciences, 70n1
Brown, Barbara, 26–27
Bull Brook site (Massachusetts), xviii,
21, 61, 111
Bullen, Adelaide Kendall, 25–28, *53*, 111
Bullen, Dana Ripley, 26
Bullen, Pierce Kendall, 26

Bullen, Ripley Pierce, 26–28, 53, 54, 72n8, 111

Bulletin of the Massachusetts Archaeological Society, 70n1, 111

Bureau of American Ethnology, 16, 42–43

Bureau of Indian Affairs, 13

Bureau of Indian Arts and Industries, 13

Busé, Rudy, 92–93, 178

Bush, George H. W., 31, 150

Bushey Cavern (Maryland), 7, 47–48

Byers, Douglas Swain: career of, xviii, 18–20, 28, 52–53; Maine fieldwork by, 19, 52, 54, 62–63, 109–11, 117, *118*; Massachusetts fieldwork by, *21*, 21–22, 54, 56, 61, 66, 112; Mesoamerican fieldwork by, 53, 64, 72n8; on Moorehead's approach, 10–11, 99–100; Phillips Academy coursework by, 189; professional affiliations of, 69n1; publications by, 19–20, 112; RSPM work of, 23–24; SAA presentation by, 16, 20

Cahokia IL, 10, 11

Calf Island (Maine), 51

Callen, Eric, 124, 126

Canada, xviii, 22–23, 24, 33, *60*, 61, 63

Carnegie Institution, 14, 17, 52

Central Yucatan Archaeological Cave Project (Mexico), 191, 197–98, *198*

ceramics, *31*; Guthe's study on, 18; by Julian and Maria Martinez, 18; Kidder's study of, 49–50, 86–87, 88, 89, 91, 94; from Lucy Foster site, 26; of Maine sites, 117–19; from Pecos National Historic Park, 215; Petrie's study of, 86; and stratigraphy, 49, 50, 88

Chaco Canyon (New Mexico), 26, 87

Chan Chan (Peru), 195

Chandler, Joseph Everett, 192

Chapman, Kenneth, 89

Chase, Barbara Landis, 164, *165*, 218

Chavín de Huántar (Peru), 195

Chetro Ketl (New Mexico), 87

Chicago World's Fair (1893), 4, 9, 44

Chichén Itzá (Mexico), 63

Chile, 68

classification system, 54, 86, 91

Clovis Barrier, 58, 62

Clovis culture, xviii, 58, 59, 61, 63–68

collections management system, 24–25, 33–34, 109

Colorado, 58

Committee for the Recovery of Archaeological Remains (CRAR), 23, 69n1

Conaway, Mary Ellen, 30, 72n7

Cook, Ángel García, 28

corn. *See* maize

Corn Hills on Cape Cod: Archaeological Investigations at Sandy's Point, Yarmouth, Massachusetts (exhibition), 32

Coxcatlán Cave (Mexico), 28, 124, 125, 126, *127*, 128

Coxcatlán phase, 126

cranial morphology, *186*

CRAR. *See* Committee for the Recovery of Archaeological Remains (CRAR)

crop domestication, 123, 126–30. *See also* agricultural origins of Mesoamerica

crude stone tools, 42–43, 45, 65. *See also* projectile points

Cutler, Hugh, 124, 126

Cutler, Mark, 194, 215

F1 and F2 teosinte-*Tripsacum*, 122–24, 132–36, *133. See also* teosinte; *Tripsacum*

Farquharson, Lois, 134

faunal evidence. *See* animals

Field Museum of Natural History (Chicago), 25

Figgins, Jesse D., 56, 58

Flannery, Kent, 28, 137

Fletcher, John Gould, 84

Florida Museum of Natural History (formerly Florida State Museum), 27

fluted point discoveries, 56–58, *57, 59,* 61

Folsom (New Mexico), 56–58, *57,* 92

Ford Foundation, 124

Forensic Anthropology (unit at Phillips Academy), 187

Fort Ancient (Ohio), 8, 10, 11, 43

Foster's Cove (Massachusetts), 54

Founder's Collection, Robert S. Peabody Museum, 9, 24–25, 44, 58, *59*

France. *See* Piette Program

Fulfilling a Prophecy: The Past and Present of the Lenape in Pennsylvania (exhibition), 221, 224

Gachupin, Raymond, *165,* 167

Gachupin, Stuart, 169

Gainey points, 58

Galinat, Walton C., 122, 125, 128, *133,* 135–36, *141*

Galisteo Basin (New Mexico), 88

genetic studies, 130, 138–41. *See also* DNA analysis

genomics, 130–32, 138

genotyping, 138

Gilleon, Kristi, *xvii, 214*

GIS (Global Information System), 119, 195, 197

Goujon, M. Guillaume, 210

GPS (Global Positioning System), 195

grave-lot seriation technique, 86

grid system, unit-delineated, 6

Griffin, James B., 113

Guatemala archaeological sites, 18, 25, 53, 124, 195

Guernsey, Samuel, 88

Guernsey-Pitman Studios, 23–24

Guila Naquitz cave (Mexico), 128

Guthe, Carl, 18, 50, 91, 92

Hadlock, Wendell S., 62

Hamilton, Nathan D., xvi, *xvii,* 117

Hartley, Gary, 167

Harvard Peabody Museum of Archaeology and Ethnology, xv, 2, 31–32, 164

Hewett, Edgar Lee, 84–85, 87

Hollis, Christiana, 188

Holmes, William Henry, 12, 16, 43, 148

Honduras archaeological sites, 72n8, 124

Hooton, Earnest, 18

Hopewell Mounds (Ohio), 14, 43, 44, 99

Hornblower site (Massachusetts), 54

Howard, Edgar, 58

Hrdlička, Aleš, 7, 70n4

HUACA. *See* Human Understanding through Archaeology and Cultural Awareness (HUACA)

Human Origins (course at Phillips Academy), xxiv, 186, 188–89, *189*

Human Understanding through Archaeology and Cultural Awareness (HUACA), 191, 195–97, *196*

MacNeish, Richard Stockton "Scotty,"
29, *141*; award for, 63; career of, xi,
xxi, 18, 28–30, 218; funding for, 148,
150–51; and Kidder, 63; Mesoamerican fieldwork by, xviii, 28, 29–30,
122–24, 140, 148; *The Origins of
Agriculture and Settled Life*, 121,
122; and pre-Clovis debate, xviii,
63–68; professional affiliations of,
70n1; work with Phillips Academy,
xxi, 148, 149, 189. *See also* Tehuacán
Archaeological-Botanical Project
(Mexico)
Madalena, Joshua, 166, 167–68
Maine archaeological sites: Calf Island,
51; Jones Cove site, 110; Marks
collection from, 12; Moorehead's
work at, xx–xxi, 12, 54, 100–101,
101, 107–9; Nevin site, 19, 23, *52*, 54,
109–10, 117–19; Richards site, 19,
117–19, *118*; site survey of, 27–28;
Smith Farm, 62–63; Stevens site,
109; Sunkhaze Ridge site, 108–9;
Tafts Point, 110; Waterside site, 110
Maine Archaeological Society, 20
Maine Historic Preservation Commission, 28
Maine State Museum, 107, 108
maize: evolutionary pathway for origin
of, xxi, 28, 122–24, 130–40; Phillips
Academy curriculum on, 186–87;
specimen images of, *123*, *130*, *133*, *135*,
137; from Tamaulipas, 64, 122–23;
from Tehuacán Valley, 126–30, *127*, *130*
mammoth and Clovis point discovery,
58, *59*
Mangelsdorf, Paul, 122–24, 125, 128,
130–31

Man in Northeastern North America
(Johnson), 22, 54
Manitonquat, *208*
*Maps and Dreams: Native Americans
and European Discovery* (exhibi-
tions), 32
Marks, A. E., 12
Marks, Copeland H., 25
Martin, Louis Henri, 7
Martinez, Julian, 18
Martinez, Maria, 18
Le Mas d'Azil site (France), 202,
210–13, *211*
Mashantucket Pequot Reservation,
178, *180*
Mashpee Wampanoag Tribe, 32
Massachusetts archaeological sites:
Andover town dump, 50, 72n7, 148,
149; Bolyston Street Fish Weir, 21–22,
54–56, *55*, 112; Bull Brook, xviii, *21*, 61,
111; Foster's Cove, 54; Hornblower
site, 54; Lucy Foster site, 26–27, 111;
Shattuck Farm site, *105*; Shawsheen
Valley, 26, 27; site survey data on,
27–28; Squibnocket site, 54
Massachusetts Archaeological Society,
53; and Bullen, 27; *Bulletin of the
Massachusetts Archaeological Society*,
70n1, 111; founding of, xvi, 20, 111,
218; lecture series of, 198, 214
Massachusetts Historical Commission,
27, 30
Maya Cosmos (course by Slater), xxiv,
196–97
McBride, Kevin, 178
McNemar, Donald W., 30
Meadowcroft Rockshelter (Pennsylva-
nia), 68

IN THE CRITICAL STUDIES IN THE HISTORY OF ANTHROPOLOGY SERIES

To order or obtain more information on these or other University
of Nebraska Press titles, visit nebraskapress.unl.edu.